HOW THE
ELL
Brain Learns

HOW THE ELL Brain Learns

David A. Sousa

CORWIN
A SAGE Company

For information:

Corwin
A SAGE Company.
2455 Teller Road
Thousand Oaks, California 91320
(800) 233-9936
Fax: (800) 417-2466
www.corwin.com

SAGE India Pvt. Ltd
B 1/I 1 Mohan Cooperative Industrial Area
Mathura Road, New Delhi 110 044
India

SAGE Ltd.
1 Oliver's Yard
55 City Road
London EC1Y 1SP
United Kingdom

SAGE Asia-Pacific Pte. Ltd.
33 Pekin Street #02-01
Far East Square
Singapore 048763

Printed in the United States of America.

Library of Congress Cataloging-in-Publication Data

Sousa, David A.
How the ELL brain learns / David A. Sousa.
    p. cm.
Includes bibliographical references and index.
ISBN 978-1-4129-8834-6 (pbk.)
    1. English language—Study and teaching—Foreign speakers. 2. Language and languages—Study and Teaching. 3. Second language acquisition. I. Title.

PE1128.A2.S5954 2011
428.2′4 019—dc22   2010031504

This book is printed on acid-free paper.

10 11 12 13 14 10 9 8 7 6 5 4 3 2 1

Acquisitions Editor:	Carol Chambers Collins
Associate Editor:	Megan Bedell
Editorial Assistant:	Sarah Bartlett
Production Editor:	Cassandra Margaret Seibel
Typesetter:	C&M Digitals (P) Ltd.
Proofreader:	Cheryl Rivard
Cover Designer:	Anthony Paular
Permissions Editor:	Adele Hutchinson

Contents

List of Teaching Tips

About the Author

**David A. Sousa,** Ed.D., is an international consultant in educational neuroscience and author of more than a dozen books that suggest ways that educators and parents can translate current brain research into strategies for improving learning. He has conducted workshops in hundreds of school districts on brain research, instructional skills, and science education at the PreK–12 and university levels. He has made presentations to more than 100,000 educators at national conventions of educational organizations and to regional and local school districts across the United States, Canada, Europe, Australia, New Zealand, and Asia.

Dr. Sousa has a bachelor's degree in chemistry from Massachusetts State College at Bridgewater, a Master of Arts in Teaching degree in science from Harvard University, and a doctorate from Rutgers University. His teaching experience covers all levels. He has taught senior high school science, served as a K–12 director of science, a supervisor of instruction, and a district superintendent in New Jersey schools. He has been an adjunct professor of education at Seton Hall University and a visiting lecturer at Rutgers University.

Dr. Sousa has edited science books and published dozens of articles in leading journals on staff development, science education, and educational research. His most popular books for educators include: *How the Brain Learns,* third edition; *How the Special Needs Brain Learns,* second edition; *How the Gifted Brain Learns; How the Brain Learns to Read; How the Brain Influences Behavior;* and *How the Brain Learns Mathematics,* which was selected by the Independent Publishers' Association as one of the best professional development books of 2008. *The Leadership Brain* suggests ways for educators to lead today's schools more effectively. His books have been published in French, Spanish, Chinese, Arabic, and several other languages.

Dr. Sousa is past president of the National Staff Development Council. He has received numerous awards from professional associations, school districts, and educational foundations for his commitment to research, staff development, and science education. He recently received the Distinguished Alumni Award and an honorary doctorate from Massachusetts State College (Bridgewater), and an honorary doctorate from Gratz College in Philadelphia.

Dr. Sousa has been interviewed by Matt Lauer on NBC's *Today* show and by National Public Radio about his work with schools using brain research. He makes his home in South Florida.

Acknowledgments

The author and Corwin gratefully acknowledge the contributions of the following individuals:

Irma Guadarrama, Ph.D.
Professor, Department of Curriculum and Instruction
College of Education, University of Texas-Pan American

Sharon Latimer
ESL PreK Teacher
Plano ISD
Plano, TX

Herbert Pérez-Vidal
Freelance Writer
Retired Professor of French and Spanish
Palm Beach State College
Lake Worth, FL

Elizabeth Scaduto
K–12 Director of ESL and Bilingual Programs
Riverhead Central School District
Riverhead, NY

Sue Summers
Elementary ELL teacher
Boise School District
Boise, ID

Introduction

WHO ARE ENGLISH LANGUAGE LEARNERS?

For the purposes of this book, the term *English language learner* (ELL) refers to a diverse group of students who have one common feature—they are all learning English as other than their native language. There are other labels for these students. Official documents may refer to them as *limited English proficient (LEP),* and the terms *language-minority* and *bilingual* are common. Various government entities and national organizations favor some terms over others. They argue, for example, that the term *language-minority students* does not make sense in those communities where they outnumber their native English-speaking peers. Others suggest that the term *limited English proficient* places too much emphasis on what the student cannot do, hardly a positive approach. Even the term *second-language learner* is not accurate for students who may be learning English as their third or fourth language. To avoid these labeling problems, some organizations are referring to these students as *English as a new language (ENL)* learners and *English as an additional language*, denoting that these learners are adding English to their existing linguistic repertoire. Labels are evolving, so stay tuned.

By all available estimates, the population of school-age children who are English language learners is more than 5 million (NCELA, 2006). It may come as a surprise to many readers that most English language learners (ELLs) in American schools were actually born in the United States. About 76 percent of elementary-age ELLs and 56 percent of middle and high school ELLs were born in the United States. However, about 80 percent of ELLs' parents were born outside of the United States. As shown in Figure I.1, more than 80 percent

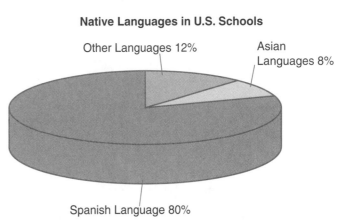

Native Languages in U.S. Schools

Other Languages 12%

Asian Languages 8%

Spanish Language 80%

Figure I.1 This chart illustrates the percentage of students in U.S. schools who are native speakers of Spanish, Asian, and other languages (Capps et al., 2005).

of ELLs are Spanish speakers and many of these come from lower economic and educational backgrounds than either the general population or other immigrants and language minority populations (Capps et al., 2005). Furthermore, fewer than 40 percent of immigrants from Mexico and Central America have the equivalent of a high school diploma, in contrast to between 80 and 90 percent of other immigrants (and 87.5 percent of U.S.-born residents). As a result, most ELLs are at risk in school not only because of language but also because of socioeconomic factors. The next largest group of ELLs are the speakers of Asian languages (e.g., Chinese, Hindi, Hmong, Khmer, Korean, Laotian, Tagalog, and Vietnamese) who comprise about 8 percent of the ELL population. Students of Asian origin typically come from families with higher income and education levels than do other immigrant families.

Academic Achievement of ELLs

Despite the increased awareness among educators that ELLs need support to acquire the English proficiency to succeed in school, the academic achievement of ELLs tends to be low when compared to their non-ELL peers. Furthermore, as shown in Figures I.2 and I.3, the gaps in achievement between ELLs and non-ELLs have remained stubbornly unchanged from the 2005 to the 2009 National Assessment of Educational Progress (NAEP) tests in mathematics (NCES, 2009b; Perie, Grigg, & Donahue, 2005a) and reading (NCES, 2009c; Perie, Grigg, & Donahue, 2005b). These gaps are not really a surprise because ELLs are limited in their English

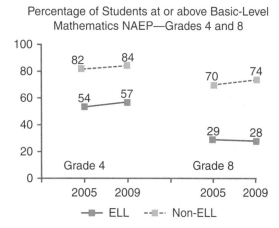

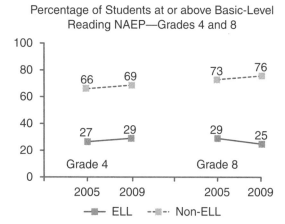

Figure I.2   The graph shows the percentage of ELL and non-ELL students at or above the basic achievement level in mathematics in Grades 4 and 8 on the 2005 and 2009 National Assessment of Educational Progress tests (NCES, 2009b; Perie et al., 2005a).

Figure I.3   The graph shows the percentage of ELL and non-ELL students at or above the basic achievement level in reading in Grades 4 and 8 on the 2005 and 2009 National Assessment of Educational Progress tests (NCES, 2009c; Perie et al., 2005b).

proficiency and the NAEP tests are in English. But the test data do not reveal the causes of the achievement gaps. Did the ELLs test low because of limited English proficiency, or because of lagging content knowledge and skills, or because of other factors that interfere with their test performance—or some combination of these? Apart from the reasons for these discrepancies, the scores do not suggest a promising picture for the ELLs' level of achievement in school or for their future. Schools, then, must reexamine their curriculum, instruction, and assessment to ensure they understand our current state of knowledge regarding how to improve the achievement of ELLs.

ABOUT THIS BOOK

Let's face it: Teachers of students who are English language learners have an exceptionally difficult job. Most of them are responsible not only for delivering curriculum content but doing so in a way that students struggling to learn a new language will understand it. These teachers are more likely to be successful if they have a deeper understanding of the cognitive, emotional, and cultural challenges their students are facing while trying to learn English and course content simultaneously. It is a formidable task, and teachers of ELLs need all the help they can get.

In recent years, teachers who work with ELLs can access a growing number of professional texts, articles, and online resources. However, the sheer volume of information is sometimes overwhelming. Consequently, teachers can succumb to the allure of strategy books. But selecting strategies from books without an understanding of the ELLs' unique language and learning needs is like driving a car without knowing the basic rules of the road. You may crash into something before you get very far. Teachers also need to be knowledgeable about the scientifically based evidence that underlies their instructional decisions. In this age of accountability, they not only have to make informed decisions about teaching their ELLs, they have to be ready to justify their decisions to administrators, parents, and teacher colleagues as well. This responsibility can be particularly difficult because few teachers are professionally prepared to serve students who are

> *This is not just a "how-to" book. It is a "why-because-how-to" book.*

simultaneously learning English and academic content. That is why I wrote this book. There are plenty of "how to" books available with instructional strategies aimed at ELLs. But few, if any, delve into explaining what new research in cognitive neuroscience is telling us about how the brain of an English language learner deals with the linguistic reorganization needed to acquire another language after the age of 5 years. This is not just a "how to" book. It is a "why-because-how-to" book.

Questions This Book Will Answer

This book will answer questions such as these:

- What are we learning from neuroscience about how the brain acquires language?
- Why is learning the first language so easy but learning a second language later so difficult?
- Are there differences between male and female brains in learning language?
- Can learning a second language too young interfere with learning the first language?
- What roles do memory and transfer play when acquiring a second language?
- Why is learning English particularly difficult compared to some other languages?
- What role does culture play in second-language acquisition?
- How effective are immersion programs for ELLs?
- How can content-area teachers help ELLs learn academic English successfully?
- How can we tell if an ELL is just having difficulty with language acquisition or has a developmental learning disability?
- What are the basics of an effective research-based program for ELLs?
- How can we identify gifted and talented ELLs?

Many examples in the text will refer to Spanish-speaking ELL students, although they can apply to other native language groups as well. I refer to Spanish more frequently because—as mentioned earlier—Spanish-speaking ELLs represent the largest non-English-speaking minority in the U.S. school population, and their numbers are growing.

Chapter Contents

Chapter 1 — Learning the First Language(s). Humans learn language effortlessly. This chapter discusses how and why young children can acquire spoken language easily and without direct instruction. It explores the structure of language and examines whether male and female brains learn language differently. How can the brain learn two languages at once? That is also explained in this chapter.

Chapter 2 — Learning a New Language (English) Later. Children's innate ability to learn language begins to decrease as they get older. How does this affect learning a new language after the age of 5 years? What impact does the first language have on learning the second? What roles do memory and transfer play? Why is English a difficult language to learn for speakers of Romance languages? These and other related questions are addressed in this chapter.

Chapter 3 — Teaching English Language Listening and Speaking. Are immersion programs for ELLs as successful as some people claim? This question is explored along with research evidence on other program formats. But the focus here is on ways of developing ELLs' listening and speaking skills in English.

Chapter 4 — Teaching English Language Reading and Writing. Learning to read is a real challenge for many ELL students. Research is telling us more about how the brain learns to read and suggests ways we can apply these findings to helping ELLs learn to read and write English faster and with understanding. This chapter investigates the research and applications.

Chapter 5 — Teaching Language Arts and Social Studies. Many ELLs have difficulties acquiring the academic English they need to succeed in the content areas. This chapter explores ways of helping ELLs learn the academic English and content in language arts and social studies. It also discusses ways of working with the culture differences among ELLs from various countries.

Chapter 6 — Teaching Mathematics and Science. Despite the notion that mathematics and science use universal symbols and languages, ELLs still have difficulty mastering these subjects. That is because language plays an important role in describing mathematical and scientific operations. Among other ideas, this chapter suggests ways of helping ELLs with word problems in mathematics and working successfully with the scientific method.

Chapter 7 — Recognizing and Addressing Problems in Learning English. How can we tell if an ELL is just having difficulty with language acquisition or has a developmental learning disability? Not knowing the difference may misidentify ELLs so that those without a learning disability get special services while those who need extra support do not. This chapter offers some ways that can help teachers avoid misidentification while helping struggling ELLs to succeed.

Chapter 8 — Putting It All Together. This chapter pulls together the main ideas of the book. It debunks some common misconceptions about ELLs and discusses the basics of an effective ELL program, including professional development for teachers of ELLs. It also explores ways of incorporating technology into ELL instruction and suggests ways to identify and support gifted and talented ELLs.

Other Helpful Tools

Applications. At the end of most chapters are the **Teaching Tips.** These suggestions stem from the major concepts and research discussed in the chapter and represent ways of translating the research into practical classroom applications. Many of them have been used successfully by teachers of ELL students at the elementary and secondary levels. A few teaching strategies are found in several sections of the book because it is possible that some readers will go to only those sections that interest them.

Key Points to Ponder. This page at the very end of each chapter is an organizing tool to help you remember important ideas, strategies, and resources you may wish to consider at a later time.

Glossary. Many of the neuroscientific and specialized terms used in the text are defined in a glossary.

References. Many of the citations in this extensive section are the original research reports published in peer-reviewed journals. These references will be particularly helpful for researchers and for those who would like more specific information on how the research studies were conducted.

Resources. This section offers some valuable Internet sites that will help teachers at all grade levels find many additional strategies for working with ELL students.

The value of this book can be measured in part by how it enhances your understanding of how ELLs acquire the English language and of the strategies that are more likely to help them succeed in that challenging task. Take the following true-false test to assess your current knowledge in this area.

WHAT DO YOU ALREADY KNOW?

Directions: Decide whether the statements are generally true or false and circle T or F.

1. T   F   Exposing ELLs to English and having them interact with native English speakers will result in learning English.

2. T   F   All ELLs learn English in the same way and at the same rate.

3. T   F   Teaching methods that are successful with native English speakers also will be successful with ELLs.

4. T   F   Using visuals and other nonverbal tools in instruction helps ELLs avoid the language demands in school.

5. T   F   Assessments of ELLs' native language proficiency provide an accurate picture of linguistic proficiency.

6. T   F   The more time ELLs spend in receiving English instruction, the faster they will learn it.

7. T   F   Errors in English may cause problems and should be avoided.

8. T   F   Using technology regularly in the classroom will reduce the ELL students' attention span.

9. T   F   Intelligence and nonverbal tests are reliable methods for identifying gifted and talented ELLs.

The answers to these items will be found throughout Chapter 8.

Chapter 1

Learning the First Language(s)

One of the most extraordinary features of the human brain is its ability to acquire spoken language quickly and accurately. We are born with an innate capacity to distinguish the distinct sounds (phonemes) of all the languages on this planet, with no predisposition for one language over another. Eventually, we are able to associate those sounds with arbitrary written symbols to express our thoughts and emotions to others.

Other animals have developed sophisticated ways to communicate with members of their species. Birds and apes bow and wave appendages, honeybees dance to map out the location of food, and even one-celled animals can signal neighbors by emitting an array of various chemicals. The communicative systems of vervet monkeys, for instance, have been studied extensively. They are known to make up to ten different vocalizations. Amazingly, many of these are used to warn other members of the group about *specific* approaching predators. A "snake call" will trigger a different defensive strategy than a "leopard call" or an "eagle call." Apes in captivity show similar communicative abilities, having been taught rudimentary sign language and the use of lexigrams—symbols that do not graphically resemble their corresponding words—and computer keyboards. Some apes, such as the famous Kanzi, have been able to learn and use hundreds of lexigrams (Savage-Rumbaugh & Lewin, 1994). However, although these apes can learn a basic syntactic and referential system, their communications certainly lack the complexity of a full language.

By contrast, human beings have developed an elaborate and complex means of spoken communication that many say is largely responsible for our place as the dominant species on this planet. To accomplish this required both the development of the anatomical apparatus for precise speech (i.e., the larynx and vocal cords) along with the necessary neurological changes in the brain to support language itself. The enlargement of the larynx probably occurred as our ancestors began to walk upright. Meanwhile, as brain development became more complex, regions emerged that specialized in sound processing as well as musical and arithmetic notations (Vandervert, 2009). Somewhere along the way, too, a gene variation known as *FOXP2* appeared. Geneticists believe it contributed significantly to our ability to create precise speech. Evolutionary anthropologists are still debating whether language evolved slowly as these physical and cerebral capabilities were acquired, resulting in a period of semilanguage, or whether it emerged suddenly once all these capabilities were available.

SPOKEN LANGUAGE COMES NATURALLY

Spoken language is truly a marvelous accomplishment for many reasons. At the very least, it gives form to our memories and words to express our thoughts. A single human voice can pronounce all the hundreds of vowel and consonant sounds that allow it to speak any of the estimated 6,500 languages that exist today. (Scholars believe there were once about 10,000 languages, but many have since died out.) With practice, the voice becomes so fine-tuned that it makes only about one sound error per million sounds and one word error per million words (Pinker, 1994). Figure 1.1 presents a general timeline for spoken language development during the first three years of growth. The chart is a rough approximation. Some children will progress faster or slower than the chart indicates. Nonetheless, it is a useful guide to show the progression of skills acquired during the process of learning any language.

Before the advent of scanning technologies, we explained how the brain produced spoken language on the basis of evidence from injured brains. In 1861, French physician Paul Broca noticed that patients with brain damage to an area near the left temple understood language but had difficulty speaking, a condition known as aphasia. About the size of a quarter, this region of the brain is commonly referred to as Broca's area (Figure 1.2).

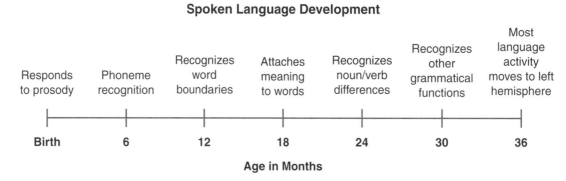

Spoken Language Development

Responds to prosody	Phoneme recognition	Recognizes word boundaries	Attaches meaning to words	Recognizes noun/verb differences	Recognizes other grammatical functions	Most language activity moves to left hemisphere
Birth	6	12	18	24	30	36

Age in Months

Figure 1.1   An average timeline of spoken language development during the child's first three years. There is considerable variation among individual children as visual and auditory processing develop at different rates.

In 1881, German neurologist Carl Wernicke described a different type of aphasia—one in which patients could not make sense out of words they spoke or heard. These patients had damage in the left temporal lobe. Now called Wernicke's area, it is located above the left ear and is about the size of a silver dollar. Those with damage to Wernicke's area could speak fluently, but what they said was quite meaningless. Ever since Broca discovered that the left hemisphere of the brain was specialized for language, researchers have attempted to understand the way in which normal human beings acquire and process their native language.

Processing Spoken Language

Recent research studies using imaging scanners reveal that spoken language production is a far more complex process than previously thought. When preparing to produce a spoken sentence, the brain uses not only Broca's and Wernicke's areas but also calls on several other neural networks scattered throughout the left hemisphere. Nouns are processed through one set of patterns; verbs are processed by separate neural networks. The more complex the sentence structure, the more areas that are activated, including some in the right hemisphere.

In most people, the left hemisphere is home to the major components of the language processing system. Broca's area is a region of the left frontal lobe that is believed to be responsible for processing vocabulary, syntax (how word order affects meaning), and rules of grammar. Wernicke's area is part of the left temporal lobe and is thought to process the sense and meaning of language. However, the emotional content of language is governed by areas in the right hemisphere. More recent imaging studies have unexpectedly found

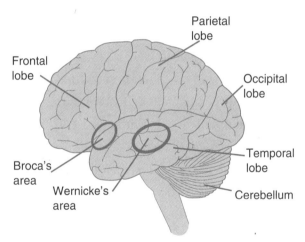

Figure 1.2 The language system in the left hemisphere is comprised mainly of Broca's area and Wernicke's area. The four lobes of the brain and the cerebellum are also identified.

that the cerebellum—long thought to be involved mainly in the planning and control of movement—also seems to be involved in language processing (Booth, Wood, Lu, Houk, & Bitan, 2007; Ghosh, Tourville, & Guenther, 2008). Four decades ago, researchers discovered that infants responded to speech patterns (Eimas, Siqueland, Jusczyk, & Vigorito, 1971). More recently, brain imaging studies of infants as young as 4 months of age confirm that the brain possesses neural networks that specialize in responding to the auditory components of language. Dehaene-Lambertz (2000) used electroencephalograph (EEG) recordings to measure the brain activity of 16 four-month-old infants as they listened to language syllables and acoustic tones. After numerous trials, the data showed that syllables and tones were processed primarily in different areas of the left hemisphere, although there was also some right-hemisphere activity. For language input, various features, such as the voice and the phonetic category of a syllable, were encoded by separate neural networks into sensory memory.

Subsequent studies have supported these results (Bortfeld, Wruck, & Boas, 2007; Friederici, Friedrich, & Christophe, 2007). These remarkable findings suggest that even at this early age, the brain is already organized into functional networks that can distinguish between language fragments and other sounds. Other studies of families with severe speech and language disorders isolated a mutated gene—the *FOXP2* mentioned earlier—believed to be responsible for their deficits. This discovery lends further credence to the notion that the ability to acquire spoken language is encoded in our genes (Gibson & Gruen, 2008; Lai, Fisher, Hurst, Vargha-Khadem, & Monaco, 2001). The apparent genetic predisposition of the brain to the sounds of language explains why most young children respond to and acquire spoken language quickly. After the first year in a language environment, the child becomes increasingly able to differentiate those sounds heard in the native language and begins to lose the ability to perceive other sounds (Conboy, Sommerville, & Kuhl, 2008).

> *The ability to acquire language appears to be encoded in our genes.*

Gestures appear to have a significant impact on a young child's development of language, particularly vocabulary. Studies show that a child's gesturing is a significant predictor of vocabulary acquisition. The daily activities for children between the ages of 14 and 34 months were videotaped for 90 minutes every four months. At 42 months, children were given a picture vocabulary test. The researchers found that child gesture use at 14 months was a significant predictor of vocabulary size at 42 months, above and beyond the effects of parent and child word use at 14 months. These results held even when background factors such as socioeconomic status were controlled (Rowe, Özçaliskan, & Goldin-Meadow, 2008).

Brain Areas for Logographic and Tonal Languages

Functional magnetic resonance imaging (fMRI) and magnetoencephalography (MEG) studies have shown that native speakers of other languages, such as Chinese and Spanish, also use these same brain regions for language processing. Native Chinese speakers, however, showed additional activation in the right temporal and parietal lobe regions. This may be because Chinese is a logographic language and native speakers may be using the right hemisphere's visual processing areas to assist in processing language interpretation (Pu et al., 2001; Valaki et al., 2004). Additional evidence for this involvement of visual areas in the brain comes from imaging studies of Japanese participants reading both the older form of Japanese logographs (called *kanji*) and the simplified syllabic form (called *hiragana*). Kanji showed more activation than hiragana in the right-hemisphere visual processing areas, while hiragana showed more activation than kanji in the left-hemisphere areas responsible for phonological processing

(Buchweitz, Mason, Hasegawa, & Just, 2009). Another interesting finding among native Chinese speakers was that the brain area processing vowel sounds was separate from the areas processing variations of tone because Chinese is a tonal language (Green, Crinion, & Price, 2007; Liang & van Heuven, 2004).

Role of the Mirror Neuron System

To some degree language acquisition is dependent on imitation. Babies and toddlers listen closely to the sounds in their environment as their brain records those that are present more frequently than others. Eventually the toddler begins to repeat these sounds. Whatever response the toddlers get from adult listeners will affect their decision to repeat, modify, or perhaps discard the sounds they just uttered. This ongoing process of trying specific sounds and evaluating adult reactions is now believed to be orchestrated by the recently discovered *mirror neuron system.*

It seems the old saying "monkey see, monkey do" is truer than we would ever have believed. Scientists using brain imaging technology recently discovered clusters of neurons in the premotor cortex (the area in front of the motor cortex that plans movements) firing just before a person carried out a planned movement. Curiously, these neurons also fired when a person saw someone else perform the same movement. For example, the firing patterns of these neurons that preceded the subject grasping a pencil was identical to the pattern when the subject saw someone else do the same thing. Thus, similar brain areas process both the *production* and *perception* of movement (Fadiga, Craighero, & Olivier, 2005; Iacoboni et al., 2005). Neuroscientists believe these mirror neurons are responsible for helping babies and toddlers imitate the movements, facial expressions, emotions, and sounds of their caregivers. Subsequent studies suggest that the mirror neuron system also helps infants develop the neural networks that link the words they hear to actions of adults they see in their environment (Arbib, 2009).

Gender Differences in Language Processing

One of the earliest and most interesting discoveries neuroscientists made with functional imaging was that there were differences in the way male and female brains process language. Male brains tend to process language in the left hemisphere, while most female brains process language in both hemispheres. Figure 1.3 shows representational fMRIs with the solid white areas indicating areas of the brain that were activated during language processing

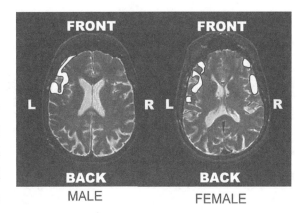

Figure 1.3 These are combined representational fMRIs showing the solid white areas of the male and female brains that were activated during language processing (Clements et al., 2006; Shaywitz et al., 1995).

(Burman, Bitan, & Booth, 2008; Clements et al., 2006; Shaywitz et al., 1995). A study of native Chinese speakers yielded similar findings (Hsiao & Shillcock, 2005).

Another interesting gender difference is the observation that the large bundle of neurons that connects the two hemispheres and allows them to communicate (called the *corpus callosum*) is proportionately larger and thicker in the female than in the male. Assuming function follows form, this difference implies that information travels between the two cerebral hemispheres more efficiently in females than in males. The combination of dual-hemisphere language processing and more efficient between-hemisphere communications may account for why most young girls generally acquire spoken language easier and more quickly than most young boys.

Nonetheless, the gender-difference debate continues. Some researchers suggest that these gender differences are minimal and of little importance as we age (e.g., Sommer, Aleman, Somers, Boks, & Kahn, 2008; Wallentin, 2009). But others maintain that these differences continue to affect the way each gender uses and interacts with language, even as adults (e.g., Guiller & Durndell, 2007; Jaušovec & Jaušovec, 2009).

STRUCTURE OF LANGUAGE

At first glance, the title of this section, "Structure of Language," seems like an impossible task when one considers that there are more than 6,000 distinct languages—not counting dialects—spoken on this planet. Although the structures of these languages vary widely, there are some common elements. Obviously, all spoken language begins with sounds, so we will begin this discussion looking at sound patterns and how they are combined to make words. Our next step is to examine the rules that allow words to be combined into sentences that make sense and communicate information to others.

Many of the examples used will come from English to make it easier for the reader to follow the discussion. However, a few examples from other languages will also be used to explain deviations from English, particularly the Romance languages (these include French, Italian, Portuguese, Romanian, and Spanish). The main task here is to explain how *spoken* language is acquired because for most children, they speak their native tongue at least several years before they face having to learn to *read* it. This is an important point to remember because, although there are many different ways to write language—such as the Roman, Greek, Cyrillic, Arabic, and Hebrew alphabets as well as the logograms of Japanese and Chinese—all beginning language speakers face the same task: making sense of sounds.

> *Despite the many different ways to write language, all beginning language speakers face the same task: making sense of sounds.*

Learning Phonemes

All languages consist of distinct units of sound called *phonemes*. Although each language has its own unique set of phonemes, only about 150 phonemes comprise all the world's languages. These phonemes consist of all the speech sounds that can be made by the human voice apparatus. Phonemes combine to form syllables. For example, in English, the consonant sound "t" and the vowel sound "o" are both phonemes that combine to form the syllable *to-*, as in *tomato.* Although the infant's brain can perceive the entire range of phonemes, only those that are repeated get attention, as the neural networks reacting to the unique sound patterns are continually stimulated and reinforced.

At birth, or some researchers say even before birth (Pocaro et al., 2006), babies respond first to the prosody—the rhythm, cadence, and pitch—of their mothers' voice, not to the words. Around the age of 6 months or so, infants start babbling, an early sign of language acquisition. The production of phonemes by infants is the result of genetically determined neural programs; however, language exposure is environmental. These two components interact to produce an individual's language system and, assuming no abnormal conditions, sufficient competence to communicate clearly with others. Their babbling consists of all those phonemes, even ones they have never heard. Within a few months, however, pruning of the phoneme networks begins, and by about one year of age, the surviving neural networks focus on the sounds of the language being spoken in the infant's environment (Beatty, 2001).

Learning Words and Morphemes

The next step for the brain is to detect words from the stream of sounds it is processing. This is not an easy task because people do not pause between words when speaking. Yet the brain has to recognize differences between, say, *green house* and *greenhouse.* Studies show that parents help this process along by slipping automatically into a different speech pattern when talking to their babies than when speaking to adults. Mothers tend to go into a teaching mode with the vowels elongated and emphasized. They speak to their babies in a higher pitch, with a special intonation, rhythm, and feeling. Researchers refer to this maternal speaking pattern as *motherese,* and suggest that mothers are instinctively attempting to help their babies recognize the sounds of language. Mothers use this pattern in other languages as well, such as Russian, Swedish, and Japanese (Burnham, Kitamura, & Vollmer-Conna, 2002).

Remarkably, babies begin to distinguish word boundaries by the age of 8 months even though they don't know what the words mean (Singh, 2008; Yeung & Werker, 2009). They now begin to acquire new vocabulary words at the rate of about 7 to 10 a day. By the age of 10 to 12 months, the toddler's brain has begun to distinguish and remember phonemes of the native language and to ignore foreign sounds. For example, one study showed that at the age of 6 months, American and

Japanese babies are equally good at discriminating between the "l" and "r" sounds, even though Japanese has no "l" sound. However, by age 10 months, Japanese babies have a tougher time making the distinction, while American babies have become much better at it. During this and subsequent periods of growth, one's ability to distinguish native sounds improves, while the ability to distinguish nonnative speech sounds diminishes (Cheour et al., 1998). Soon, *morphemes,* such as *-s, -ed,* and *-ing,* are added to their speaking vocabulary. At the same time, working memory and Wernicke's area are becoming fully functional so the child can now attach meaning to words. Of course, learning words is one skill; putting them together to make sense is another, more complex skill.

Vocabulary Gaps in Toddlers

In the early years, toddlers acquire most of their vocabulary words from their parents. Consequently, children who experience frequent adult-to-toddler conversations that contain a wide variety of words will build much larger vocabularies than those who experience infrequent conversations that contain fewer words. The incremental effect of this vocabulary difference grows exponentially and can lead to an enormous word gap during the child's first three years.

A particularly significant two-part longitudinal study (Hart & Risley, 2003) documented the vocabulary growth of 42 toddlers from the age of 7 to 9 months until they turned 3 years old. Because parental vocabulary is closely associated with their socioeconomic status (SES), part one of this study looked at toddlers in families from three different groups. On the basis of occupation, 13 of the families were upper SES, 23 were middle-lower SES, and 6 were on welfare. By the time the children were 3 years old, the researchers had recorded and analyzed over 1,300 hours of casual conversations between the children and their parents. To their surprise, the analysis showed a wide gap in the number of words present in the vocabularies of the children based on their SES. Children from the welfare families had an average recorded vocabulary size of just 525 words. Those from the middle-lower SES had 749 words, while the children in the upper SES had average vocabularies of 1,116 words (see Table 1.1). Furthermore, the children from welfare families were adding words to their vocabulary more slowly than the other children throughout the length of the study.

Table 1.1 English Vocabulary Size at Three Years of Age in Various Economic Groups

Socioeconomic Group	Average Number of Words in Vocabulary
Upper	1,116
Middle-Lower	749
Welfare	525

SOURCE: Hart & Risley, 2003

Part two of the study was conducted six years later. The researchers were able to test the language skills of 29 of these children who were then in third grade. Test results showed that the rate of early vocabulary growth was a strong predictor of scores at ages 9 to 10 on tests of vocabulary, listening, speaking, syntax, and semantics. This study points out how important the early years are in developing a child's literacy and how difficult it is to equalize children's preschool experiences with language.

In the United States, early literacy problems can be addressed successfully through the publically funded birth-to-school programs now available in several states. In these programs, school district personnel meet regularly with parents of infants in low SES households and provide them with inexpensive, age-appropriate resources to use with their children during the preschool years. The idea is to build the child's vocabulary and exposure to enriched language before entering school.

As for young children who speak languages other than English, the size of their mental lexicon will also be determined largely by the richness and breadth of the exposure they have had to vocabulary words in their native language. This in turn will have an impact on how well they learn English because their brain will usually attempt to match a new English word with its counterpart stored in the child's native language lexicon. Furthermore, one of the most reliable predictors of how well youngsters will learn to *read* is the size of their mental lexicons (Sousa, 2005).

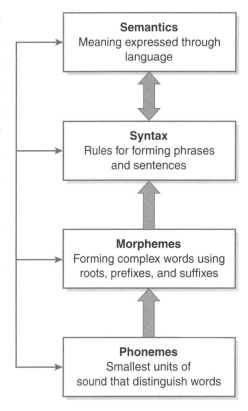

Figure 1.4 The diagram represents the levels of hierarchy in language and in language acquisition. In early language learning, the process usually flows from the bottom to the top, as indicated by the white arrows. But as the learner becomes more fluent in language, recycling from the top to lower levels also occurs, as indicated by the arrows to the left.

Syntax and Semantics

Language Hierarchy

With more exposure to speech, the brain begins to recognize the beginnings of a hierarchy of language (Figure 1.4). Phonemes, the basic sounds, can be combined into morphemes, which are the smallest units of a language that have meaning. Through a set of conventions, morphemes are combined into words. These words may accept prefixes, suffixes, and infixes (insertions), and may undergo a change of consonants or vowels. A part may be repeated as, for example, in Malay where the plural of *orang* ("person") becomes *orang-orang*.

In many languages words are modified for person, number, tense, definiteness (as in English, the difference between *a* and *the*), and mood (e.g., indicative, imperative, subjunctive). Word inflection can be relatively easy, as in Turkish, or it can be a combinational nightmare, as in Russian. Yet some languages, for instance, Chinese, do not inflect words at all because their morphology consists of compounding and a few derivations. Many languages sort verbs into categories, usually "regular" and "irregular." Words can be put together according to the rules of syntax (word order) to form phrases and sentences with meaning. In English, the difference in meaning (semantics) between the sentences "The woman chased the dog" and "The dog chased the woman" results from a different word order, or syntax. Toddlers show evidence of their progression through the syntactic and semantic levels in English when simple statements, such as *Candy,* evolve to more complex ones, *Give me candy.* They also begin to recognize that shifting the words in sentences can change their meaning.

The Syntactic Network

Syntax refers to the rules and conventions that govern the *order* of words in phrases, clauses, and sentences. Each language has its own rules of syntax. This chapter presents a few differences in syntax found among common world languages. Chapter 2 describes how English syntax can pose problems for non-English-speaking individuals who are attempting to learn English.

SVO, SOV, and VSO Strings. One of the rules of sentence word order common to many languages involves the placement of the subject, verb, and object. In some languages, such as English, German, and the Romance languages, the common word order is subject-verb-object—or SVO. An example in English, German, French, and Spanish, respectively: *I see the train, Ich sehe den Zug, Je vois le train,* and *Veo el tren.* Other languages, such as Japanese, use a subject-object-verb order—or SOV (*I the train see*). Actually, until a few centuries ago, English also allowed the SOV sequence in certain formal settings. This can be recognized in archaic expressions that still exist today, such as *With this ring I thee wed* and *Till death do us part.* Still other languages, such as Modern Irish (Gaelic), use the VSO string (*See I the train*).

Some languages, such as Latin and Finnish, avoid the word order problem by adding prefixes and suffixes to verbs and nouns to identify the subject and object. For example, in Latin, the verb forms *amo* (I love), *amas* (you love), and *amat* (he/she loves) use the suffixes *-o, -as, -at* to identify the subject of the sentence. In Finnish, the English word *school* when used as the subject of a sentence is *koulu,* but when used as the object as in *to school,* it becomes *kouluun,* while *in school* becomes *koulussa.*

Adjective-Noun Order. In English and German, the adjective precedes the noun it modifies; in Romance languages, the adjective generally follows the noun. The English phrase *white hat* becomes *weißer Hut* in German, but *chapeau blanc* in French, *cappello bianco* in Italian, and *sombrero blanco* in Spanish. However, there are infrequent occasions when the adjective will be placed before the noun for special emphasis as in French, *Oh, le pauve homme* (Oh, the poor man!).

Subject-Prominent and Topic-Prominent Languages. Some languages, like the Romance languages and English, are subject prominent in that every sentence must have a subject in the initial position, even if the subject plays no role, as in *It is snowing* or *It is possible that the sun will shine today.* Other languages, like Japanese, Mandarin, and Korean, are topic prominent in which the topic holds the initial position and there may or may not be a subject. For example, *It is cold in here* becomes in Mandarin *Here very cold.* In Korean, *The 747 is a big airplane* becomes *Airplanes* (topic) *the 747 is big.* As for Japanese, *Red snapper is my favorite fish* translates to *Fish* (topic) *red snapper favorite it is* (note the SOV string). Topic-prominent languages also downplay the role of the passive voice and avoid "dummy subjects," such as the *It* in *It is snowing.*

Grammatical Gender. Nouns in English are gender neutral, except for the few personal pronouns *he, him, his* and *she, her, hers.* But in languages with grammatical gender, nouns can be masculine, feminine, or neuter. In French, Italian, Portuguese, and Spanish, for example, nouns are either masculine or feminine; German adds neuter as well. Moreover, in the Romance languages, personal pronouns agree in gender with the *noun* they modify, not with the *subject.* In English, however, the personal pronoun agrees with the gender of the subject. English speakers say, *John forgot his pen,* but the French say, *John a oublié sa plume.* The personal pronoun *sa* is feminine because the word for pen, *plume,* is feminine.

The gender of the noun can be different from the gender of the individual the noun describes. In German, a young girl is neuter, *das Mädchen.* In his essay, "That Awful German Language," Mark Twain (1876) observed: ". . . a tree is male, its buds are female, its leaves are neuter; horses are sexless, dogs are male, cats are female—tomcats included, of course." He also noted that foreigners "would rather decline two drinks than one German adjective." Although this may seem bizarre, young children learning German or other gender languages acquire gender marking quickly with few errors. Further, they do not associate the nouns' gender markings with human maleness or femaleness. Their brains just form the needed neural networks in the language processing areas, that then become more robust as the children continue to learn and practice their native tongue.

The Semantic Network

As phonemes combine into morphemes, and morphemes into words, and words into phrases, the mind needs to arrange and compose these pieces into sentences that express what the speaker wants to say. Meanwhile, the listener's language areas must recognize speech sounds from other background noise and interpret the speaker's meaning. This interaction between the components of language and the mind in search of meaning is referred to as *semantics.* Meaning occurs at three different levels of language: the morphology level, the vocabulary level, and the sentence level.

Morphology-Level Semantics. Meaning can come through word parts, or morphology. The word *biggest* has two morphemes, *big* and *-est.* When children can successfully examine the morphology of words, their mental lexicons are greatly enriched. They learn that words with common roots often have common meaning, such as *nation* and *national,* and that prefixes and suffixes alter the meaning of words in certain ways. Morphology also helps children learn and create new words, and can help them spell and pronounce words correctly.

Vocabulary-Level Semantics. A listener who does not understand many of the vocabulary words in a conversation will have trouble comprehending meaning. Of course, the listener may infer meaning based on context, but this is unreliable unless the listener understands most of the vocabulary. Children face this dilemma every day as adults around them use words they do not understand.

Sentence-Level Semantics. The sentence "Boiling cool dreams walk quickly to the goodness" illustrates that morphology and syntax can be preserved even in a sentence that lacks semantics. The words are all correct English words in the proper syntactic sequence, but the sentence does not make sense. Adults recognize this lack of sense immediately. But children often encounter spoken language that does not make sense to them. To understand language, the listener has to detect meaning at several different levels. Because adults do not normally speak sentences that have no meaning, a child's difficulty in finding meaning may result from a sentence having meaning for one person but not another. At this level, too, the listener's background knowledge or experience with the topic being discussed will influence meaning.

The cerebral processes involved in producing and interpreting meaning must occur at incredible speed during the flow of ordinary conversation. How it is that we can access words from our enormous storehouse (the mental lexicon) and interpret the meaning of conversation so quickly? What types of neural networks can allow for such speed and accuracy? Although linguistic researchers differ on the exact nature of these networks, most agree that the mental lexicon is organized according to meaningful relationships between words. Experimental evidence for this notion comes from numerous studies that involve word priming. In these studies, the subjects are presented with pairs of words. The first word is called the prime and the second word is the target. The target can be a real word or a nonword (like *spretz*). A real-word target may or may not be related in meaning to the prime. After being shown the prime, the subject must decide as quickly as possible if the target is a word. The results invariably show that subjects are faster and more accurate in making decisions about target words that are related in meaning to the prime (e.g., *swan–goose*) than to an unrelated prime (e.g., *tulip–goose*). Researchers suspect that the reduced time for identifying related pairs results from these words being physically closer to each other among the neurons that make up the semantic network, and that related words may be stored together in specific cerebral regions (Gazzaniga, Ivry, & Mangun, 2002; Lavigne & Darmon, 2008).

Additional evidence for this idea that the brain stores related words together has come from imaging studies using PET scans. Subjects in PET scanners were asked to name persons, animals, and tools. The results (Figure 1.5) showed that naming items in the same category activated the same area of the brain (Chouinard & Goodale, in press; Damasio, Grabowski, Tranel, Hichwa, & Damasio, 1996). It seems that the brain stores clusters of closely associated words in a tightly packed network so that words *within* the network can activate each other in minimal time. Activating words *between* networks, however, takes longer.

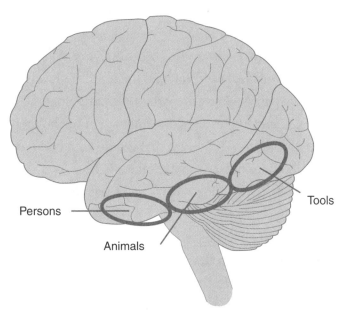

Figure 1.5 This diagram is a representation of the combined PET scan results showing that naming persons, animals, and tools mostly activated different parts of the brain (Chouinard & Goodale, in press; Damasio et al., 1996).

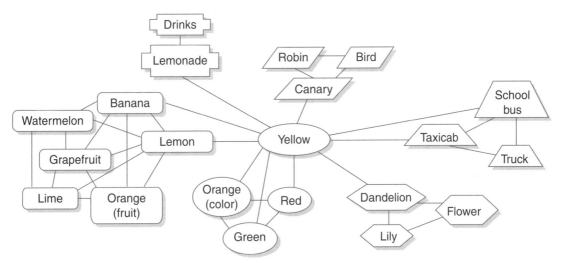

Figure 1.6 This is a representation of a semantic network. Words that are semantically related are closer together in the network, such as *lemon–yellow,* than words that have no close relationship, such as *lemon–bird.* Similar geometric figures identify semantically related words. The lines connect words from different networks that are associated, such as *lemon–yellow.*

How can we best represent these networks? Several different models have been proposed. One that seems to garner substantial support from contemporary neuroscientists is based on an earlier model first proposed by Collins and Loftus (1975) in the mid-1970s. In this model, words that are related are connected to each other. The distance between the connection is determined by the semantic relationship between the words. Figure 1.6 is an example of a semantic network. Note that the word *lemon* is close to—and would have a strong connection to—the word *grapefruit,* but is distant from the word *bird.* If we hear the word *lemon,* then the neural area that represents *lemon* will be activated in the semantic network. Other words in the network such as *lime* and *grapefruit* would also be activated and, therefore, accessed very quickly. The word *bird* would not come to mind.

From Words to Sentences

We have just discussed how the brain acquires, stores, and recognizes words. But to communicate effectively, the words must be arranged in a sequence that makes sense. Languages have developed certain rules—called grammar—that govern the order of words so that speakers of the language can understand each other. In some languages, such as English, different arrangements of words in a sentence can result in the same meaning. *The girl ate the candy* has the same meaning as *The candy was eaten by the girl.* Of course, different word arrangements (syntax) can lead to different meanings, as in *The boat is in the water* and *The water is in the boat.*

As a child's syntactic and semantic networks develop, context plays an important role in determining meaning. When hearing the sentence *The man bought a hot dog at the fair,* the youngster is very likely to picture the man eating a frankfurter rather than a steaming, furry animal that barks. That is because the rest of the sentence establishes a context that is compatible with the first interpretation but not the second.

How does the young brain learn to process the structure of sentences? One prominent model suggests that words in a sentence are assigned syntactic roles and grouped into syntactic phrases (Pinker, 1999). For example, the sentence *The horse eats the hay* consists of a noun phrase (*the horse*), a verb (*eats*), and another noun phrase (*the hay*). A rule of grammar is that a verb (V) can be combined with its direct object to form a verb phrase (VP). In the preceding example, the verb phase would be *eats the hay*. The combination of the noun phrase (NP) and the verb phrase comprises the sentence (S), which can be represented by the syntactic model shown in Figure 1.7.

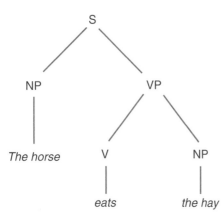

Figure 1.7 This model illustrates how the brain may process sentences to establish meaning. By grouping, or chunking, individual words into phrases, processing time is increased.

As sentences become more complicated, each module can contain another module within it. For example, the sentence *The parent told the principal her son is ill* contains a verb phrase that is also a sentence (*her son is ill*). To ensure rapid processing and accurate comprehension, the brain groups the phrases into the hierarchy as represented by the diagram shown in Figure 1.8.

How Can We Speak So Rapidly?

This module-within-a-module pattern (Figure 1.8) has two major advantages. First, by rearranging and including different phrase packets, the brain can generate and understand an enormous number of sentences without having to memorize every imaginable sentence verbatim. Second, this pattern allows the brain to process syntactic information quickly so that it can meet the demanding comprehension time required for normal conversation. The efficiency of the system is amazing! The young adult brain can determine the meaning of a spoken word in about one-fifth of a second. The brain needs just one-fourth of a second to name an object and about the same amount of time to pronounce it. For readers, the meaning of a printed word is registered in an astounding one-eighth of a second (Pinker, 1999).

Recognizing Meaning

The brain's ability to recognize different meanings in sentence structure is possible because Broca's and Wernicke's areas establish linked networks that can understand the difference between *The dog chased the cat* and *The cat chased the dog*. In an fMRI study, Dapretto and Bookheimer (1999) found that Broca's and Wernicke's areas work together to determine whether changes in syntax or semantics result in changes in meaning. For example, *The policeman arrested the thief* and *The thief was arrested by the policeman* have different syntax but the same meaning. The fMRI

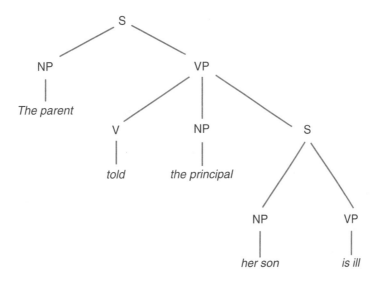

Figure 1.8 This illustrates how the brain proceeds to make additional chunks into phrases to ensure rapid processing and accurate interpretation.

showed that Broca's area was highly activated when subjects were processing these two sentences. Wernicke's area, on the other hand, was more activated when processing sentences that were semantically—but not syntactically—different, such as *The car is in the garage* and *The automobile is in the garage.*

How is it that Wernicke's area can so quickly and accurately decide that two semantically different sentences have the same meaning? The answer may lie in two other recently discovered characteristics of Wernicke's area. One is that the neurons in Wernicke's area are spaced about 20 percent farther apart and are cabled together with longer interconnecting fibers (called *axons*) than the corresponding area in the right hemisphere of the brain (Galuske, Schlote, Bratzke, & Singer, 2000). The implication is that the practice of language during early human development results in longer and more intricately connected neurons in the Wernicke region, allowing for greater sensitivity to meaning.

The second discovery regarding Wernicke's area is its ability to recognize predictable events. An MRI study found that Wernicke's area was activated when subjects were shown differently colored symbols in various patterns, whether the individuals were aware of the pattern sequence or not (Bischoff-Grethe, Proper, Mao, Daniels, & Berns, 2000). This capacity of Wernicke's area to detect predictability suggests that our ability to make sense of language is rooted in our ability to recognize syntax. The researchers noted that language itself is very predicable because it is constrained by the rules of grammar and syntax. And these findings are presumably true for any language.

The Components of Speaking and Understanding Language

Any model for speaking and understanding any language has to address the various stages of sound interpretation, beginning with the auditory input and ending with the formation of a

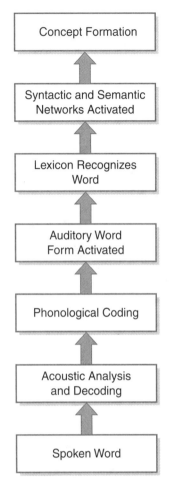

Figure 1.9 This schematic representation shows the major neural components required for spoken language processing. Feedback from higher to lower levels is possible. (Adapted from Gazzaniga et al., 2002.)

mental concept represented by the word or words. Figure 1.9 shows the various neural components that linguistic researchers and neuroscientists believe are required for spoken language comprehension. It is a complex process, but the efficient organization of the linguistic networks that was built up through practice allows it to occur very quickly.

To understand the different components, let's take the word *dog* through the model. After the spoken word *dog* enters the ear canal, the listener has to decode the sound pattern. In the word form area of the brain, acoustic analysis separates the relevant word sounds from background noise, decodes the phonemes of the word (*duh-awh-guh*), and translates them into a phonological code that can be recognized by the mental lexicon. The lexicon selects the best representation it has in store and then activates the syntactic and semantic networks, which work together to form the mental image of a furry animal that barks (concept formation). All this occurs in just a fraction of a second thanks to the extensive network of neural pathways that were established during the early years of speaking and listening.

Notice that the flow of information in this model is from the bottom up and, thus, appears linear. However, feedback from higher to lower levels is possible. For example, if the lexicon does not recognize the first set of signals, it could reactivate the phonological coding component to produce another set before they decay. It is important to understand how this spoken language processing works because the process of *reading* words shares several steps with this model of spoken language processing.

LEVELS OF LANGUAGE COMPREHENSION

Parents speak differently to their children than to other adults. Elementary teachers use different language with their students than with their principal. Speech can be formal, as in the classroom, or informal, as around the dinner table. When young children use informal language, it is often context dependent; that is, the conversation focuses on the immediate situation or activities at hand. On the other hand, formal speech may be more context independent or abstract in that the child may be relating different possible endings to a story. Sometimes people say one thing but really mean something else, and they hope that the listener will catch on to the subtler meaning. These different language forms are a recognition that there are several types and levels of spoken language and of language comprehension.

Explicit Comprehension

The most basic type of language comprehension is explicit comprehension—the sentence is clear and unambiguous. When someone says *I need a haircut,* the interpretation is unmistakable. The listener knows exactly what the speaker means and does not need to draw any inferences or elaborate further. Adults tend to use explicit sentences with children to avoid ambiguity. *Eat your vegetables* and *Please be quiet* are clear statements. Whether the child complies, of course, is another story.

Inferred Comprehension

A more sophisticated form of language comprehension requires the listener to make inferences about meanings that go beyond what the speaker explicitly said. A principal who says to a tardy teacher, *Our school really gets off to a great start in the morning when all the staff is here by 8:15,* is really saying, *Be on time.* The teacher has to infer the statement's real intent by reading between the lines of what the principal explicitly said.

Young children have difficulty with inferred comprehension. If the parent says, *Vegetables are good for you,* the child may not pick up on the underlying intent of this statement—eat your vegetables. Consequently, the child may not finish the vegetables and the parent may mistake this behavior as disobedience when it was really a lack of inferred comprehension.

> *Teachers sometimes use language requiring inferred comprehension when explicit comprehension would be much easier.*

Teachers sometimes use language requiring inferred comprehension when explicit comprehension would be much easier. A teacher who says, for example, *Do you think I should speak if someone else is talking?* may provoke a variety of responses in the minds of the students. One could think absolutely not, while another might hope she would just speak louder than everyone else so the lesson could move along. A few might get the real intent—oh, she wants us to be quiet.

Context Clues. We discussed earlier how context can be an important clue for determining the meaning of vocabulary words in a sentence. Context can also help with inferred comprehension. A first-grade teacher who is telling her spouse over dinner how crowded her classroom is and that there are too many students who need special help may just be seeking sympathy. But in having the same conversation with her principal, she is really saying she needs an instructional aide. She never says that explicitly; the principal must infer the teacher's intent from her statement and the context.

Children need to develop an awareness that language comprehension exists on several levels. It involves different styles of speech that reflect the formality of the conversation, the context in which it occurs, and the explicit as well as underlying intent of the speaker. When children gain a good understanding of these patterns in speech, they will be better able to comprehend what they read.

LEARNING TWO FIRST LANGUAGES

Some young children have the good fortune to be raised in a home where two languages are spoken, so they acquire both simultaneously. They are referred to as simultaneous bilinguals. It is already a wonder that the young brain can learn spoken language so quickly and with little effort. But the fact that it can learn two languages at the same time and in such a manner that the speaker can easily switch from one to the other is truly amazing. The very nature of this fascinating ability has been the object of research interest to neuroscientists seeking answers to questions such as the following:

- Are the brain of bilinguals different from those of monolinguals?
- Are the two languages processed by the same regions of the brain, or does each have its own networks?
- How do the processing areas interact when the person speaking is shifting from one language to the other?
- Can exposing a child to a second language too soon delay the development of the brain networks that are processing the first language?

Here is what studies have found.

Are Monolingual and Bilingual Brains Different?

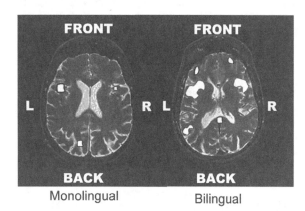

Figure 1.10 This composite fMRI image shows that the brain's language areas in the left hemisphere are activated when both the monolingual and bilingual subjects spoke language. But the bilinguals also activated the region on the right side corresponding to Broca's area when they shifted between two languages. (Adapted from Kovelman et al., 2009.)

Linguists have wondered for decades whether the brains of bilingual individuals are different from monolinguals. In a significant study, Kovelman and her colleagues used imaging technology (fMRI) to examine the brains of 21 young adults, 10 monolinguals who spoke only English and 11 bilinguals who spoke both English and Spanish since birth (Kovelman, Baker, & Petitto, 2008). The researchers found that the brains of bilinguals and monolinguals are similar, and that both process their individual languages in fundamentally similar ways. That is, there was similar increased brain activity across both monolinguals and bilinguals in the brain's classic left-hemisphere language regions, such as Broca's area (see Figure 1.2), when they were speaking in only one language (monolingual mode). However, when the bilinguals were simultaneously processing each of their two languages and rapidly switching between them (bilingual mode), they showed an increase in brain activity in both the left and the right hemisphere, with greater activation in the right hemisphere's equivalent of Broca's area, as shown in Figure 1.10.

The researchers suggest that this finding is a key indicator of the brain's bilingual signature. The results were so promising that Kovelman carried out a similar study using an optical imaging system and got similar results (Kovelman, Shalinsky, Berens, & Petitto, 2008). However, several studies have shown that this right-hemisphere involvement in language processing in bilinguals who learned both languages as toddlers is not found in individuals who learned the second language (L2) at a later time, despite their degree of fluency in the L2 (Hull & Vaid, 2007).

Building the Bilingual Brain

The Kovelman teams (Kovelman, Baker, & Petitto, 2008; Kovelman, Shalinsky et al., 2008) also proposed that bilingual language processing provides a new window into the extent of what an individual's neural architecture for language processing could be, if only we used it. It may be, the researchers continue, that the monolingual is not taking full advantage of the neural landscape for language and cognitive processing that nature has provided us. In other words, we are not born with monolingual, bilingual, or multilingual brains. Rather, the bilingual "signature" that appears is most likely the result of *environmental exposure* to several languages during the child's early years.

> *Exposing young children to other languages helps build the neural networks that will make it easier to learn a third language later in life.*

Another feature of structural differences in the brains of monolinguals and bilinguals is the thick cable of nerves that connects the two hemispheres—the *corpus callosum*—that was discussed earlier. It seems to be larger and more densely populated with neurons in bilinguals than in monolinguals, most likely to accommodate the multilanguage capacity (Coggins, Kennedy, & Armstrong, 2004). The implication here is that exposing very young children to other languages helps build the neural networks that will consolidate and process them. Furthermore, it seems that these networks will make it easier for these individuals to learn a third language later in life (Bloch et al., 2009).

Do the Two Languages Use the Same or Different Brain Regions?

Numerous studies have looked at whether each language is represented by distinct or overlapping cerebral areas. Research using neuroimaging techniques, cortical stimulation, and clinical findings seems to indicate that most bilinguals possess three different types of neural sites:

1. Multiuse sites where both languages perform multiple tasks. These are located in the frontal, temporal, and parietal areas.

2. Single-task sites that carry out one specific task for both languages. These are found in the postcentral and parietal areas.

3. Single-use sites that perform one specific task for one language. There are located in the frontal, temporal, and parietal areas.

These results support the notion that bilinguals have distinct brain regions representing both languages and different language tasks, in addition to overlapping or shared sites that support both languages and multiple tasks (Lucas, McKhann, & Ojemann, 2004; Roux et al., 2004; Serafini, Gururangan, Friedman, & Haglund, 2008). At the very least, these findings should encourage parents and educators to ensure that bilingual students receive continued support in developing both of their languages, thereby strengthening and consolidating the language processing networks.

How Do the Two Languages Interact During Speech?

When a bilingual is speaking in the first language (L1), are elements of the second language (L2) activated as well? If so, how does the bilingual brain deal with it? The answer to the first question is that considerable research evidence exists showing that both languages are active in the brain, even when only one language is spoken (Guo & Peng, 2006; Thierry & Wu, 2007). Answering the second question is a bit more involved. Two different models have emerged to explain the interaction between L1 and L2 when a bilingual is speaking in only one (target) language. In the first group of language-specific selection models, it is thought that both languages may be active but bilinguals develop the ability to selectively focus solely on word candidates in the intended language. In the alternative model, word candidates from both languages compete for selection, requiring that cross-language activity be modulated so that the speaker can select the correct word. In this model, the selection mechanism may require the speaker to inhibit word candidates in the nontarget language. Researchers have conducted a number of studies seeking behavioral and neuroimaging data to support one model or the other. As of this writing, the research evidence seems to favor the inhibiting model (Kroll, Bobb, Misra, & Guo, 2008; Rodriguez-Fornells et al., 2005; van Heuven, Schriefers, Dijkstra, & Hagoort, 2008).

Figure 1.11 illustrates how the inhibiting model is thought to work. Assume that a Spanish-English bilingual speaker has the image of a chair in mind. Instantly, vocabulary words for the object in both Spanish and English are activated in the mental lexicons and ready to be spoken. But because the speaker is using English (target language), the Spanish (nontarget language) word candidates of *silla* and *asiento* (and any others that the speaker may know) must be inhibited so that the speaker can select from the English candidates, *chair* and *seat*. In this example, the speaker chooses *chair.*

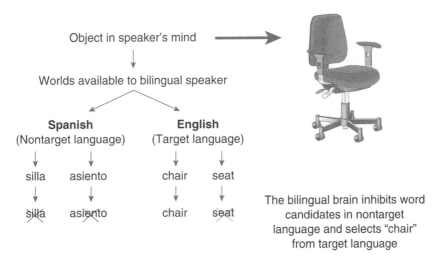

Illustraton of Bilingual Inhibiting Model

Object in speaker's mind

Worlds available to bilingual speaker

Spanish
(Nontarget language)

English
(Target language)

silla   asiento   chair   seat

silla   asiento   chair   seat

The bilingual brain inhibits word
candidates in nontarget
language and selects "chair"
from target language

Figure 1.11 In this example, the Spanish-English bilingual speaker, who is using English (target language) on this occasion, must inhibit the two Spanish word candidates and select from the English candidates—the selection here being *chair.*

Despite the time and neural effort involved in the inhibiting mechanism, bilinguals rarely make random errors of language when they speak. This is surprising if we assume that candidate words in both languages are simultaneously available and in competition for selection. Some researchers suggest that as a result of their exposure to two languages simultaneously, bilinguals possess a formidable mechanism of cognitive control that develops as they become more competent in the L1 and the L2. If so, that capability should generally enhance other executive control processes that are already evident in bilingual infants (Kovács & Mehler, 2009) and continue as the individual ages (Abutalebi & Green, 2007; Bialystok, Craik, Klein, & Viswanathan, 2004).

Can Learning the Second Language Too Soon Delay the First Language?

We have already seen that the infant human brain can begin to develop cerebral regions that manage the acquisition of more than one language simultaneously. We have also noted that some of these regions do not appear in the monolingual brain, giving the bilingual toddler distinct advantages for current and future language processing. As long as both languages are learned simultaneously from or soon after birth, the brain seems able to acquire them with little or no impact on the development of either language. However, if the second language is acquired around the age of 5 years or later, then problems may arise, as we shall discuss in Chapter 2.

WHAT'S COMING

The child's brain has now acquired the fundamentals of its native language(s). Neural networks are developing rapidly in Broca's and Wernicke's areas, and every day brings new vocabulary and understanding to the expanding mental lexicon. How will these acquired native language skills and knowledge help the child accomplish the next major cognitive task: learning another language later? All the steps the brain must go through to progress from the native language to another language at a later age—in this case, English—are unveiled in the next chapter.

CHAPTER 1

Key Points to Ponder

Jot down on this page key points, ideas, strategies, and resources you want to consider later. This sheet is your personal journal summary and will help to jog your memory.

_____

_____

_____

_____

_____

_____

_____

_____

_____

_____

_____

_____

_____

_____

_____

Chapter 2

Learning a New Language (English) Later

L et's make clear at the outset that we are not discussing here the process of learning two languages *simultaneously*. That was already presented in Chapter 1. Rather, our task now is to explore the cognitive, emotional, and social changes that occur when learning a second language—in this case, English—at a later time, say, after the age of 5 years. Regardless of the age of the learners, acquiring a second language later on still involves the language regions of the brain used by the first language, namely, Broca's and Wernicke's areas. And, likewise, most L2 processing is done in the left hemisphere (Newman-Norlund, Frey, Petitto, & Grafton, 2006).

THE CHALLENGE OF ACQUIRING A NEW LANGUAGE LATER

Teachers of students who are English language learners should have a deep understanding of the mental demands these students face. Acquiring a new language later can definitely be a challenge.

> Most researchers agree that acquiring language within the language-specific areas of the brain diminishes during the middle years of adolescence.

One of the major factors determining just how difficult this challenge will be seems to be the age of the learner. How long the brain retains its responsiveness to the sounds of language is still open to question. However, there does seem to be general agreement among researchers that the window of opportunity for acquiring language within the language-specific areas of the brain diminishes during the middle years of adolescence. Obviously, one can still acquire a new language after this period, but it takes more effort because learning the L2 recruits brain regions not generally involved in native language acquisition (Midgley, Holcomb, & Grainger, 2009). Furthermore, PET scans show that when children grow up learning two languages, all language activity is found in the same areas of the brain. But those who learn a second language at a later age show that the two language areas are spatially separated (Bloch et al., 2009; Hernandez & Li, 2007).

Further evidence of the drop-off in English language acquisition as a child ages is seen in a study of the parents of ELLs (Bleakley & Chin, 2008). The researchers looked at how well the parents from non-English-speaking countries learned English as compared to the age they arrived in the United States. They found that parents who had arrived between 1 to 5 years of age were able to reach a higher level of English proficiency than those who arrived at a later age. Proficiency dropped somewhat at 6 years of age, but significantly at 9 years of age.

Why should there be a decrease in language learning ability at all? Plausible explanations include the decline in the metabolic rate and in the number of new connections between brain cells that occurs around puberty. Also, the child's brain has much more plasticity. Even children whose left hemisphere of the brain is severely damaged or removed can still learn or recover language. But such damage in an adult usually results in some degree of permanent aphasia (Crosson et al., 2007).

Evolutionary biologists would add another possible explanation. The genetic predisposition for learning language was probably coded in primitive humans so that it became a one-shot skill. Once a youngster acquired the necessary particulars of the local language from surrounding adults, there was no further need to develop language ability, except for acquiring vocabulary. Furthermore, primitive humans stayed with their tribe so there was little exposure and no incentive to learn the language of their neighbors (Pinker, 1994).

Not all researchers agree that there is a critical or sensitive period in the early years for learning language or that the ability to acquire a second language becomes more difficult with age. For example, one study showed that older learners were more nativelike in their L2 pronunciation than younger learners (Abu-Rabia & Kehat, 2004). A few others have shown no age effects for later learners of L2 (e.g., Hirsh, Morrison, Gaset, & Carnicer, 2003; Trofimovich & Baker, 2006). These inconsistencies, however, may not mean that a sensitive period does not exist. Rather, they may indicate that some other mechanism is involved that explains the variations that researchers find when examining the degree of ease or difficulty in acquiring a second language. One likely explanation may well be the effects of the first language's presence.

Impact of the First Language on Acquiring the Second Language

As we discussed in Chapter 1, all languages are composed of phonemes, morphemes, syntax, and semantics. Differences between languages are the result of differences among these components. Remember that the second-language learner already has a well-established vocabulary and a fully operational set of grammar rules for the first language. So the challenge is to determine the degree to which the language components of the learner's first language (L1) correspond to the components of the target language (L2). The learner needs to find out the answers to questions such as the following:

- How are words put together in the L2?
- What are the rules governing syntax and how are they different from those in the L1?
- Which grammatical forms are optional and which are obligatory, and what makes them obligatory?

The Influence of Transfer

This tendency of the learner's brain to compare aspects of L2 to what it has already learned about L1 represents the cognitive operation known as transfer. The process goes something like this: Whenever we are learning something new, long-term memory searches our brain's long-term storage sites for any past learnings that are similar to, or associated with, the new learning. If the experiences exist, the memory networks are activated and the associated memories are reconsolidated in working memory (Sousa, 2006). In other words, we depend on our past learnings to associate with, make sense of, and treat new information. This recycling of past information into the flow not only reinforces and provides additional rehearsal for already-stored information but also aids in assigning meaning to new information. The degree of meaning attributed to new learning will determine the connections that are made between it and other information in long-term storage.

In the context of learning a second language, the transfer process is attempting to determine how the essential language components of L2 are consistent with, or different from, those of the individual's L1. Transfer can occur in two ways (see Figure 2.1).

Positive Transfer. When past learning *helps* the learner deal with and acquire new learning, it is called *positive transfer.*

Negative Transfer. Sometimes past learning *interferes* with the learner's understanding of new learning, resulting in confusion or errors. This process is called *negative transfer.*

Transfer is an important factor in language learning at all levels and is probably a major contributor to what linguists call the "Interaction Hypothesis." This holds that L1 and L2 will exert

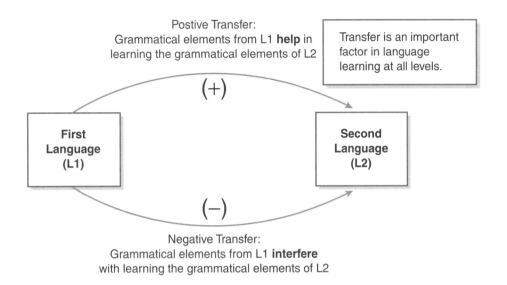

Figure 2.1   The diagram illustrates the impact of transfer on new learning. If the learner is acquiring the second language in the primary grades and later, then the firmly established elements of L1 can either help or interfere with the acquisition of L2, or both. The effect of negative transfer is greatly reduced when the child is of preschool age because the grammatical networks are still plastic and not yet firmly consolidated.

influences on each other when the L2 is acquired at a later age. Typically learners begin by transferring sounds (phonetic transfer) and meanings (semantic transfer), as well as various rules including word order and sentence structure. As learners progress and gain more experience with the target language, the role of transfer typically diminishes. Thus, language transfer can be considered as the initial state of second-language acquisition rather than its developmental stage.

Teachers of Romance languages to native English speakers are frequently helped by positive transfer and plagued by negative transfer. Words like *rouge* in French and *mucho* in Spanish help to teach *red* and *much,* respectively, but when students see the French word *librairie* and are told it is a place where books are found, experience (i.e., transfer) prompts them to think that it means "library." It really means "bookstore." (The French word for library is *bibliothèque.*) Never underestimate the power of transfer. Past learning *always* influences the acquisition of new learning. Thus, the grammatical networks of the learner's L1 will always influence—positively and negatively—the acquisition of the grammatical networks of L2.

> *Never underestimate the power of transfer. Past learning (L1) always influences the acquisition of new learning (L2).*

Of course, the degree to which positive and negative transfer affect the acquisition of L2 depends largely on how closely the grammatical components of the two languages align. A native

Italian speaker, for example, will most likely find it easier to learn Spanish than Finnish. Italian and Spanish are both Romance languages that contain many vocabulary words with the same roots as well as similar morphology and rules of syntax. Finnish, on the other hand, is related to Hungarian. Both are from the Uralic language group (originating from the Ural mountains area) whose grammar contains many declensions, cases, and vocabulary not found in the Romance languages.

The effects of negative transfer are greatly reduced if the learner is acquiring the L2 at a very early (preschool) age. That is because the grammatical networks are still very plastic, not yet firmly consolidated, and open to new linguistic structures. As time goes on, however, these networks become more established and the opportunities for negative transfer increase. This explains why it takes more effort and motivation for a middle-aged adult to learn a new language. All the grammatical rules of the adult's native language have been practiced so often that these neural networks are robust and resistant—but not impervious—to change.

As for positive transfer, research evidence suggests that whenever second-language acquirers encounter a grammatical element of L2, they quickly search for any similarity to the elements they have learned about L1 (Lardiere, 2009). If they find close similarities (e.g., Italian to Spanish), then the lexical networks for L2 can be more easily established in the brain than if there were no similarities (e.g., Italian to Finnish).

Some researchers in second language acquisition suggest that transfer helps determine how much the learner has to examine and reassemble the grammatical features of L2 in order to learn them. Slabakova (2009), for example, uses a "line of difficulty" to illustrate how much mental effort the learner has to expend when comparing similar grammatical features of L1 to L2. Think of a continuum with "easier to acquire" at one end and "harder to acquire" at the other. Here are three possible scenarios:

- If the learner can match L1 morphemes to L2 morphemes with no mental reassembly, then such an L2 would be easier to acquire, as in, perhaps, Italian to Spanish. That would place this scenario at the "easier to acquire" end of the continuum. An example would be the Italian and Spanish words for *unforgivable: im-per-don-a-bi-le* (Italian) to *im-per-don-ab-le* (Spanish).

- A situation where the learner can match L1 morphemes to L2 morphemes with some mental reassembly would, naturally, be somewhat harder to acquire, as, say, German to Dutch. This situation would be located near the center of the continuum. An example would be the German and Dutch words for *unforgivable: un-ver-zeih-lich* (German) to *on-ver-geef-lijk* (Dutch).

- But when the learner cannot make an L1 to L2 morpheme-to-morpheme comparison, even with mental reassembly, then comprehension comes mainly from matching the L1 *context* to the L2 morpheme, making it a much more difficult language to acquire as in English to Finnish. This situation would be placed at the "harder to acquire" end of the continuum. An example would be the words *un-for-giv-able* (English) to *an-teek-si-an-tam-aton* (Finnish).

Age and the Second Language's Phonology

One measure of how well an individual is acquiring a second language is the sensitivity the learner has to those sound patterns (phonology) in the L2 not found in the L1. That sensitivity is generally revealed not so much by pronunciation but by the learner's ability to distinguish those new patterns when listening to the L2. Because of transfer, the L1 and L2 always influence each other to some degree in all learners (Baker & Trofimovich, 2005). However, the nature of the L1–L2 interaction changes depending on the state of development of the L1 phonetic system at the time L2 learning begins. Long-term memory representations for vowels and consonants of the L1 develop slowly through childhood and into adolescence (Hazan & Barrett, 2000). Over time, the L1 categories become robust with practice. As a result, L2 vowels and consonants are increasingly likely to be treated as variations of an L1 category as the L1 phonetic system develops, even when L1–L2 differences can be detected auditorily.

Numerous studies of adults have shown that the L1 indeed exerts a powerful influence on their ability to learn L2 sounds (Baker, Trofimovich, Flege, Mack, & Halter, 2008). Consequently, the adult variations from native L2 speech and sound detection are often traceable to their L1 (Flege, Bohn, & Jang, 1997). With children, however, the influence of the L1 on their ability to learn L2 sounds is not so evident. They seem more likely than adults to overcome the influences of the L1 and to approximate more closely native L2 speakers in speech production and sound perception. It seems, then, that the differences in L2 phonological learning observed between children and adults depend on how much the L1 and L2 interact. The degree of interaction is weaker in younger learners and is more pronounced in older ones. In other words, the extent to which the L1 and the L2 phonetic systems interact in learners is a result of prior learning itself, or transfer, which we discussed earlier.

Impact of Acquiring the Second Language on the First Language

We observed in Chapter 1 the benefits of learning two languages simultaneously from birth. But what happens if a person acquires the second language after the age of 5 when the cerebral networks for the L1 are already getting established? Does the L2 have any impact on the development of the L1 as the child grows older? Studies looking at the impact of later learning of an L2 reveal, not surprisingly, that the impact of acquiring the L2 on the development of L1 depends on the age of the learner and environmental factors. Several different scenarios have been studied.

Incomplete or Interrupted Acquisition of L1. This scenario refers to bilinguals who never fully acquired one of the languages they were exposed to as children. They are either simultaneous bilinguals or early child L2 learners who were exposed to the second or majority language early in childhood (preschool or early school years), and this language later becomes dominant. Exposure to, or use of, the L1was either interrupted or significantly reduced. In the United States, for instance, these would typically be second- and third-generation immigrants. Because bilingual school-age children are very vulnerable to abrupt shifts in their dominant language (Kohnert, Bates, & Hernández, 1999), the lack of use of L1 may result in some loss of its language features and fluency, with the L1 processing networks finally stabilizing in an incomplete state as the acquisition of L2 progresses.

> *Young children lose more of their first language than older children after moving to a new environment.*

Other studies' findings confirm that immigrant children tend to give up their L1 more quickly and completely than adult immigrants, and young children lose more L1 than older children after moving to a different language environment (Anderson, 2001). Such a dramatic decline of the L1 in young children may be related to the incomplete acquisition of the L1 or a still incomplete identification with the L1 culture. Researchers have also noted that many immigrant children avoid the L1 and express a desire to assimilate, sometimes under pressure from their peers and teachers (Ecke, 2004).

L2 Acquisition as a Postadolescent. These are first-generation immigrants whose L1 is firmly in place, who learn the L2 in their postadolescent years, and who live almost exclusively in an L2 environment. They begin to forget aspects of their L1 as time goes on and they improve speaking fluency in the L2. However, their forgetting is not because the L1 linguistic components have disappeared from the mind, which is highly unlikely given the early age they acquired it. Rather, the forgetting here equals reduced L1 access and retrieval due to the low levels of activation and weakening neuronal connections for L1 items stored in long-term memory. This first language attrition, then, is not a sweeping disintegration of the L1 components, but more of a decline in its usage and retrievability as the individual gains knowledge of the competing L2 (Opitz, 2004).

The apparent decrease in accessability to the L1 can be quite dramatic for some individuals. For instance, studies of adults who had been adopted from Korea to France as monolingual Korean children between the ages of 3 and 8 years appeared unable to access their childhood language memory. They could neither discriminate among certain Korean speech sounds nor identify Korean sentences from a series of sentences in unfamiliar languages. Instead, they performed just like native French speakers who were never exposed to Korean. More surprisingly, the fMRI brain activation patterns of the adoptees revealed no signs of recognition of Korean. That is, their imaging patterns did not differ while listening to Korean versus a completely unfamiliar language, and their patterns for French versus Korean looked just like those of native French speakers (Pallier et al., 2003; Ventureyra, Pallier, & Yoo, 2004). Dramatic and rapid first-language loss has also been documented in other studies of international adoption. It may be that their first language was so closely associated with traumatic and unpleasant memories of their birthplace that they blocked the networks that would access the L1.

There are also many examples of recovery of the L1. For example, adult learners of Spanish who had overheard Spanish regularly only before the age of 7 years spoke it with a more native-like accent than those without such experience. This advantage was evident by acoustical analyses and by rating the native-speaker accent (Au, Knightly, Jun, & Oh, 2002). Adult relearners of Korean who had spoken Korean regularly only as young children had a similar advantage over adult novice learners for both production and perception of Korean speech sounds (Oh et al., 2003). It seems that speaking a language regularly for several years during early childhood has a lasting and measurable benefit for retaining both grammar and phonology of the L1 for future use.

LEARNING ENGLISH IS NOT EASY

I am so glad that I never had to learn English as a second language. It is a rich and versatile language, yet those very characteristics make it difficult for a nonnative speaker to learn all the grammar and pronunciation exceptions, not to mention the idioms and slang. Sure, all languages have these anomalies, but English is exceptional in that it has absorbed words from so many *other* languages. Knowing a little about the evolution of English helps us understand why this fertile language can be so difficult for a nonnative speaker to learn.

A Brief History of English

Over the course of history languages continually infiltrate each other as words are spread by conquest, empire, trade, religion, and in modern times through technology. As we shall see, the evolution of Old English into Modern English was mostly the result of conquest. English is a West Germanic language (along with Dutch, German, Flemish, and the Scandinavian group) with its roots in northern Germany, close to what is now the Netherlands. This land was inhabited by the Angles, the Saxons, the Frisians, and the Jutes. When the Roman Empire collapsed in the middle of the fifth century, these tribes invaded what was to become England (Angle-land), displacing the Celts to Scotland and Ireland. Old English was a mix of diverse dialects, but Late Saxon emerged as the dominant one. This dialect was influenced by two later invasions: the Scandinavians, who colonized England in the eighth and ninth centuries, and then the Norman invasion from France in 1066 (Shay, 2008).

Living with the Scandinavians—who spoke Norse—simplified the Anglo-Saxon grammar, eliminating noun genders and case endings. The later Norman occupation introduced elements of the Romance (Latin-based) languages. For the ensuing 150 years, Norman French became the language of the aristocracy and government supplying English with French words, including many verbs. As a result, English developed into a "borrowing" language of immense flexibility with an enormous and varied vocabulary. Furthermore, introducing the Romance language vocabulary and more restrictive syntax led to the variety of quirks in grammar and pronunciation that still exist today. For instance, single-syllable Anglo-Saxon words such as *send, stop,* and *build* were now joined by the polysyllabic Latin-based words of *transmit, desist,* and *construct.* Thus, Anglo-Saxon evolved into Anglo-Norman and for the next 300 years shifted into what was called Middle English—the language of Geoffrey Chaucer's works.

Early Modern English is generally dated from the mid-15th century to the 1700s. At this time, a sudden and distinct change in pronunciation—known as the Great Vowel Shift—occurred whereby vowels were being pronounced shorter and shorter. English continued to adopt foreign words, especially from Latin and Greek as Christianity spread. The language was further transformed by the increased use of a London-based dialect in government and administration and by the standardizing effect of the printing press.

By the time of William Shakespeare (mid-late 16th century), the language had become clearly recognizable as Modern English. In 1755, Samuel Johnson published the first significant English dictionary. The language continued to evolve and grow, mainly because the Industrial Revolution and subsequent technology created a need for new words. Furthermore, the British Empire at its height covered one-quarter of the Earth's surface, and the English language adopted foreign words from many countries.

Some Considerations of Learning English

Verbal- and Image-Based Words

How quickly a child understands words of another language may be closely related to whether the word can generate a clear mental image. A word like *elephant* generates a picture in the mind's eye and thus can be more easily understood than an abstract word like *justice*. Could it be that the brain maintains two distinct systems to process image-loaded words and abstract words?

To further investigate this point, Swaab and her colleagues used numerous electro-encephalographs (EEGs) to measure the brain's response to concrete and abstract words in a dozen young adults (Swaab, Baynes, & Knight, 2002). EEGs measure changes in brain wave activity, called *event-related potentials* (*ERPs*), when the brain experiences a stimulus. The researchers found that image-loaded words produced more ERPs in the front area (frontal lobe—the part thought to be associated with imagery) while abstract words produced more ERPs in the top central (the parietal lobe) and rear (the occipital lobe) areas. Furthermore, there was little inter-action between these disparate areas when processing any of the words (Figure 2.2). The results support the idea that the brain may hold two separate stores for *semantics* (meaning), one for verbal-based information and the other for image-based information. This discovery has implications for language instruction. Teachers should use concrete images when presenting an abstract concept. For example, teaching the idea of justice could be accompanied by pictures of a judge in robes, the scales of justice, and a courtroom scene.

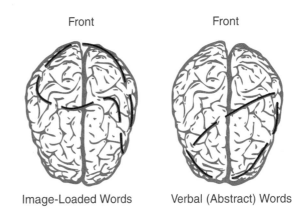

Figure 2.2 The dotted regions represent the areas of highest event-related potentials when subjects processed image-loaded words or verbal (abstract) words (Swaab, et al., 2002).

The Syntactic Network

The rules of syntax in English prohibit the random arrangement of words in a sentence. The simplest sentences follow a sequence common to many languages, that of subject-verb-object (or SVO) format, as in *He hit the ball.* In more complex sentences, syntax imposes a stringent structure on word order to provide clarity and reduce ambiguity. Just look at what happens to meaning when writers neglect to follow the rules of syntax. The following examples are taken from actual headlines that appeared in U.S. newspapers (Cooper, 1987).

> *Teachers should use concrete images when presenting an abstract concept.*

- "Defendant's speech ends in a long sentence"
- "Sisters reunited after 18 years in checkout line at supermarket"
- "Dr. Ruth talks about sex with newspaper editors"

Over time, the child hears more patterns of word combinations, phrase constructions, and variations in the pronunciation of words. Toddlers detect patterns of word order—person, action, object—so they can soon say, *I want cookie*. They also note statistical regularities heard in the flow of the native tongue. They discern that some words describe objects while others describe actions. Other features of grammar emerge, such as tense. By the age of 3, over 90 percent of sentences uttered are grammatically correct because the child has constructed a syntactic network that stores perceived rules of grammar. For example, the child hears variations in the pronunciation of *walk* and *walked, play* and *played,* and *fold* and *folded.* The child isolates the *-ed* and eventually recognizes it as representing the past tense. At that point, the child's syntactic network is modified to include the rule: "add *-ed* to make the past tense." The rule is certainly helpful, but causes errors when the child applies it to some common verbs. Errors are seldom random, but usually result from following perceived rules of grammar such as the add *-ed* rule. If "I *batted* the ball" makes sense, why shouldn't "I *holded* the bat"? After all, if *fold* becomes *folded,* shouldn't *hold* become *holded*? Regrettably, the toddler has yet to learn that over 150 of the most commonly used verbs in English are irregularly conjugated (Pinker, 1999).

Why do these common past tense errors occur in a child's speech and how do they get corrected? Once the add *-ed* rule becomes part of the syntactic network, it operates without conscious thought (Figure 2.3). So when the child wants to use the past tense, the syntactic network automatically adds the *-ed* to *play* and *look* so that the child can say, "I *played* with Susan and we *looked* at some books." If, however, the child says "I *holded* the bat," repeated adult corrections, repetition, and other environmental encounters will inform the syntactic network that the add *-ed* rule is not appropriate in this case and should be blocked, and that a new word *held* should be substituted and added to the child's lexicon. This principle of *blocking* is an important component of accurate language fluency and, eventually, of reading fluency (Post, Marslen-Wilson, Randall, & Tyler, 2008).

> Most common verbs in English and many other languages are irregular.

So how does the child eventually learn the irregular forms of common verbs? Long-term memory plays an important role in helping the child learn the correct past tense forms of irregular verbs. The more frequently the irregular verb is used, the more likely the child will remember it. Take a look at Table 2.1, which shows the 10 most common verbs in English as computed by researchers at Brown University. The verbs are drawn from a million-word database of text used in magazines, newspapers, textbooks, popular books, and other sources (Francis & Kucera, 1982). Note that all of these most common verbs are irregular. Interestingly enough, this tends to be true in many other languages. Pinker (1999) explains that irregular forms have to be repeatedly memorized to survive in a language from generation to generation, otherwise the verbs will be lost. He cites several infrequently used irregular verbs whose past tenses have slipped from common usage: *cleave–clove, stave–stove,* and *chide–chid.*

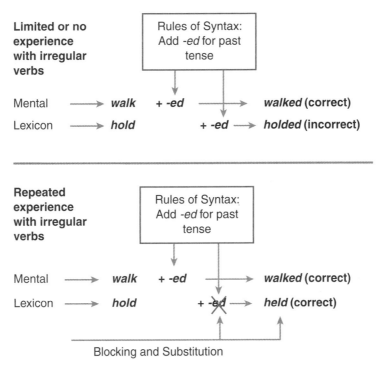

Figure 2.3 The diagrams illustrate how blocking becomes part of the syntactic network. Before a child encounters an irregular verb, the add -ed rule applies. Thus *walk* becomes *walked* and *hold* becomes *holded*. After several instances of adult correction and other environmental exposures (repetition is important to memory), the syntactic network is modified to block the rule for the past tense of *hold* and to substitute *held,* a word that now becomes part of the child's lexicon (Pinker, 1999).

| Table 2.1 Frequency of Common Verbs in English in a Million Words of Text ||
Verb	Number of Occurrences
1. *be*	39,175
2. *have*	12,458
3. *do*	4,367
4. *say*	2,765
5. *make*	2,312
6. *go*	1,844
7. *take*	1,575
8. *come*	1,561
9. *see*	1,513
10. *get*	1,486

SOURCE: Francis & Kucera, 1982

The ability of children to remember corrections to grammatical errors—including blocking—would be impossible without some innate mechanism that is genetically guided. No one knows how much grammar a child learns just by listening, or how much is prewired. What is certain is that the more children are exposed to spoken language in the early years, the more quickly they can discriminate between phonemes, recognize word boundaries, and detect the emerging rules of grammar that result in meaning.

Syntax and English Language Learners. Each language has its own rules of syntax. Consequently, children learning English as an additional language often have problems with English syntax. For example, unlike English, adjectives in Spanish, French, and other similar languages are typically placed *after* the noun they modify. <u>*Blue* sky</u> in French becomes *ciel bleu.* German verbs usually are placed at the end of a clause and rarely follow the subject-verb-object (or SVO) sequence so common in English. For these beginning English language learners, special attention has to be paid to understanding how English rules of syntax differ from those of their native tongue.

> *Beginning English language learners need to understand how English rules of syntax differ from those of their native tongue.*

Syntax refers to the rules and conventions that govern the *order* of words in phrases, clauses, and sentences. Each language has its own rules of syntax. However, languages that evolved from similar linguistic origins often have similar rules of syntax. For example, in the related Romance languages of Italian, French, Spanish, and Portuguese, adjectives usually follow the noun they modify rather than precede it as, for example, in English and German. English speakers say *green house* and the Germans say *grünes Haus,* but the Italians, Spanish, and Portuguese say *casa verde,* and the French say *maison verte.* Thus, when translating a sentence from Spanish to English, word order can be a problem. For example, *el niño rubio tiene nueve años* in Spanish means *the blond boy is nine years old.* But the literal translation is *the boy blond has nine years.* A Spanish-speaking child who mistakenly says *the boy blond* rather than *the blond boy* or *he has nine years* rather than *he is nine years old* would be transferring knowledge of Spanish word order and verb meaning to English. Native speakers of Romance languages will need to remember this noun-adjective inversion when learning English.

> *Native speakers of Romance languages will need to remember the noun-adjective inversion when learning English.*

The rules of syntax are designed to ensure that the speaker conveys the correct meaning. Take the classic example of *Dog bites man* (not newsworthy) and *Man bites dog* (newsworthy). In the first sentence, *dog* is the subject and *man* is the object. In the second sentence, those grammatical roles are reversed. Hence, the word order in many English sentences is critical because it informs us that the biter and the bitten in one sentence are different from those in the other sentence. Of course, English does allow for some flexibility of word order in prepositional phrases with no change in meaning as, for example: *The letter was mailed from Detroit to London by John,* or *The letter was mailed to London from Detroit by John,* or *The letter was mailed by John from Detroit to London.*

In many languages, different prefixes or suffixes—called *cases*—are placed on nouns to identify the subject and object of the sentence, thus making word order less important for meaning. Pinker (1994) uses the Latin version of the dog (*canis*) and man (*homo*) biting story to illustrate this point. The endings of these words change depending on who is biting whom. *Canis hominem mordet* is not newsworthy, but *Homo canem mordet* might raise eyebrows in the local forum. Because the case endings clearly identify the subject and object in each sentence, word order loses its importance. Thus, *Canis hominem mordet* and *Hominem canis mordet* have the same meaning as do *Homo canem mordet* and *Canem homo mordet.* In Latin and other languages with case endings (sometimes called "scrambling" languages), the speaker does not need to pay much attention to word order and is free to move words around for emphasis and know that the interpretation will be the same. Native speakers of these "scrambling" languages will need to pay close attention to word order when learning English.

> *Native speakers of "scrambling" languages will need to pay close attention to word order when learning English.*

Impact of Culture on Learning a New Language

A majority of immigrant students entering the public schools in the United States today come from Spanish-speaking backgrounds, although other significant language groups exist. As discussed earlier, the students' first language (LI) can contribute to the challenges encountered in mastering English. In addition, the relative prestige of the L1 has a clear impact on how the students are being perceived by their peers and teachers. It can be difficult for students to feel proud of their cultures if they suffer from low status in the majority culture, which, in turn, affects the rate of their second language (L2) acquisition (Diaz-Rico, 2000).

Learning a new language also involves learning the culture associated with it. The greater the social distance between the learner's native culture and that of the L2, the more difficulty the learner experiences in acquiring the second language. Obviously, L2 students who are motivated and have a positive attitude toward the target language and culture are more likely to be successful than those whose feelings toward the L2 culture are negative or fearful. It is not difficult to imagine, for example, that an immigrant student from an Arab culture today might feel uncomfortable with the American culture, given the prolonged and continuing American military involvement in Arab and Muslim countries.

Apparently, identifying with the new culture and developing a new identity filled with tension is a conflict that not all L2 learners can resolve (Chiang & Schmida, 2002). To be successful in learning English, English language learners need to be taught not only the language of the culture but also the sociocultural behaviors and beliefs of the school community. Without this knowledge, the second-language learners cannot find their social status in the school context. That, in turn, affects their participation and status as well as opportunities to access more language and interaction. Educators, then, need to pay close attention to the messages that are

> *Educators need to pay attention to their beliefs, values, and status pertaining to the cultures of their ELLs.*

embedded in their schools regarding their beliefs, values, and status pertaining to the cultures of their non-English-speaking students.

Other Considerations for ELLs

There are, of course, other considerations regarding how successfully ELL students will acquire English. Among those considerations, the following four appear often in the research literature (Verdugo & Flores, 2007).

1. Roles of Home and Community

The home and community play an important role in English language acquisition for several reasons. First, as discussed in Chapter 1, children in their early years are collecting and sifting through an enormous amount of data about language. During these formative years, children internalize and examine information that will affect their later written and oral language skills. Consequently, those children who come from literate households—that is, whose parents have been formally educated and where conversation and literacy are practiced on a regular basis—are much more likely to become successful speakers and readers (August & Hakuta, 1997). Second, the level of language proficiency a child develops at home in the native language can have a direct positive relationship to the acquisition of another language because the child has built robust language networks and a rich mental lexicon that can increase the likelihood of positive transfer during L2 acquisition. Thus, the greater the proficiency a child has in the native language, the greater the likelihood of English language acquisition and proficiency.

Another consideration is the way ELLs interact with their home community as they get older. Do they tend to socialize almost exclusively with peers whose native language is the same as theirs?

If so, there will be few if any occasions to practice English. Does the school community afford opportunities for the ELLs to mix in social and nonacademic situations with peers who are native English speakers? These events give ELLs a chance to practice conversational English in a more relaxed environment. Acquiring English as a second language in U.S. schools goes beyond instructional and program considerations and spills over into the area of complex social relationships between native-English-proficient and limited-English-proficient students. Although communities and schools cannot force favorable social interaction between these two groups in question, they can design different and appropriate ways for this to happen.

2. Degree of Language Fluency

How long it takes students to become fluent in the English language is a major and complex issue and, thus, the subject of much controversy. The time it takes to become proficient in English is based on numerous factors: uprooting experience, socioeconomic status, the students' time in the United States (or other English-speaking country), the time they have been in school, and their length of time in a particular language program. For instance, Thomas and Collier (1997) indicated that the number of years of formal schooling in the ELL's home language, including schooling in the home country, is a strong predictor for academic achievement in English. Immigrant students who have had 2 to 3 years of first-language schooling in their home country usually take between 5 and 7 years to perform like typical native English speakers. Similar students with no schooling in their native language take 7 to 10 years to reach the age and grade-level norms of their English-speaking peers.

Given these variables, placing a specific time for students to become English proficient is arbitrary and generally not helpful to students, educators, or schools. Rather, research suggests that educators should assess and evaluate students prior to drawing any conclusions about their English-language proficiency. By identifying the developmental stage of language proficiency among ELLs, educators can tailor instructional strategies to meet their specific language needs.

McLaughlin et al. (1995) have identified the following four stages in this language development process:

Stage 1: The children use their native language.

Stage 2: The nonverbal period during which children attempt to communicate by using nonverbal cues. This is also the stage where children begin to crack the L2 code. Some children will practice their L2 by repeating what they hear others speak, but in a low voice and by playing with sounds.

Stage 3: As the children are now ready to speak in public, their speech can take two forms: telegraphic traits and the use of formulas. In telegraphic traits, speakers use only a few content words without functional words or morphological markers. For instance, children may say *toy,* *here* when they mean *I want my toy over here with me.* In formula speech, children use large bits of words that they hear. These bits of words are used over and over long before the children know their meaning.

Stage 4: In the final stage of this process, children begin to use the new language productively. They use words that they understand and in the proper syntactical form. Children eventually develop productive control over the new language.

Naturally, these stages are not clear-cut, and some children stay in one stage longer than others. Furthermore, there is considerable variability in how children proceed through these stages. Nonetheless, an understanding of these stages is essential for educators of ELL students.

3. Differences Between Academic and Everyday Language

For ELLs to achieve academically in the L2 environment, they must have academic language fluency. Distinguishing between academic and everyday language is important for improving the academic progress of ELL students. Individuals can easily learn basic conversational language skills, but it takes longer to acquire academic language skills. Estimates for developing academic English proficiency range from four to seven years. In this context, *academic English* (sometimes referred to as *content obligatory language*) is described as the ability to use spoken English with such complexity that one's academic performance is not impaired. It includes the technical vocabulary, special expressions, syntactic features, and language constructions that are inherent to the various academic content areas. An important component of this description is the idea that English-language proficiency is not static but is continually changing, depending on grade level and teachers' and educators' expectations. A second significant component is the link between academic fluency and socioeconomic status. The greater the students' socioeconomic status, the more likely they are to master academic English.

4. Isolating Language from Other Needs

Isolating language from other factors that affect academic performance—such as knowledge, ability, and skill—is an important yet difficult task. ELL students should be evaluated on a regular basis to determine if modifications are needed in the content of their programs to meet their language and educational needs. It is not so much the means by which students are evaluated, but rather that English language proficiency is viewed as a continuum, with gradual, individual progress as the major goal. Educators need to plan the time students need to progress so they will eventually be able to function in the school without supports.

Before moving on to how we can teach English to ELLs, it helps to know ways in which we can assess these students' current knowledge of English, or any other language of interest. See the **Resources** section for suggestions regarding instruments that can be considered to assess a student's language competency.

WHAT'S COMING

Learning any language at any age begins by listening to it for some time. After the brain becomes familiar with the new language's phonology, grammar, and syntax, the learner may attempt to speak it. Exactly what teachers of ELLs can do to build listening and speaking skills of English learners is the subject of our next chapter.

CHAPTER 2

Key Points to Ponder

Jot down on this page key points, ideas, strategies, and resources you want to consider later. This sheet is your personal journal summary and will help to jog your memory.

_____

_____

_____

_____

_____

_____

_____

_____

_____

_____

_____

_____

_____

_____

Chapter 3

Teaching English Language Listening and Speaking

SEARCHING FOR THE BEST MODEL

Sorry, but there is no *one* best way to teach the English language to nonnative speakers. Now there are a number of existing instructional models, such as total and partial immersion, bilingual instruction in English and the learner's native language, the whole-language model, and separate skills instruction (based on listening, speaking, reading, and writing). The many programs can be divided into two basic categories: (1) those that focus on developing the students' literacy in two languages, and (2) those that focus on developing the students' literacy solely in English. Table 3.1 shows the types of programs that exist in each of these categories.

But we know that students come with their own unique set of cerebral language networks, mental lexicons, literacy abilities, and culture that will defy any narrow pedagogical approach. Chapter 2 discussed a few of the phonological, morphological, syntactic, and semantic hurdles that an English language learner (ELL) will face during the acquisition process. And we know that the more unlike the student's native language is in phonology and orthography (writing) from those of English, the more difficult the learning process may be. Learning a new language later is a complex process, so teaching that language is complex, too. Thankfully, extensive research in recent years on second-language acquisition has revealed some valuable insights that could make the teaching and learning processes easier and more successful.

A major study of instructional programs for ELLs was carried out by the Center for Research on Education, Diversity, and Excellence (CREDE) and completed in 2006. Its review of the research favored instruction that combines interactive and direct approaches.

Table 3.1 Some Common Types of Language Instruction Programs		
Name	**Goal**	**Main Characteristics**
1. Programs that focus on developing literacy in two languages:		
Two-way immersion or *Two-way bilingual*	Develop high proficiency in both L1 and English	• Includes ELL and English-speaking students. • Instruction in both languages, starting with a smaller portion in English, and gradually moving to half of the instruction in each language.
Developmental bilingual or *Late-exit transitional*	Develop some proficiency in L1 and high proficiency in English	• Content taught in both languages. • Teachers fluent in both languages. • Instruction at lower grades in L1, gradually transitioning to English as students move into classes with English-speaking peers.
Transitional bilingual program or *Early-exit transitional*	Develop English proficiency as soon as possible without delaying learning of academic content	• Instruction begins in L1, but rapidly moves to English. • Students are transitioned into mainstream classrooms with English-speaking peers as soon as possible.
2. Programs that focus on developing literacy solely in English:		
Sheltered English instruction or *Content-based English as a second language (ESL)*	Proficiency in English while learning content in an all-English environment	• Students from various linguistic and cultural backgrounds in same class. • Instruction adapted to students' proficiency in English with visual aids and L1 support as available.
Structured English immersion (SEI)	Develop fluency in English	• Typically, only ELLs in classroom. • All instruction in English, adjusted for students' proficiency level so subject matter is comprehensible. • Teachers have some understanding in students' L1 and use sheltered instructional methods.
Pull-out ESL	Develop fluency in English	• ELLs leave mainstream classroom for part of day for ESL instruction, focusing on grammar, vocabulary skills, and communication, not on academic content.

SOURCE: NCELA, 2005

By interactive, it referred to instruction with ongoing exchanges between learners and teacher, wherein the teacher is actively promoting students' progress by encouraging higher levels of thinking, speaking, and reading at their instructional levels. Examples of interactive teaching include structured discussions, brainstorming, and editing and discussing student or teacher writing. Direct approaches emphasized explicit and direct teaching of skills or information, for example, letter-sound associations, spelling patterns, vocabulary words, or mathematical algorithms. Direct instruction generally uses techniques such as modeling, instructional input, corrective feedback, and guided practice to help students acquire the knowledge and skills as efficiently as possible. The CREDE report notes that it is important for teachers to provide direct instruction of specific skills to help ELLs gain mastery of the literacy-related skills that are often embedded in complex literacy or academic tasks (Genesee et al., 2006).

How Effective Are Immersion Programs?

During the 1970s and 1980s, educators thought that placing ELLs in an English-only program would be the best and fastest way for them to learn to speak and write English. The notion here was that this challenging classroom context would trigger students' survival mechanisms with the result that their brain's language networks would turn most of their attention to processing English. However, studies of the effectiveness of this total English immersion approach for young children were mixed. Educators began to focus on determining what L1-to-English combination of classroom instruction would provide most ELLs with the academic proficiency in English in the shortest amount of time, so they could succeed in school and not fall too far behind their classmates whose first language is English.

Many different variations of immersion programs were developed that increased by different degrees the amount of time devoted to instruction in the ELLs' first language. During this period, hundreds of studies appeared comparing instructional methods and evaluating various programs designed to help ELLs to speak and read English. Researchers attempted to compile these studies to determine if any particular approach was particularly successful. Several large meta-analyses were conducted over a 17-year span (Baker & de Kanter, 1981; Greene, 1998; Rossell & Baker, 1996; Willig, 1985). Their results on which instructional approaches were most effective continued to be mixed. Research studies since 2000 have indicated that instruction through the ELLs' first language is more effective in facilitating their learning to read English (Francis, Lesaux, & August, 2006; Rolstad, Mahoney, & Glass, 2005; Slavin & Cheung, 2005). However, for developing oral proficiency, transitional bilingual and immersion programs appear to be similarly effective (Tong et al., 2008).

Various bilingual and immersion programs have emerged based on competing ideologies, conflicting theories of language development, and political directives, and they carry a confusing array of titles. The two most common program types currently found in the United States, though they are known by numerous names, are *transitional bilingual education* and *structured English immersion.*

Transitional Bilingual Education (TBE) is the most common L1 instructional model in the United States. In the TBE approach, teachers initially provide instruction provided in the ELLs' first language; later, the instruction transitions to English. Once instruction in English begins, the ELL students are expected to achieve basic English language proficiency within two to three years and to be mainstreamed into English-only classrooms (Ovando, Combs, & Collier, 2006). Some TBE programs transition students into English instruction relatively early, sometimes within two years. Others are late-exit bilingual programs and maintain L1 as the language of instruction throughout the elementary grades. In both early-exit and late-exit bilingual programs, all the ELL students share the same minority language background.

Structured English Immersion (SEI) is typically used for all ELL students in a school or district, regardless of their language background. SEI programs dedicate significant amounts of the school day to the explicit teaching of the English language, and students are grouped according to their level of English proficiency. English language is the main content of instruction and academic content is secondary. Teachers and students are expected to speak, read, and write in English and strict timelines are set for students to exit the program.

Students in the SEI model do not necessarily share the same language background. In those states where most ELLs are native Spanish speakers, students with a first language other than Spanish may be enrolled in SEI programs because their parents do not want their children in bilingual programs or because there are not enough students with the same native language to establish a TBE program. In an increasing number of school districts, SEIs are required by voter initiatives or state policies mandating English-only approaches.

Studies of the effectiveness of current immersion programs continue to be mixed, further validating the notion that there is no *one* best way to teach English language acquisition. This is not surprising, given the large number of linguistic, cultural, and social variables involved. However, we know enough about language acquisition to say that there are certain curriculum decisions and instructional strategies that are more likely to be effective than others, regardless of the framework within which they are implemented. Let's explore them.

The Value of Direct Instruction

One question that ELL educators wonder about is whether English language development should be taught to young ELLs as a separate subject at a specific time of day or if it should be integrated throughout the day and taught alongside the regular curriculum. Several reliable studies have examined this question. One study of ELLs in kindergarten found that when a separate block for teaching oral English language development was used, students scored higher on a standardized measure of English oral language (Saunders, Foorman, & Carlson, 2006). Teachers in this time block spent more time on oral English and were more efficient and focused in their use of time. In contrast, when there was no separate block, less time was spent focusing on the English language and more on other language arts activities, such as reading. The findings in this study suggest that the cumulative effect of a separate block of instruction on English language development over many years could be significant.

> *Direct instruction in oral English language is an effective component of ELL programs.*

Other studies also showed similar effects of directly teaching the sounds that make up words (phonemic awareness), how letters represent those sounds (phonics), and how letters combine to form words (morphology). They continue to provide evidence of the benefits of directly teaching phonological and decoding skills to ELLs (Vaughn et al., 2006). Research studies also show that learners can increase their vocabulary size effectively with explicit study of vocabulary. The learning of a particular word through speaking is likely to occur when a carefully developed activity is focused on it. The same is also true with learning vocabulary through listening (Nation, 2001).

Acquiring English as a new language later (i.e., after the age of 5 years) requires the learner first to *listen* carefully to the prosody of the language, that is, its rhythm, cadence, accent patterns, and pitch. After listening to the language, the learner needs to *speak* it so that the speech apparatus can practice its prosody and any phonemes not found in the learner's native language. To *read* English, the learner needs to accurately match its sounds (phonemes) to the letters of the alphabet (graphemes) that represent those sounds, and vice versa. Mastery of the phoneme-to-grapheme skill becomes more evident when the learner can *write* the language correctly. In essence, language consists of these four skills, two for output (speaking and writing) and two for input (listening and reading).

Figure 3.1 shows how these four skills are related. In this chapter, we will look at the spoken skills of listening and speaking. In Chapter 4, we will examine the written skills of reading and writing. Although any instructional approach for helping ELLs acquire English needs to contain components for developing all four skills, some focus mainly on the spoken skills. Programs that do so might consider using some of the following strategies for listening and speaking. Each strategy should be adjusted so that it is appropriate for the learner's age and competency in English.

Figure 3.1 Language skills are related to each other by the direction of the communication (input or output) and by the method of communication (spoken or written).

LISTENING

Chapter 1 explained how the infant's brain carefully processes sounds from the environment, sifting out those that seem random and retaining those that are repeated by the caregivers. Even though the baby probably does not understand the sounds or words, this process continues. The more often sounds are repeated, the greater the likelihood that they will become part of the infant's fledgling lexicon and available for use later when the infant begins to make conscious attempts to communicate. Listening, then, is the very first step to successful language acquisition, regardless of the learner's age.

Parents who are fluent in English, but do not speak it at home, can contribute greatly to building the toddler's mental lexicon in English. Studies have found that when parents read and explained stories in English to their preschoolers at least three times a week, the children had a more sophisticated English vocabulary than those students whose parents did little reading to them (Collins, 2010).

Of course, this is a valuable strategy for preK and primary-grade teachers as well, especially when accompanied later by visual images to explain vocabulary. One study compared traditional and multimedia-enhanced read-aloud vocabulary instruction and investigated whether the effects differed for ELLs and non-ELLs (Silverman & Hines, 2009). The results showed that although there was no added benefit of multimedia-enhanced instruction for the non-ELLs, there was significant improvement for ELLs on a measure of general vocabulary knowledge. Furthermore, for children in the multimedia-enhanced instruction, the gap between non-ELLs and ELLs in knowledge of instructional words was closed, and the gap in general vocabulary knowledge was narrowed. The multimedia support did not have a negative impact on non-ELLs, indicating the potential for using multimedia-enhanced vocabulary instruction for ELLs in inclusive settings. Another study found that concentrating on listening comprehension with a group of ELL kindergartners improved their reading comprehension more than the control group who did not get this extra instruction (Solari, 2007).

We listen considerably more than we speak, read, or write. So listening is a skill to be taught along with strategies to help ELLs become successful. ELLs should be encouraged to listen to native English whenever they can because listening does the following:

- Trains the learner's attention
- Allows the learner's brain to recognize and mentally practice English vocabulary words
- Allows the learner to recognize and practice accented syllables
- Helps the learner hear differences in intonation
- Allows the learner to identify and understand different grammatical constructions
- Helps the learner acquire new words and expressions that are heard frequently
- Gives the learners the confidence to imitate what is heard and to say it aloud

Technology is a real help when looking for authentic materials for use in the classroom; an Internet connection is all that is needed to gain access to many examples of native-English speech. Nevertheless, ELL teachers still need to prepare appropriate activities for working with native English-speakers using audio and video clips that will maximize comprehension and minimize frustration on the part of the learners. Internet materials are just one source of native-English speech, but some studies have shown them to be particularly effective. Verdugo and Belmonte (2007) conducted a study with more than 200 6-year-old native Spanish speakers to determine if Internet-based technology could improve listening comprehension in English. About one-half of the group listened to several dozen digital stories on the Internet while the control group received standard instruction from classroom teachers. After 22 weeks, all the students were tested for listening comprehension and the Internet group significantly outperformed the control group.

Assessing Listening Skills

Because good listening skills are essential for accurate English language acquisition, teachers should regularly assess an ELL's progress in listening comprehension. Teachers can use checklists, rubrics, or anecdotal records to document this progress. Gottlieb (2006) suggests that listening skills can be assessed at the following five levels of language proficiency:

- Level 1: Student matches oral commands to learning strategies represented visually. (e.g., Write a word in the blank.)
- Level 2: Student follows oral directions involving learning strategies that are represented visually. (e.g., Choose the best one out of four possible answers.)
- Level 3: Student practices learning strategies with visual representation from oral directions. (e.g., Answer the easy questions first.)
- Level 4: Student selects and uses learning strategies that are presented orally with familiar material. (e.g., Use a Venn diagram to compare the traits of two characters from the teacher's oral reading.)
- Level 5: Student applies multiple learning strategies to new material through an oral presentation. (e.g., Reenact or dramatize a narrative text that is read aloud.)

There are a number of assessment strategies that teachers can use. Here are just a few possibilities.

Using Audio Clips to Assess Listening Skills

Audiotapes or CDs of conversations in English are handy tools for assessing how well ELLs are developing their listening skills. These media are available commercially or can be made in the school district with native English-speaking students reading the scripts. Videotapes and DVDs can also be used but only after the ELLs have had experience with the audiotapes. The idea is to get them to focus first on the *sounds* of the language and not be distracted by visual images. See **Teaching Tip 3.1** for some suggested questions for assessing the listening skills of ELLs with audio passages.

Using Photographs to Check Understanding

An interesting multimodal method to check for understanding when listening to English is to show the ELL student some photographs. For each photograph, you orally read four descriptions and ask the student to choose the one description that best describes what is pictured. **Teaching Tip 3.2** shows some examples of how to use this strategy.

Metacognitive Component of Developing Listening Skills

Developing the listening skills of ELLs should not be limited to simply listening to audio or watching video passages and completing sentences or answering comprehensive questions. These activities are fine in the beginning to teach ELLs how to focus and attend to the sound patterns of English. But they should not be the *only* instructional strategy that teachers of ELLs employ because they contribute little to helping the ELL *internalize* the language. Once ELLs can comfortably express themselves in basic English, the next step is to help them to *think* about how they are learning English. This is a big cognitive step for ELLs involving metacognition and one that requires considerable planning on the teacher's part. Although metacognition is certainly not a new concept, its application to developing second-language listening skills is recent. Several decades ago, Flavell (1979) noted that metacognition involved three dimensions of declarative knowledge, and they represent the areas that ELLs should develop:

- *Person knowledge:* the way ELLs learn to listen to the L2 (English) as well as the factors that influence one's own listening.
- *Task knowledge:* the nature and the demands of the ELL's listening tasks.
- *Strategy knowledge:* the ELL's effective methods for learning or accomplishing a listening task.

Our current understanding of how the brain constructs meaning—even when acquiring a new language—tells us that learners need to internalize and reflect on the various cognitive components that their brain is processing. ELLs can become better listeners when they also reflect on how well their skills as a listener are progressing. This metacognition allows them to monitor their own thinking about how they listen and solve listening problems.

Research evidence suggests that language learners who are aware of the benefits of listening strategies use these strategies to improve their listening comprehension during communication. ELLs who are aware of their

> *ELL instruction should also focus on developing metacognitive skills.*

own listening problems are motivated to find ways of addressing them (Zhang & Goh, 2006). Studies show that metacognitive strategies also have benefitted young ELLs with weak listening skills (Goh & Yusnita, 2006). When teachers offer instructional opportunities for ELLs to manipulate and think about their new language and their listening skills, they are

- Improving the ELLs' affect in listening (by becoming more confident, more motivated, and less anxious);
- Improving the ELLs' listening performance; and
- Helping weak listeners benefit the most.

Furthermore, the teachers are aiding their ELLs in building robust neural networks for successful English language acquisition. Obviously, metacognitive strategies can be employed at all stages of language acquisition. But because listening is the first skill that must be mastered before an ELL can acquire a new language, it is very important to use metacognitive strategies to develop excellent listening skills.

Types of Metacognitive Activities

There are several different approaches that teachers can use to include metacognitive activities for developing listening skills. Based on recent research studies, Goh (2008) suggests that two types of activities appear effective. One type is called *integrated experiential listening tasks*. These tasks allow ELLs to experience the social-cognitive processes of comprehension while working on specific listening activities. The activities focus mainly on the extraction of information and construction of meaning. Integrating everyday listening activities with metacognitive materials helps learners become aware of the various processes involved in listening carefully to English. At the same time, they learn how to apply this knowledge to their listening development beyond the classroom, whether it be to explore their own self-concept as listeners or to identify factors that affect their own performance during different listening tasks.

Goh refers to the second type of activity as *guided reflections on listening*. The purpose of these activities is to draw out the ELLs' implicit knowledge about listening to English while encouraging them to construct new knowledge as they make sense of their own listening experiences. When ELLs engage in these reflections, they not only think back to events that have taken place, but they also plan ahead in order to manage their own learning.

Both types of metacognitive learning activities are appropriate for encouraging self-appraisal and self-regulation of English language comprehension because they provide explicit guidance on how to listen. To keep the activities fresh and interesting, teachers should use a wide range of learning materials. See **Teaching Tip 3.3** for suggestions on how to use these two types of metacognitive activities.

Learning to listen in a new language is not easy and it can be frustrating. Teachers play an important role in guiding and supporting the ELLs' efforts to achieve success in listening to English. Listening instruction has gone beyond just listening to written texts read aloud slowly and completing comprehension exercises. With the current attention given to teaching and researching L2 listening and our increasing knowledge about human cognition, teachers should consider including metacognitive strategies to improve ELLs' listening skills.

SPEAKING

Speaking a language that is not your native tongue takes courage. I know from experience. In my mid-twenties, I accepted a science teaching position at the American School of Paris. I knew no French. This was not an employment problem because the teaching was in English. However, it became an immediate practical problem when I was plunged into a different culture and unknown language. What seemed at first like a great adventure suddenly turned into an unsettling experience. I had to find an apartment, negotiate rent, and purchase necessities. Buying food was a particular challenge because there were no supermarkets, and pointing got me only so far. I carried an English-French dictionary with me everywhere, but my pronunciation was not accurate. To add to the frustration, the French seemed to have little tolerance for my mumbling and hand signals.

Outside the school, I was a French language learner—an FLL, if you will. I kept my mouth shut (unless absolutely necessary) to avoid embarrassment and aggravation. But I listened very carefully to French conversations, television, radio, and the occasional movie. After about six months, I mustered up enough courage to start speaking French, first with patient teachers at the school and more frequently in shops. What a relief it was when people actually seemed to understand me! And that gave me the motivation to work harder at practicing and improving my spoken French, especially my pronunciation of those phonemes that do not exist in English.

> *ELLs often socialize with other speakers of their native language to avoid the frustration of trying to speak English.*

I can empathize with how ELLs must feel trying to become part of an English-speaking school and community. Granted, I was learning a new language as an adult, so my coping skills were more developed than a child's. Plus, it was my native language that got me through most of the workday. This experience has helped me understand why ELLs often retreat to their homes and socialize mainly with others who speak their native language, thus avoiding the frustration and embarrassment of trying to speak English. Similarly, I met quite a few Americans in Paris who had lived there for years and barely spoke elementary French. By choice, their work and social life centered almost exclusively around English. In a city like Miami, Spanish speakers can carry out all of their daily activities and find entertainment in their native language, so there is little motivation or need to learn English.

Overcoming Reluctance to Speak English

The emotional system of the brain does not handle embarrassment or frustration well. Consequently, we tend to avoid situations that have the potential to embarrass us. Speaking a foreign language in a foreign land is one of those situations. Even fluent speakers of a foreign language can suffer embarrassment by inadvertently using a word that may have suddenly acquired a vulgar or profane connotation.

ELL students may be more withdrawn in middle and high school than in elementary school. They want to move away from just translating and become autonomous with English. The pressure to fit in, especially for adolescents, may make them reluctant to ask questions or participate in class for fear of exposing weaknesses in English fluency. That is why it is imperative for teachers to help ELLs feel safe and supported in the classroom and help them acquire a rich academic vocabulary to complement the basic English vocabulary skills they have learned in order to survive. ELLs need to be encouraged to speak English even if they make mistakes. People learn from their mistakes, so they should think of them as useful and positive.

Some ELLs worry about speaking English with the accent of their native language. An accent is the result of a language's unique sound patterns, including intonation, timing, and stress. Remind them that practice is the key to speaking more like a native English speaker. With practice, L2 language learners can acquire a more nativelike accent. Here is one teaching activity that may help ELLs feel more confident when they speak English.

Tell Me a Story

One activity for assessing ELL students' competency level in speaking English is to ask them to tell you a story. Sit down together and ask the student to talk to you in English for a few minutes about any topic of interest. You should make notes during this time regarding the student's use of English. See **Teaching Tip 3.4** for suggestions on how to use this strategy.

Vocabulary

As we discussed in the previous chapters, the young human brain is prewired to acquire spoken vocabulary, but that predisposition begins to wane around puberty. Of course, that does not mean older ELLs *cannot* acquire vocabulary, but that it will take *more mental effort* to do so. The message here is that the younger the ELLs are when learning vocabulary, the easier it will be. In the primary grades, for example, by the end of second grade, there is a 4,000-word difference in vocabulary size between readers in the upper quartile and those in the lowest quartile of the class, and this gap widens in later school years (Biemiller & Boote, 2006).

Direct instruction of vocabulary is a major benefit for ELLs. Studies of vocabulary instruction also show that ELLs are more likely to learn new words when they are directly taught. Just as with English speakers, ELLs learn more vocabulary when the words are embedded in meaningful contexts and when students are provided with frequent opportunities for their repetition and use, rather than looking up their dictionary definitions or presenting words in single sentences. A study of fifth graders found that explicit vocabulary instruction led to improvements in word learning and reading comprehension (Carlo et al., 2004). The ELLs used words from texts appropriate for and likely to interest them, combined with exposure to and use of the words in numerous contexts, such as reading and hearing stories, discussions, posting target words, and writing words and definitions for homework. Also, a preschool study showed that explaining new vocabulary helped Portuguese-speaking children acquire vocabulary from storybook reading. Although children who knew more English words learned more words, explaining the new words was helpful for all children, regardless of how much English they already knew (Collins, 2005).

An important variable here, of course, is motivation. Older ELLs who are socializing with English-speaking peers are more motivated and will devote the extra effort to acquire English vocabulary, especially idioms and slang. The school can help here by sponsoring and encouraging events that get ELLs to mix with their native English-speaking peers. Remember, too, that the greater the number of English words in the ELL's mental lexicon, the easier it will be to learn to *read* English.

How Much Vocabulary Does the ELL Need to Succeed?

One obvious question to ask at this point is: How much vocabulary does an ELL need to be able to communicate successfully? Linguists usually express this amount as a range of *word families*. A word family includes the root form (*regulate*), its inflections (*regulates, regulating, regulated*), and regular derivations (*regulative, regulation*). The generally accepted range is between 2,000 and 3,000 word families to understand conversational English, and a range of 8,000 to 9,000 word families to read a wide variety of texts without unknown vocabulary becoming a problem (Schmitt, 2008). Students will need guidance about which vocabulary items to learn as well as help in developing effective learning techniques. Teachers are the natural source for this guidance, but their experience may not be sufficient to provide the guidance without help. For example, research studies indicate that the intuitions of native speakers regarding word frequency appear limited to differentiating between very frequent and very infrequent words (McCrostie, 2007). Apparently, even native-speaking teachers cannot always trust their intuition to identify more frequent—and thereby generally more useful—words of English, and so they should consult frequency lists along with their intuitions. These lists should be adapted to the age level and context in which this vocabulary learning is occurring.

Acquiring a vocabulary is not enough, of course. ELLs must also know what the word *means.* Further adding to the difficulty is the fact that English is a strongly contextual language—a word can have many different meanings, depending on context. For example, look up the simple word *run* in an unabridged dictionary and you will find more than 120 definitions! Knowing the word is great; knowing its meaning in the context is which it is used is critical to full understanding.

Can the L1 Help in English Vocabulary Acquisition?

One controversial topic in L2 vocabulary instruction is whether teachers should use the learner's L1 in helping to explain the L2's new word form-to-meaning link. Recent research seems to indicate yes. Here is why. Studies show that the initial form-to-meaning link consists of the new L2 word form being attached to a representation of the corresponding L1 word that already exists in the ELL's long-term memory (Hall, 2002). Consequently, an L1

> *Using the ELL's L1 to explain the meaning of English words is an effective strategy.*

translation is a natural vehicle for achieving this cerebral match, perhaps through using English-to-L1 word cards. Furthermore, we know that learning English word forms can be challenging, so using the L1 to facilitate the English form-to-meaning linkage may allow more of the brain's cognitive resources to be focused on the English form itself (Barcroft, 2002). As soon as the English-L1 link is established, more of the brain's language processing resources will be freed up to focus on learning the more contextualized types of word knowledge.

Because of the cognitive constraints that accompany learning English, it is unlikely that ELLs will absorb much contextualized knowledge at the beginning stages anyway, which suggests that there is little disadvantage to using the ELL's native language to establish initial meaning. After this initial stage, however, the advantages of using the new English word form in different contexts becomes important in order to enhance contextual word knowledge. Thus, the research results imply that using the ELL's L1 may be appropriate at some stages along the vocabulary learning process. This process will be easier if all ELLs in the class have the same L1. However, in a mixed scenario where many L1s are present in the class, the teacher needs to consider the time and logistics required to try this approach.

Some experienced teachers report that it is more efficient and effective to teach grammar rules and basic information in L1 because trying to have students understand this in English is very difficult. Time in the classroom is too limited, they say, to get ELLs to grasp the conjugation of verbs and so on in the target language. Using just English works better after the ELLs have sufficient proficiency to converse comfortably in English. See **Teaching Tip 3.5** for some suggestions for helping ELLs acquire English vocabulary and **Teaching Tip 3.6** for in-depth vocabulary comprehension.

Idioms

Idioms add to the richness of any language, conveying meaning through figurative speech. But they are also difficult to understand because ELLs are still struggling with the *literal* meaning of English words. Take the common idiom, *It's raining cats and dogs.* A native English speaker thinks: *It's raining hard.* But an ELL is thinking: *Rain + cats? + dogs? That doesn't make sense. What can it mean?* The challenge, then, is to help ELLs uncover the hidden meaning of idioms. There are several Internet sites that list hundreds of English idioms and their meaning (see the **Resources** section). See **Teaching Tip 3.7** on how to help ELLs cope with idioms.

Pronunciation

Pronunciation describes the uttering of the sound (phoneme) or sounds of a word. Perhaps the most difficult thing for ELLs to realize is that English is *not* a phonetic language. That is, words are not always pronounced the way they are spelled. (To illustrate this point, one has only to recall George Bernard Shaw's complaint that the word *fish* could also be spelled *ghoti,* and yet still comply with English pronunciation. In *ghoti,* the *gh* is from *tough,* the *o* from *women,* and the *ti* from *nation.* He also suggested that English adopt a more spell-it-like-it-sounds system but, of course, that never happened.)

Table 3.2 Language Sounds of Some Languages	
Language	**Number of Sounds**
French	32
Italian	33
Spanish	35
English	44+

There are about 44 different sounds that make up all the words of English. This reality can pose a problem for ELLs whose native language has fewer sounds. Let us look at some examples. Table 3.2 lists the number of phonemes in English compared to three Romance languages. Subtracting out the phonemes in their native language that do not exist in English, this means that French, Italian, and Spanish speakers will have to learn about 20 or more phonemes in order to pronounce English words similar to a native English speaker. To accomplish this, teachers have to identify these new sounds for the ELLs and provide them with sufficient practice in pronunciation.

An additional challenge is that certain consonants that look alike in both the L1 and English may be pronounced quite differently. For example, the sound of /p/ is aspirated in English as in *Peter Piper picked a peck* . . . but much less aspirated in Spanish and French. The sound of /d/ in English requires the tip of the tongue on the forward palate. However, in Spanish this sound requires the tip of the tongue placed between the upper and lower teeth, similar to the /th/ sound in English. Even vowel sounds in English, which are often diphthongs, are pronounced differently than in the Romance languages.

The good news is that with sufficient practice, ELLs can begin to discriminate the phonemes of English through several different methods. One method is through meaning. For instance, realizing that the words *cold* and *gold* have different meanings may provide the ELL with sufficient information to determine that their initial sounds, /k/ and /g/, are different in English. Another method is for the ELL to simply listen to selected English passages containing the target phoneme pairs during extended sound-training sessions. Listeners were able to infer the different phonemes of a language from the statistical patterns they heard in the input speech. These patterns alone influenced the listeners' ability to discriminate differences in closely related phonemes even without the benefit of word meanings. This feedback method has been particularly successful in helping native Japanese speakers distinguish between the /l/ and /r/ sounds in English (Hayes-Harb, 2007).

Stress on Words and Sentences

Unlike some languages, such as French and Japanese where each syllable is said with equal force, speakers of English put strong force (stress) on some syllables and none on others. The brain's language processing regions use stress to help the listener or speaker make sense of what is being spoken. Variations in word stress can make it difficult for ELLs to understand English, especially if it is spoken quickly. Nonetheless, mastering English stress patterns is a learned language skill that develops by listening and practicing speaking English consistently. Not surprisingly, studies indicate that the more ELLs practice English word stress patterns, the more likely they are to develop this skill (Tremblay, 2009).

Sentence stress is a main contributor to the prosody of English, especially its rhythm. In sentence stress, some words in the sentence are stressed (said louder) while others are weak (said softer). Once again, how well ELLs pick up on English sentence stress will depend on the role that stress has in the pronunciation of their native language. Their brain's language networks have already consolidated that role and the degree it helps in comprehension. Now these networks have to accommodate different patterns of stress that are essential if the ELL is to understand and speak English correctly. This capability to hear and to produce stress patterns is important because how words are stressed in an English sentence can alter its meaning. See **Teaching Tip 3.8** for some strategies to practice word stress and **Teaching Tips 3.9, 3.10,** and **3.11** for practice activities regarding sentence stress.

Intonation

Another component of speech that is related to word stress is *intonation.* Intonation refers to the rise and fall in the pitch of one's voice while speaking. Intonation is present in every language and can be used to mark gender, number, tense or time, and quantity. For instance, the pitch of a native English speaker tends to rise when asking a question and fall when making a statement. Romance languages have similar patterns. Tonal languages, like Chinese and Vietnamese, however, have different patterns of intonation. Consequently, their early attempts at English conversation will have intonation patterns during speech that are quite different from those of a native English speaker. Native Chinese speakers do understand, however, that rising and falling pitches in English speech can change a statement's meaning, even if they cannot translate it into English (Grabe, Rosner, García-Albea, & Zhou, 2003).

Intonation is best taught, preferably in conversation, rather than within isolated sentences (Jenkins, 2004). For example, modeling conversation when being friendly versus angry or assertive versus shy. However, this more subtle aspect of conversational speech should probably be avoided until there has been substantial direct instruction and ELLs' practice on word and sentence stress.

WHAT'S COMING

As the ELLs develop their English listening and speaking skills, they are building the vocabulary store they will need to learn to read in English. Reading is a significant challenge for learners even in their native language. Learning to read a second language can be daunting. What approaches work best with ELLs learning to read English? Should they be allowed to use their native language? Writing is even more of a challenge, especially if the ELL's native writing system uses another alphabet. How does the teacher help the ELL with that problem? The answers to these and other related questions are in the next chapter.

Teaching Tip 3.1: Assessing Listening Skills in English

Listening involves not only understanding the words and phrases that are used in English speech but their meaning as well. Here is one multistep process for assessing how well ELLs are listening and understanding what they hear. You can modify this activity for the age and competency level of the ELL. These audio passages are usually conversations between two or more people using simple English. Passages can be divided into segments that for more advanced ELLs should contain more sophisticated vocabulary. Students are allowed to take notes as they listen to the segment and you can replay the segment as many times as you feel is appropriate.

After listening to the audio segment, select from the following questions:

1. **Understanding the Gist.** This tests the ELL's ability to understand the main idea and purpose of what was contained in the audio segment. These questions are not about specific details but focus on purpose and content.
   * What is the main topic of this selection?
   * What are the speakers mainly discussing?
   * Why does (insert speaker's name) ask the question about (insert topic) . . . ?

2. **Details.** The ELLs can use their notes to answer the detail questions. Encourage them to take down important facts as they listen. Avoid asking questions about minor details.
   * According to (insert speaker's name), what is the problem with . . . ?
   * What does (insert speaker's name) say about . . . ?
   * What caused (insert description) . . . ?

3. **Understanding Attitude.** This requires listening to the sound of the speakers' voices for hints about their attitudes and opinions about the topic.
   * What is (insert speaker's name) impression of . . . ?
   * How does (insert speaker's name) feel about . . . ?
   * What does (insert speaker's name) mean when s/he says . . . (listen again)?

4. **Deep Understanding.** Part of the listening segment can be replayed in these questions.
   * What does (insert speaker's name) imply when s/he says this . . . (listen again)?
   * Why does the speaker mention/discuss (insert topic)?
   * What is the sequence of events in this passage?

You may wish to provide a checklist or chart to help the ELLs answer the questions requiring deeper understanding. See also **Teaching Tip 3.3** on using metacognitive strategies.

Teaching Tip 3.2: Using Photographs
to Check for Understanding in English

The teacher shows the ELLs a photograph and then says aloud four descriptions. The students must select the one that best describes what is pictured. For example:

A. The girl is holding her shoe.

B. The girl is leaning on her bag.

C. It is raining.

D. The girl is wearing short pants.

A. The teacher is writing.

B. The teacher is wearing a hat.

C. There are six people in the picture.

D. The teaching is wearing glasses.

A. There are three people in the picture.

B. The girl on the left is wearing a hat.

C. The girl on the right is smiling.

D. The computer is behind the boy.

Teaching Tip 3.3: Metacognitive
Strategies to Develop Listening Skills

Metacognitive strategies have been shown to develop listening skills even in ELLs in the primary grades. Goh (2008) suggests two types of activities. The integrated tasks on this list focus on extraction of information and construction of meaning.

Integrated Experiential Listening Tasks	
Learning Activity	**Description**
Metacognitive listening sequence	Guide ELLs through a sequence of listening activities that they discuss with peers, followed by a personal evaluation of what they learned.
Self-directed listening	Help ELLs make prelistening preparations, evaluate their performance in order to plan future listening tasks.
Listening buddies	ELLs work in pairs or small groups, selecting resources and identifying strategies for their listening practice.
Peer-designed listening programs	A small group of ELLs design a listening task for the rest of the class, and during that process they: • Identify listening problems, causes, and possible solutions • Discuss factors that influence listening performance • Identify ways they can improve their listening skills outside of school • Differentiate various types of listening skills • Identify strategies that may not be appropriate for their culture
Postlistening perception activities	Provide activities after a listening task that raise the ELLs' awareness of the phonological features of the passage they listened to.

These reflections (Goh, 2008) include sample self-report items (Vandergrift et al., 2006).

Guided Reflections on Listening	
Learning Activity	**Description**
Listening diaries (for ELLs who can write basic English)	Ask questions that cause ELLs to reflect on a listening activity and record their responses as, for example, • Did they have any listening problems, and if so, what are possible solutions? • What listening skill did they use the most: listening for the gist, for details, or to infer information? Why? • Did anything in the passage affect their listening performance? Why?
Anxiety and motivation charts	ELLs draw line or bar diagrams to show changes in their anxiety and motivation levels both in and out of school.
Process-based discussions	These are small-group or whole-class discussions on learning to listen and related matters, such as useful social strategies when speaking with others, ways for using Internet resources to enhance listening skills, and language-related problems that occur when listening.
Self-report checklist	ELLs evaluate their own knowledge and performance using a list of preselected items regarding their metacognitive activities when listening. Sample self-report items could be: • I translated in my head as I listened. • Listening in English is still more difficult than speaking, reading, or writing in English. • Before listening, I thought of similar texts that I have listened to. • As I listened, I adjusted my interpretation when it was not correct. • As I listened, I asked myself if I was satisfied with my level of comprehension. • After I listened, I think back to how I listened and what I would do differently next time.

Teaching Tip 3.4: Tell Me a Story

This activity helps you assess the ELL student's level of competency in speaking English.

- Sitting down together, you ask the student to talk to you in English about any topic of interest.
- Topics can include a recent vacation, a hobby, a movie, sports event, or a book.
- During the student's description, you should make notes of specific speaking errors, using a format that will help you select future instructional strategies for correcting the speaking errors.
- Avoid interrupting the description, so as not to break the flow or intimidate the student.
- Here is one possible format:

Student's Name:	Topic:	
Skill	**Degree of Competency**	**Follow-Up Help**
Vocabulary:	Did the student use the correct words to convey meaning? How many incorrect words were used?	
Pronunciation:	How understandable was the student's pronunciation? Did the student make specific pronunciation errors that need to be corrected?	
Stress:	Did the student stress the appropriate words while speaking? Were there specific stress patterns that need to be corrected?	
(Other)		
(Other)		

- After the story, point out errors and discuss ways to improve speaking in English.
- Develop a follow-up program to help the student increase competency in those areas of need that are identified above.

Teaching Tip 3.5: Acquiring English Vocabulary

Here are some suggestions for helping ELLs acquire English vocabulary (Swanson & Howerton, 2007).

- Remember that ELL students can engage in conversational English long before they can function with academic proficiency. Peer-appropriate language skills develop in about two years, but academic proficiency takes much longer.
- Provide opportunities for students to say new words. Consider using choral reading in Grades 1 through 6 to provide good models of academic English. In the upper grades, repeated readings of passages containing new words provide opportunities for additional practice in pronunciation and in grasping meaning from context.
- Use key words and pictures to help ELLs make connections between the sound of the word and its meaning. This works particularly well with nouns that are easily matched with pictures. You can present both examples and nonexamples of the word to enhance understanding and meaning.
- Try to match common sounds in English that correspond to the ELL's first language. English has deep orthography, which means that irregular letter-to-sound correspondences are common. On the other hand, Spanish contains more regular letter-to-sound correspondences. Therefore, initially select vocabulary words that are easy for ELLs to pronounce correctly in English. For example, the following consonant sounds exist in both languages: *p, t, b, k, d, g, m, n, f, s, w, y, ch, l*. However, the following English consonant blends do not appear in Spanish: *st, sp, sk, sm, sl, sn, sw, tw, qu, scr, spl, spr, str, squ* (Helman, 2004).
- Encourage students to use new vocabulary words in different settings outside of class. Consider challenging students to find the ways in which new vocabulary words are used outside of school and ask them to report their discoveries during class.
- Use cognates to help students see the connections between their language and English through roots, prefixes, and suffixes. Many words in the Romance languages have roots similar to the same word in English. These comparisons also help students move from known words to acquiring new ones. See the chart on the next page for some common English/Spanish cognates.
- Expose students to words that will be useful for understanding content in other academic areas.
- Ensure that you have a safe environment where vocabulary can be practiced free of criticism from others.
- Teach comprehension monitoring skills so that students recognize when they do not understand and are able to ask for help.
- When working on conversation skills, ask students what words they would like to learn in English. This generates interest that motivates the students to increase their vocabulary.

Some Common English/Spanish Cognates		
English and Spanish nouns ending in *-or* are often identical.	actor color doctor	actor color doctor
English and Spanish nouns ending in *-al* are often identical in meaning.	animal general hospital	animal general hospital
Many English nouns ending in *-ist* exist as Spanish nouns ending in *-ista*.	artist socialist tourist	artista socialista tourista
Many English nouns ending in *-ism* exist as Spanish nouns ending in *-ismo*.	idealism organism optimism	idealismo organismo optimismo
Many English nouns ending in *-tion* exist as Spanish nouns ending in *-ción*.	association combination instruction	asociación combinación instrucción
English and Spanish adjectives ending in *-ble* are often identical in meaning.	favorable impossible terrible	favorable imposible terrible
Many English adjectives ending in *-ous* exist as Spanish adjectives ending in *-oso*.	ambitious delicious generous	ambicioso delicioso generoso
Most English verbs ending in *-ate* exist as Spanish verb infinitives ending in *-ar*.	associate demonstrate participate	asociar demostrar participar
Many English verbs ending in a vowel + consonant + *t* exist as Spanish infinitive verbs ending in *-ar* or *-ir*.	import present insist	importar presentar insistir
Many English adverbs ending in *-ly* exist as Spanish adverbs ending in *-mente*.	correctly exactly finally	correctamente exactemente finalmente

Teaching Tip 3.6: In-Depth
Vocabulary Comprehension and Use

When learning a new vocabulary word, the form-to-meaning link is very important and usually sufficient for beginning conversation. But for reading and writing, ELLs will eventually need to know other forms of the word, their meaning, and how to use them correctly to communicate. This range of word knowledge can be described as follows (Nation, 2001):

Forms of the word:

- What does the word sound like?
- How do we pronounce the word?
- What does the word look like?
- How do we write and spell the word?
- What word parts are needed to express this meaning?

Meanings of the word:

- What meaning does this word form imply?
- What word form(s) can be used to express this meaning?
- What is included in the word's concept?
- What other words does this make us think of?
- Are there other words we could use instead of this one?

Uses of the word:

- Are there other patterns in which this word occurs?
- Are there patterns in which we must use this word?
- Are there other words or types of words that are used with this one?
- When, where, and how often would we expect to see this word?
- When, where, and how often can we use this word?

Teachers can use instructional strategies to teach word forms and meanings, but the various word patterns and colloquial uses of the word are difficult to teach directly. They are more likely to be acquired through extensive exposure to a variety of English language sources.

Teaching Tip 3.7: Coping With Idioms

Idioms can be very confusing for ELL students, so be aware of the idioms used in casual classroom conversation. When teaching idioms, ask students what idioms are common in their language so they can recognize the differences between literal and figurative language.

- Select a common idiom appropriate for the age level of the ELLs and ask them what they think it means. Take the idiom, *It's a piece of cake*. Students might suggest its literal meaning and other alternatives. Then tell them the figurative meaning that it is a task that can be accomplished very easily. Repeat this process with other common idioms, such as *A smart cookie, All in the same boat,* or *Can't cut the mustard.*

- Ask students to think about idioms in their native language and compare them to those in English. This helps build a common language in the class and strengthens the class community, because students are able to discuss their challenges in mastering English through their own idioms. For example, the English idiomatic expression for an expensive item is *It costs an arm and a leg.* A similar expression in Spanish is *Cuesta un oto de la cara,* or *It costs an eye of your face.* When being duped, one might say, *Don't pull my leg,* but in Spanish the same sentiment becomes *No me tomes el pelo,* or *Don't take my hair.*

- Encourage students to visit Internet sites (see **Resources** section) that explain the meaning of hundreds of English idioms.

- Invite students to bring to class an English idiomatic expression they hear elsewhere in the school, on television, or in popular music. Ask the class if they can explain its meaning. (Important Note: Have the student share the expression first with you to ensure that it is appropriate.)

- Consider asking students to deliver a short speech to the class that uses at least four (or some other number) idioms they had learned in class. During the speech, ask the other students to write down the meaning of the idioms to improve their listening skills.

- For students who can read and write English, suggest they keep an idiom journal whose entries are regularly discussed in class. This discussion helps students realize that they are not alone in their struggle with complex and hidden meanings. Consider even creating an idiom wall using input from the idiom journals. The wall bolsters student confidence because they can see their growth in English language acquisition.

Teaching Tip 3.8: Word Stress

Stress is an important part of speaking in English as meaning is often conveyed through stressing of a word or particular words in a sentence. Yet stress is often a difficult listening and speaking skill for ELLs to acquire without substantial practice. Here are a few important characteristics about stress, and each one can be turned into individual lessons, depending on the ELL's age and competency in spoken English.

- Point out that stress occurs in all words of two or more syllables.
- The stress is always on the vowel. *CAN-a-da, a-BOVE, TU-lip, TEACH-er.*
- One word can have only one stress. If you hear two stresses, you are hearing two words.
- Demonstrate how stress can move among syllables even in words that are similar. For example: *PHO-tograph, pho-TOG-rapher,* and *photo-GRAPH-ic.*
- Words that can be both nouns and verbs are often stressed differently and can have different meanings. Usually, the stress is on the first syllable for the noun and on the second syllable for the verb.

Examples: *His CON-duct was excellent.* *He will con-DUCT the orchestra.*
　　　　　　 The OB-ject is made of glass. *I ob-JECT to that comment.*
　　　　　　 This PRES-ent is for you. *He will now pre-SENT the gift.*

A few other common words in this category are: *contest, contract, convict, insult, permit, perfect, produce, project, protest, recall,* and *reject.* Use these words in sentences as both a noun and a verb so that the ELLs can hear the differences in stress.

Examples: *I want to preSENT you this PRESent.*
　　　　　　 I hope my father will perMIT me to get a driver's PERmit.
　　　　　　 If you perFECT your stress, your accent will be PERfect.
　　　　　　 He is a REBel who wants to reBEL against the world.

- In compound words (words with two parts), the stress depends on the word's grammatical usage (but there are exceptions).

  For compound nouns, the stress in on the first part: *FIREproof, GREENhouse, SKYscraper, SNOWdrift, UPdate*

  For compound adjectives, the stress is in the second part: *kind-HEARTed, old-FASHioned, left-HANDed, sure-FOOTed*

  For compound verbs, the stress is on the second part: *foreTELL, overCOME, underSTAND, upHOLD*

Teaching Tip 3.9: Basics of Sentence Stress

Sentence stress can be a difficult aspect of learning English, because stress affects meaning and also because many words in English have multiple meanings that vary with context. Practicing stress in sentences, then, is an important part of learning spoken English.

- Point out that in sentence stress some words are said louder (stressed) than others.
- Distinguish between **content** words and **structure** (or function) words in a sentence. Content words convey meaning while structure words make the sentence grammatically correct. Content words are usually nouns, main verbs, adjectives, adverbs, negative auxiliaries (*aren't, can't, don't*), demonstratives (*that, this, those*), and question words (*who, what, where*). Structure words are articles (*a, some, the*), conjunctions (*and, because, but*), pronouns, prepositions, and auxiliary verbs (*be, can, do, have, must*). In the sentence: *I am going to California because I am buying a house*, the content words are *I, going, California, buy,* and *house,* while the structure words are *am, to, because,* and *a.* Usually, content words are stressed and structure words are unstressed.
- In certain instances, structure words ARE stressed in order to clarify a statement. For example, in reply to: *Didn't they go to the party last night?*, one might say, *No, THEY didn't go, but WE did.*
- Note that an English sentence will always have a certain number of beats. Stressed words will always take up a beat while unstressed words fall between the beats. The time between beats is always the same.
- Explain that changing which words in a sentence are stressed can change the meaning that the speaker is convening.

For example, start with the sentence: *We have to go to school.*
Show how stress words in this simple sentence can vary and thus change its implied meaning:

WE have to go to school. (We, rather than anyone else, must go.)

We HAVE to go to school. (There is no other choice.)

We have to GO to school. (We must leave now.)

We have to go to SCHOOL. (We are off to school rather than any other place.)

Teaching Tip 3.10: Teaching Sentence Stress to ELLs in Elementary Grades

Teaching sentence stress in the elementary grades can be done with all ELLs but is likely to be more successful with those who are able to read and/or write basic English sentences. Each point below can include several lessons, depending on the age and English competency of the students.

- Using simple sentences, ask the students to repeat them after you slowly, with extra emphasis on the stressed words.
- After repeating the sentences, ask the students to start clapping out a rhythmic beat, and to insert the sentences into this rhythm. The goal here is to get their brain to establish associations between English vocabulary words and their stress in usage.
- Next, tell the students how many beats they are allowed for each sentence. For example, for the sentence, *The boy is running with his dog,* the students should fit this sentence into three claps, representing the stressed words (*boy, running,* and *dog*). First say the sentence without the clapping and then have them repeat it with the clapping.
- Explain differences in stress by using words such as *loud* and *quiet,* or *big* and *small,* so students understand the notion of opposites. Then write the sentence on the board and have them say it while clapping out the rhythm. Ask them which words are loud/big and which are quiet/small. Their brain is now associating word usage with variations in stress.

Practice on sentence stress can include a number of activities and games, such as:

- Working in pairs, one student pronounces sentences (where the stress has been indicated) while the partner listens and writes down only the stressed words. They are awarded a point for each accurate response. They exchange roles and repeat the activity.
- Divide the class into two teams. A student from each team stands at each end of the board. The teacher pronounces a sentence and the student who writes down all the correct stressed words first wins the game.
- For primary grades, students can be given word cards that when combined in the right sequence create a sentence. The stressed words are in a different color from the unstressed words. This activity combines sentence stress with word order.
- For upper-elementary grades, students can be given a grid where each square represents a word. Certain squares are a different color or highlighted for the stressed words. They refer to a word list or word cards and try to put them into a sentence in the correct order with the correct stress pattern.
- In a total-physical-response (TPR) activity, ask students to pronounce sentences as a team. Create sentences with a beat/rhythm corresponding to the number of students in the classroom

or in a small group. For example, a class or group of seven students could be given the sentence, ***What's** [your] **name** [and] **how** [are you] **today**?* This sentence has four stressed and three unstressed beats (total of seven). Distribute these seven elements to the students and have the stressed-beat students stand. The stressed-beat students should speak loudly and clearly, but the unstressed-beat students should speak softer and faster.

As a follow-up, ask the students to create sentences with stressed and unstressed beats. To make the activity more challenging, ask the students to judge for themselves which beats are stressed and unstressed after hearing the teacher say the sentence. They then decide as a team who should be standing and sitting when they reproduce the sentence as a class or group.

- Sentence stress can also be taught and practiced with drawing. Students can write stressed words on big balloons or balls and unstressed words on small ones. These sorts of activities can also incorporate key language structures and vocabulary by using words related to content units they are currently studying.

Sentence stress is not difficult to teach to young children, and it can be surprising how quickly they learn the pattern of it. Introduce it with simple conceptual terms and make it an ongoing activity in the classroom. When ELLs can clearly identify the stressed and unstressed elements in a sentence, and practice producing it in focused activities, they are on the way to producing natural English rhythm on their own (adapted from www.englishraven.com).

Teaching Tip 3.11: Teaching Sentence Stress to ELLs in Secondary Grades

Many of the activities presented in **Teaching Tip 3.10** can be adapted for middle and high school students. However, learning sentence stress at these grade levels can be both easier and more difficult at the same time. It is easier for older students because of their cognitive ability, experience, and familiarity with the patterns and rules that are characteristic of learning grammar. Moreover, they can also usually read and write English with some proficiency, which is useful in identifying and sorting words as units. But learning sentence stress may be more difficult because the ELLs may already have been taught to pronounce English orally with little or no sentence stress, thus creating the flat-sounding English characteristic of students in this age bracket. This means that the teacher must rectify what may be entrenched errors in the ELLs' pronunciation.

The first step is to assess the ability of the students. Students of very low ability will find many of the activities listed in **Teaching Tip 3.10** very useful, as long as they are carefully adapted to suit this older age bracket. Once the conceptual idea of stressed and unstressed words in a sentence has been conveyed to the students, it can be practiced and expanded through some of the following activities.

- **Sentence Stress Bingo:** Create a list of sentences incorporating key language and vocabulary, perhaps from a regular English textbook the ELLs are using. From these sentences make up a vocabulary list that includes only the stressed words. Students choose words from this list and fill it into their Bingo grid (usually a 5 × 5 grid). Read the sentences aloud while the students listen for the stressed words and cross off the ones they have chosen. This listening-based activity is helpful in encouraging and practicing identification of stressed words in a sentence. Students will focus on stressed words only, and may even repeat the sentence they hear in a similar pattern in an attempt to remember the words they heard spoken. You can make the activity more challenging by incorporating minimal pairs into the sentences. Another option is to deliberately play on words and word combinations that sound alike but vary in the stress pattern. For example: *I am **running** in the **field*** and *I **run** in the **field.***

- Give students worksheets that have lists of sentences containing only unstressed elements (such as pronouns, prepositions, conjunctions, etc.) and spaces for stressed words. It is up to the students to fill in the gaps with stressed words, either from a word bank or by creating their own. They can challenge each other by writing sentences and then removing the stressed words, which a partner must then try to produce to make them complete again. This kind of activity can be used very effectively with lessons emphasizing pronouns and auxiliary verbs because the students are gaining practice in combining appropriate nouns, verbs, and adjectives with unstressed elements. As a variation, reverse the activity by giving the students sentences containing only stressed words and ask them to fill in appropriate unstressed words.

- Give students lists of sentences incorporating key language where neither stressed nor unstressed elements are indicated. The students compile a two-column list wherein stressed and unstressed words are clearly separated. The list can be based on listening to you or listening to each other.

- Memory games can be an enjoyable way to practice sentence stress. Distribute to the students lists of five or more sentences where the stressed elements are missing. After listening to you (or to each other), they attempt to remember and write down all the stressed words they heard and complete the sentences.

- As students gain in proficiency with sentence stress, incorporate activities that encourage an actual work product on the part of the students. For instance, they can write or fill in sentences and decide which elements should be stressed and which ones should not. Then they read the sentence aloud and you and/or the rest of the class decide whether sentence stress was used correctly. You can also give the students lists of words that are stressed in sentences, and ask them to produce a sentence on the spot using those words.

- Another interesting activity involves listening to English pop songs. As long as the song chosen has a relatively consistent stress pattern, the students can practice identifying the stressed words they hear. Note that sometimes in songs unstressed elements are given more length or emphasis than in natural speaking (adapted from www.englishraven.com).

- **Intonation.** Show a video scene of a film and draw the students' attention to the intonation used by the actors. Ask them to concentrate on the emotions, the mood, and the body language to identify the intonation used. Then give them the script of that scene, have them choose characters, and ask them to be the voice of the film. Watch the scene without volume first, then watch it again so that the students act the story with their voice. This can be a very interesting and humorous opportunity for the ELLs to compare the nonnative speech with the native one and to identify differences in intonation.

CHAPTER 3

Key Points to Ponder

Jot down on this page key points, ideas, strategies, and resources you want
to consider later. This sheet is your personal journal summary and will help
to jog your memory.

_____

_____

_____

_____

_____

_____

_____

_____

_____

_____

_____

_____

_____

_____

_____

Chapter 4

Teaching English Language Reading and Writing

I n the previous chapter we looked at how to help ELLs develop listening and speaking skills. These skills are essential for establishing the cerebral networks that will be processing the phonemic, morphological, syntactic, and semantic properties of English. Through targeted practice the ELLs' phonemic awareness in English can be firmly established, a necessary prerequisite if we expect the ELL to be successful in learning to read English accurately and to write it correctly. It may be very helpful to get some background information on the ELLs in the class regarding their native language proficiency in reading and writing. See **Teaching Tip 4.1** for one method for getting this information. Now we turn to the skills of reading and writing.

READING

Humans have been speaking for tens of thousands of years. During this time, genetic changes have favored the brain's ability to acquire and process spoken language, even setting aside specialized areas of the brain to accomplish these tasks. Consequently, the brain's proficiency at hearing and quickly remembering words is natural, though no less remarkable. Speaking is a normal, genetically hardwired capability; reading is not. No areas of the brain are specialized for reading. In fact, reading is probably the most difficult task we ask the young brain to undertake.

Speaking is a normal, innate ability; reading is not.

Reading is a relatively new phenomenon in the development of humans. As far as we know, the genes have not incorporated reading into their coded structure, probably because reading, unlike spoken language, has not emerged over time as a survival skill. If reading were a natural ability, everyone would be doing it. But in fact, there are nearly 40 million adults in the United States alone who are functionally illiterate. Before we look at the challenges ELLs face when learning to read English, let us look first at what the ELLs' brain had to do in order to learn to read their first language.

Early Stages of Reading

Before children learn to read, they acquire vocabulary by listening to others and by practicing the pronunciation and usage of new words in conversation. Adult correction and other sources help to fine-tune this basic vocabulary. Because the ability to read is strongly dependent on the word forms learned during this period, a child's beginning reading will be more successful if most of the reading material contains words the child is already using. The phoneme-grapheme connection can be made more easily. Reading, of course, also adds new words to the child's mental lexicon. Consequently, there must be some neural connections between the systems that allow the brain to recognize spoken words and the system that recognizes written words.

Learning to read starts with the awareness that speech is composed of individual sounds (phonemes) and a recognition that written symbols represent those sounds. The neural systems that perceive the phonemes in any language are more efficient in some children than in others. To some extent, neural efficiency is related to genetic composition, but these genetic factors can be modified by the environment. Nonetheless, being aware of sound differences in spoken language is crucial to learning to read written language.

Phonological Awareness

This is the recognition that oral language can be divided into smaller components, such as sentences into words, words into syllables and, ultimately, into individual phonemes. In children, phonological awareness usually starts with initial sounds and rhyming, and a recognition that sentences can be segmented into words. Next comes segmenting words into syllables and blending syllables into words.

Phonemic Awareness

This is a subdivision of phonological awareness and refers to the understanding that words are made up of individual sounds (phonemes) and that these sounds can be manipulated to create new words. It includes the ability to isolate a phoneme from the rest of the word, to segment words into their component phonemes, and to delete a specific phoneme from a word. This awareness does not easily develop into the more sophisticated phonemic awareness, which is so closely related to a child's success in learning to read.

Sounds to Letters (Phonemes to Graphemes)

To be able to read in any language, the brain must memorize a set of arbitrary squiggles—such as the Roman, Cyrillic, or Arabic alphabet, Japanese or Chinese logograms—and identify which symbols, called *graphemes,* correspond to the phonemes already stored in the mental lexicon. ELLs whose native language uses a nonalphabetic writing system will have a particularly difficult time learning to read English. Aside from the obvious challenge of switching from a nonalphabetic to an alphabetic system, there is also the problem of identical phonemes in both the L1 and in English being represented by different symbols in each language. Many European languages use abstract letters (i.e., an alphabetic system) to represent their sounds so that the words can be spelled out in writing. The rules of spelling that govern a language are called its *orthography.* How closely a language's orthography actually represents the pronunciation of the phoneme can determine how quickly one learns to read that language correctly. Some languages, like Spanish, Italian, and Finnish, have a very close correspondence between letters and the sounds they represent. This is known as a *shallow* orthography. Once the rules of orthography in these languages are learned, a person can usually spell a new word correctly the first time because there are so few exceptions.

English, on the other hand, often has a poor correspondence between how a word is pronounced and how it is spelled. This is called a *deep* orthography. It exists because English does not have an alphabet that permits an ideal one-to-one correspondence between its phonemes and its graphemes. Consider that just when the brain thinks it knows what letter represents a phoneme sound, it discovers that the same symbol can have different sounds, such as the *a*'s in *cat* and in *father.* Consider, too, how the pronunciation of the following English words differs, even though they all have the same last four letters, and in the same sequence: *bough, cough, dough,* and *rough.*

This lack of sound-to-letter correspondence makes it difficult for the brain to recognize patterns and affects the learner's ability to spell with accuracy and to read with meaning. Eventually, the brain must connect the 26 letters of the alphabet to the 44-plus sounds of spoken English (phonemes) that the learner may have already been using. Table 4.1 illustrates the complexity of English orthography, compared to some Romance languages. There are more than 1,100 ways to spell the sounds of the 44-plus phonemes in English.

Table 4.1 Language Sounds and Their Spellings			
Language	**Number of Sounds (Phonemes)**	**Number of Ways to Spell Sounds**	
Italian	33	25	Shallow Orthography
Spanish	35+	38	
French	32	250+	Deep Orthography
English	44+	1,100+	

Matching Sounds and Symbols

Regardless of an individual's native language, reading requires that the brain match symbols with sounds. To be successful, this process requires the cooperation of three neural systems, working together to decode the sound-to-symbol relationships peculiar to the language. This is not an easy skill to develop and it does not occur for most people without direct instruction. Figure 4.1 illustrates the three basic neural systems that the brain uses to read. For an alphabetic writing system, the visual processing system records the word *dog*. Working with Broca's area, these networks analyze the word for its component phonemes. If that phoneme combination of */d/aw/g/* exists in the mental lexicon, the information is consolidated by the frontal lobe into a representation of a furry animal that barks. For logographic writing systems, an area of the right hemisphere associated with graphical representations is also activated to help analyze the picture symbols.

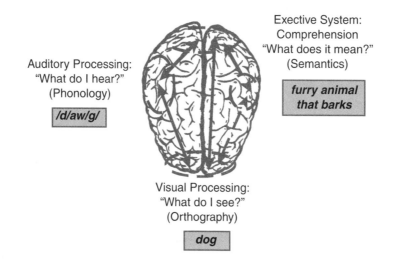

Auditory Processing: "What do I hear?" (Phonology) */d/aw/g/*

Exective System: Comprehension "What does it mean?" (Semantics) *furry animal that barks*

Visual Processing: "What do I see?" (Orthography) *dog*

Figure 4.1   The reading process begins with the visual processing of the word, in this case *dog*. The phonemes are sounded out in the auditory processing system of the left hemisphere, and the brain searches the mental lexicon for that combination of phonemes. Finally, the frontal lobe puts it all together to produce the meaning of a furry animal that barks. Readers of logographic languages, such as Chinese, also use a portion of the right hemisphere (dotted arrows) identified with processing graphical representations.

Alphabetic Principle

Unlike logographic writing systems, such as Chinese and other Asian languages, that use complex graphics to represent one or more words, alphabetic languages use separate written symbols—called letters—each of which can represent one or more sounds. The alphabetic principle (once called phonics) describes the understanding that spoken words are made up of phonemes and that the phonemes are represented in written text as letters. This system of using letters to represent phonemes is very efficient in that a small number of letters can be used to write a very large number of words. Matching just a few letters on a page to their sounds in speech enables the reader to recognize many printed words. In English, for example, connecting just four letters and their phonemes /a/, /l/, /p/, and /s/ to read *lap, pal, slap, laps,* and *pals.*

> *The human brain is not born with the insight to make sound-to-letter connections, nor does it develop naturally without instruction.*

Despite the efficiency of an alphabetic system, learning the alphabetic principle is easier in some languages than others. We already noted that Italian and Spanish have a very consistent matchup between their phonemes and the letters that represent them. But because there are about 44 English phonemes but only 26 letters in the English alphabet, each phoneme is not coded with a unique letter. There are over a dozen vowel sounds but only five letters, *a, e, i, o,* and *u* (and the occasional *y*) to represent them. Further, the ELL needs to recognize that how a letter is pronounced depends on the letters that surround it. The letter *e,* for example is pronounced differently in *dead, deed,* and *dike.* And then there are the consonant digraphs, which are combinations of two consonants, such as *ch, sh,* and *ph,* that represent a single speech sound. There are also three-letter combinations, called trigraphs, such as *tch* and *thr.* With more practice at word recognition, the ELL reader must work toward fast and accurate word recognition in order to increase reading fluency.

Whether ELL students learn the alphabetic principle for English by direct or implicit instruction, the problems of inconsistent orthography are resolved the same way other learning challenges are—through practice. With sufficient, effective practice, these students can develop a context-sensitive understanding of letter-to-sound correspondence. Eventually, they learn that *-ough* in the context of *c_ _ _ _* is pronounced differently from the context of *thr_ _ _ _.*

Letters to Words

Decoding

Phonological awareness helps the beginning ELL reader decipher printed words by linking them to the spoken English words that the learner already knows. This process is called *decoding.*

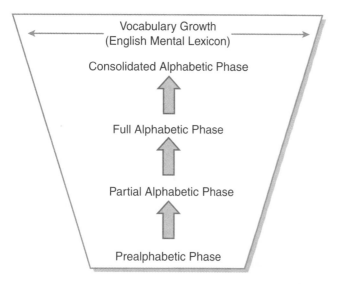

Figure 4.2   As word recognition develops over time from the prealphabetic phase to the consolidated alphabetic phase, the ELL reader's vocabulary (the mental lexicon) grows dramatically (Ehri, 1998).

It involves realizing that a printed word represents the spoken word through a written sequence of letters (graphemes) that stand for phonemes, and then blending the phonemes to pronounce the word. Exactly how the human brain developmentally makes the connections between sounds and words needed for successful decoding is still unclear. But research studies, including some that used brain scans, have helped neurolinguists gain a better understanding of how written word knowledge develops in the beginning reader of English. One model was developed by Ehri (1998), who proposed four phases of word recognition during early reading (Figure 4.2). ELLs whose native language uses a non-alphabetic writing system will need to gain competence in the alphabetic principle if they are to be successful readers of English. They, too, will need to pass through the four phases of word recognition. The phases are described as follows (Morris, Bloodgood, Lomax, & Perney, 2003):

1. *Prealphabetic phase.* In this phase, ELLs remember words by connecting visual cues in the word (such as the two *l*s in *bell* or the curve at the end of *dog*) with the word's meaning and pronunciation. There is no systematic letter-sound connection. Consequently, the learner's ability to commit new words to memory or retain old words is overwhelmed when visually similar words (such as *bell, ball, will,* or *dog, bug, dig*) are encountered in the text.

2. *Partial alphabetic phase.* In this phase, the ELL commits printed words to memory by connecting one or more printed letters with the corresponding sound(s) heard during pronunciation. For instance, the learner might remember the word *talk* by joining the beginning and ending letters (*t* and *k*) with their corresponding spoken sounds *tuh* and *kuh*. Words now become easier to remember because they can be processed through a more reliable letter-sound system rather than the unreliable visual cues used in the prealphabetic phase. This phase is sometimes called *sight-word reading* and the readers develop the ability to recognize certain familiar and high-frequency words. However, ELL readers may still confuse letters, misreading *take* or *tack* for *talk,* and usually cannot read text containing words outside their English mental lexicon.

3. *Full alphabetic phase.* As reading progresses, phonemic awareness improves and the reader moves into this phase. Here, the ELL remembers how to read a specific word by making accurate connections between the letters seen in the word and the phonemes that are used in the word's pronunciation. For example, when reading the word *trap*, the learner recognizes the initial consonant blend, */tr/,* then the medial vowel, */æ/,* and then to the final consonant, */p/.* This complete phoneme-grapheme connection will facilitate committing this word to long-term memory, thus leading to more accurate reading.

4. *Consolidated alphabetic phase.* In this phase, the beginning ELL reader notices multiletter sequences that are common to words stored in memory (such as the ending *-ake* in *cake, make,* and *take,* or the *-ent* in *bent, cent,* and *tent*). By forming a chunk for each common sequence, word reading becomes faster and more efficient. When encountering a new word containing the chunk (such as *dent*), the learner just processes the beginning consonant and the chunk, instead of processing each letter separately. Chunking is particularly helpful when reading longer, multisyllable words like *practice, measurement,* and *traditional.*

As the ELL learners master each phase, their English mental lexicons grow dramatically. Ehri's model is consistent with others, all of which describe an increasing degree of phoneme awareness that occurs in stages. The alphabetic principle is essential for success in learning to read in English.

Helping ELLs Learn to Read in English

One of the more vexing problems facing teachers of reading is whether it is better to promote reading literacy in ELL students' native language or in English. The research evidence from several separate studies indicates that initial reading instruction in a student's home language (e.g., Spanish) contributes positively to that student's ability to attain literacy in a second language, and also to the prevention of reading difficulties (Rolstad, Mahoney, & Glass, 2005; Slavin & Cheung, 2005). At first sight, this result may seem counterintuitive. How can improving reading skills in the ELLs' native language help them read in their second language? Several possible explanations exist, but the most likely one is that powerful concept of *transfer* that we discussed in detail in Chapter 2. Other research studies have suggested that literacy as well as other skills and knowledge transfer across languages. Thus, if a student learns something in one language, such as decoding or comprehension strategies, then the student can learn it in another language. Phonological awareness

It is generally counterproductive to hasten young non-English-speaking children into reading in English without adequate preparation in speaking English.

might transfer across languages, but does not appear to be helpful if the ELL's native language has a very different writing system, such as Russian, Arabic, or Chinese (Bialystok, McBride-Chang, & Luk, 2005).

It is generally counterproductive to hasten young non-English-speaking children into reading in English without adequate preparation. As we have discussed earlier, reading in any language requires a solid mental lexicon of spoken vocabulary. Thus, learning to *speak* English becomes the ELL's first priority, because it provides the foundation for hearing and reflecting on the structure of spoken words and then to learning the alphabetic principle as it applies to the sounds of English. Likewise, learning to read for meaning depends on comprehending the language of the text being read.

Can ELLs Learn Vocabulary as Well From Reading as From Speaking?

Some people contend that ELLs can learn new English vocabulary words through reading just as well as they can through speaking. They use this rationale to suggest that explicit oral vocabulary instruction is not essential as long as the ELL student sees the new written vocabulary repeatedly. Repetition of the sight words, they say, will eventually result in acquiring the word and its meaning from context. It is an interesting proposition, and perhaps it may be true for a very small number of ELLs. But our current knowledge of the different neural networks required for processing the spoken word versus the written word belies this contention. Here is why.

You will recall that in Chapter 1 we discussed the brain regions that are predisposed for acquiring and processing *spoken* language (see Figure 1.2). Over the hundreds of thousands of years that humans have been speaking to each other, these brain regions were genetically favored and have become consolidated. As a result of these genetic and neural architectural predispositions, young children learn to speak their native language without direct instruction. But reading and writing are relatively new inventions, so there are no brain areas specialized in interpreting, producing, and processing abstract symbols. Reading and writing, therefore, place a much heavier demand on neural networks than speaking.

Figure 4.3 is a schematic representation of how the spoken and written language processing systems might interact. Words can enter the system through either pathway. However, words entering through the spoken word pathway are likely to be learned easier because that process is facilitated by genetic influences and by Broca's and Wernicke's areas that specialize in spoken language processing. By contrast, the processing of written words is not facilitated at the lower levels by any brain areas specialized for reading. Consequently, reading is just another collection of stimuli that must be decoded and encoded in order to derive meaning. Several functional imaging studies have shown that both Broca's and Wernicke's areas were activated when participants were asked to generate written words (Joseph, Noble, & Eden, 2001). As can be seen from the model, the formation of visual word forms (orthographic coding) relies strongly on the ability to generate

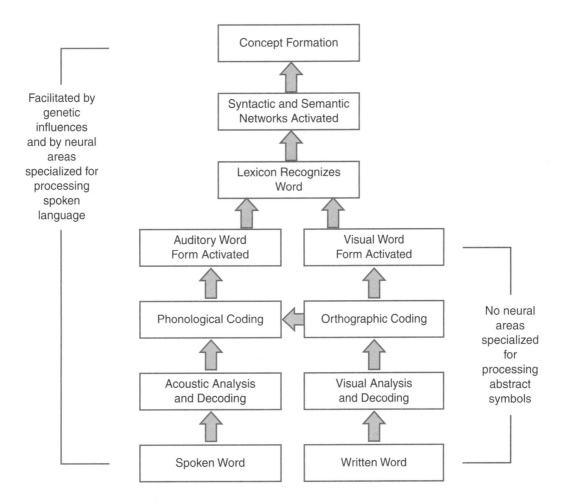

Figure 4.3 In this schematic representation of spoken and written language processing, words can enter the system through either pathway. Words entering via the spoken pathway are learned more quickly because the process is facilitated by genetic influences and specialized brain regions. Note the horizontal arrow at the third step, which indicates that the ability to encode visual words forms (orthographic coding) relies strongly on the brain's ability to generate auditory word forms (phonological coding). (Adapted from Gazzaniga et al., 2002.)

auditory word forms (phonologic coding). Thus, how quickly and how well an ELL learns to read even common words in English depends a great deal on how well that student has acquired and practices spoken English.

The report of the National Research Council (Snow et al., 1998) suggested that if children come to school with no proficiency in English but speaking a language for which there are instructional guides, materials, and locally proficient teachers, then these children should be taught how to read in their native language while acquiring oral and, eventually, reading proficiency in the English language. Those non-English-speaking children with a native language for which there are no materials should focus on developing their oral proficiency in English. Formal reading instruction should be postponed until the child can speak English with an adequate level of proficiency.

One format for providing this type of instruction is paired bilingual instruction whereby ELL students are taught to read in their native language and in English at different times of the day. This can be expanded to two-way bilingual instruction in which ELL and native English speakers both learn to read in both languages (Calderón & Minaya-Rowe, 2003). In an analysis of 17 research studies, Slavin and Cheung (2003) found that most studies showed significant positive effects of the bilingual approach, especially the two-way format, on the students' reading performance. Most of these studies evaluated the Success for All program, which is a comprehensive reading program emphasizing systematic phonics, cooperative learning, tutoring for struggling students, and family support programs. Evaluations of both the English and Spanish versions of the Success for All program have consistently found them to improve English and Spanish reading performance in beginning readers.

Reading Comprehension

Just because ELLs may be able to correctly pronounce English words in a reading passage does not mean that they actually comprehend what they are reading. Reading comprehension is more difficult for ELLs than for native speakers of English for several reasons. They are likely to lack the background knowledge necessary for understanding texts. Their prior educational experiences may have been substandard or interrupted, so reading any texts that assume certain prior knowledge becomes difficult. Even for students with good educational backgrounds, their cultural differences alone can result in a lack of background knowledge and, thus, a loss of comprehension.

The language level of the text they are reading compared to their own level of English language proficiency can also be a barrier to comprehension. Even advanced ELLs and those who have been designated as fluent in English will experience difficulty with unusual vocabulary, figurative language, very complex sentence structures, or unfamiliar styles and genres, just as many native speakers of English do.

The National Reading Panel (2000) found that teaching students comprehension strategies was important to their growth as readers. These strategies include finding the main idea, cause and effect, clarifying, comparing and contrasting, self-correction, making inferences, decoding a word, rereading a sentence, summarizing several sentences, and questioning the author and text. See **Teaching Tip 4.2** for suggestions on how to address these prerequisite needs to help with reading comprehension.

Cooperative Learning Strategies With ELL Students

For children with limited English proficiency who are beginning to acquire English, cooperative learning seems a particularly appropriate and effective instructional method. First of all, cooperative learning should improve the reading performance of students in their native language.

In an analysis of nearly 100 studies, Slavin (1995) showed that student achievement in a variety of settings using cooperative learning methods increased significantly over those of the control groups. Research on second-language learning has found that students need to engage in a great deal of oral interaction, jointly solving problems and determining meaning, if they are to achieve a high level of proficiency in the new language. Because cooperative learning provides many opportunities for ELL students to work together to share understandings, it is likely to be an especially beneficial strategy for students making the transition to reading in English.

One form of cooperative learning has been particularly successful with bilingual students. Known as Bilingual Cooperative Integrated Reading and Composition (BCIRC), this method assigns students to four-member heterogeneous learning teams. After their lesson, the students work in teams on cooperative learning activities including identification of main story elements, vocabulary, summarization, reading comprehension strategies, partner reading, and creative writing using a process writing approach. In a major study of 222 native Spanish-speaking students with limited English proficiency in Grades 2 and 3, teachers used the BCIRC model, working first with students in their native language and then helping them to make the transition to English (Calderón, Hertz-Lazarowitz, & Slavin, 1998).

The students who were part of the BCIRC program in the second and third grades performed significantly better on tests of Spanish and English reading than comparison students. Second graders taught primarily in Spanish scored significantly higher on a Spanish writing scale and somewhat higher on the reading scale than comparison students. Third-grade students who had been in the program for two years were more likely than the comparison group to meet the criteria necessary for exiting the bilingual program in language and reading. As part of BCIRC, the teachers used a total of 15 different strategies before, during, and after reading. Most of the activities were completed in a five-day cycle. Follow-up studies continue to show the efficacy of this program (Cheung & Slavin, 2005). See **Teaching Tip 4.3** for the 15 activities used in this successful program.

Monitoring Reading Progress

Just as with native English-speaking students, the ELLs' progress in reading will vary from student to student because of a number of factors. These include age, level of reading proficiency in their native language, size of their English mental lexicon, and developmental problems that may affect their ability to read. Consequently, these students' progress in reading should be monitored periodically. Studies reveal that measures of phonological processing, knowledge of letters, and word and text reading were valid for determining which ELLs may need additional support in reading (Geva & Yaghoub-Zadeh, 2006). Further, those ELL students who received early intervention in the primary grades learned to read at rates comparable to native English speakers (Lesaux & Siegel, 2003). How to develop a monitoring plan is discussed in Chapter 5.

Support From Teachers of English

Recent surveys point to a shortage of ELL teachers in U.S. schools because of the rapid increase in the ELL population (Barron & Menken, 2002). Although some ELLs get support from ELL-specialized teachers, too often many of these students find themselves in mainstream classrooms taught by teachers with little or no formal professional development in teaching ELLs. Consequently, many teachers are not adequately prepared to develop the reading skills of a linguistically diverse student population, especially in geographical areas where such populations have only recently arrived. These teachers who work with ELLs need support, and that could come from English teachers in the school. The National Council of Teachers of English (NCTE) encourages English teachers to collaborate and work closely with ELL and bilingual teaching professionals by offering classroom support, instructional advice, and general insights into learning to read a second language. See **Teaching Tip 4.4** for specific suggestions from the NCTE on how English teachers can support other teachers working with ELLs who are learning to read English.

WRITING

Writing is considered the most challenging of the four skills we have been examining. Remember that when acquiring their first language, children learn to speak first, then read and write. ELLs must do all of these simultaneously. When ELLs write, they must draw on the sum of their listening, speaking, and reading experiences. They must also use phonologic, orthographic, syntactic, semantic, and grammatical rules all at the same time. Writing in English poses several potential challenges for ELLs. These challenges fall into three major categories:

1. The mechanics of writing: How to form the letters of the English alphabet, where to place the adjective, how to spell a word, and what punctuation marks to use.

2. English proficiency: The extent of the ELL's mental lexicon and understanding of the rules of English grammar and composition.

3. Content knowledge: What the ELL knows about the subject of the writing project.

Until these students gain some mastery in English, they are likely to face numerous challenges when learning to write in English. For example:

- Because they have a limited vocabulary, they repeat the same words and phrases in their writing.
- Because their verb tenses are inaccurate, they will usually write in the present tense.

- ELLs are reluctant to use invented spelling, so their writing is limited to the words they can spell correctly.
- The complex structure of English grammar may make their writing difficult to understand.
- ELLs are not apt to share their work for peer editing for fear of embarrassment.
- Because students in many cultures are not asked for their opinions, ELLs may have little experience in their native language with creative writing. But culture will definitely have an impact on their writing. For example, well-educated Mexican students often start a narrative with long sentences containing elaborate language. To them, it is an insult to start with a succinct topic sentence. The topic is not typically approached until the embellished introduction is complete. Korean ELLs use more inductive logical structures in their writing, putting details first and then working up to a conclusion. To teachers unfamiliar with such a rhetorical approach, their style may appear indirect and unconvincing in their arguments. Students whose native language is Arabic may also love long descriptions, and may be seen as digressing from the topic at hand. Vietnamese students may focus more on setting the scene than on developing the plot. These cultural variations might give teachers false impressions about the students' writing abilities (Calderón, 2004).

ELL students often produce translated writing. This occurs when they develop their ideas in native language and then try to translate them into English. Even if they avoid writing this native language text down, they are thinking in their native language first. When this occurs, the writing is full of inaccurate verb tenses and incomprehensible sentences. Trying to edit this type of writing presents teachers with a formidable challenge. Because practice makes permanent, it is better to avoid having students write down their ideas in English through the filter of their native language. It only perpetuates poor English grammar and syntax.

Mechanics of Writing

One factor that complicates the learning of writing for ELL students is the recognition of sounds associated with the letters of the English alphabet in a specific word (phonics). Another is the physical act of reproducing the letters on a surface. The first problem is particularly vexing because although writing (that is, spelling) is a representation of spoken English, spoken English is not a representation of writing. Accents and pronunciation change over time and distance, while written English remains quite constant—although there are variations in spellings for some words in American (*center, color, behavior, program*) and British English (*centre, colour, behaviour, programme*). Furthermore, the poor correspondence between English phonemes and how they are spelled (what we earlier referred to as deep orthography in Table 4.1) makes for a high degree of uncertainty when learning to write the language.

Teachers of ELLs can lower their students' writing anxiety by focusing on the *sounds* of the language. All languages are spoken first and written later. English is not difficult to pronounce, just difficult to spell. It is not a phonetic language. The same sound can be spelled in different ways (I have *read* the book; My favorite color is *red*), and the same group of letters can have different sounds (I have *read* the book; I like to *read*).

Punctuation is also an important part of English writing, with more than a dozen primary and several ancillary marks. ELLs need to recognize each mark and its purpose because they help make a sentence's meaning clear. Perhaps you have heard the story of the college instructor who asked the class to punctuate this sentence: *woman without her man is nothing.* The men in the class wrote: *Woman, without her man, is nothing.* But the women in the class wrote: *Woman! Without her, man is nothing.* Different punctuation marks change the meaning significantly.

How well ELLs can physically write English will, once again, depend on how close the English alphabet is to the ELLs' native script. Students whose L1 uses variations of the Roman alphabet will have a high degree of crossover transfer from their L1 writing to English. Obviously, ELLs whose native language uses a writing system different from English and who have learned to write in that system will have less crossover transfer and, consequently, experience more difficulty reproducing English writing. There are a few similar letters between English and the Greek and Cyrillic alphabets, but they are usually pronounced differently. The Arabic and Hebrew alphabets have no similar letters. Japanese and Chinese logographs, of course, bear no resemblance to English letters, so the learning curve to write English letters for these ELLs is particularly steep. As is usually the case, the younger the ELLs are, the easier the task becomes.

Developing Proficiency in Writing and Composition

Recent research in this area is somewhat limited, but the consensus of researchers and practitioners is that reading and listening to read-alouds have positive effects on developing young ELLs' vocabulary and other facets of their second-language development, including writing (Krashen, 2004). In supportive contexts, ELL students in the primary grades can write productively and improve substantially over the course of a school year, especially if the teachers provide students with feedback on both content and form (Yedlin, 2003). The research study also found that ELLs often use drawing as a prewrite exercise and illustrate their stories and journal entries to support the communicative power of their writing. The ELLs' drawings serve as a basis for conversation with students and for eliciting written elaboration of journal entries and stories. Also effective are dialogue journals, in which teachers reply in writing to student entries, as well as learning logs, in which students write about their content learning, interact with their teacher, and reflect upon their learning and comprehension.

Studies also reveal the benefits of intensive teacher modeling of writing accompanied by the teacher's explicit moment-to-moment account of the thinking processes involved. Teachers model their composing processes by verbalizing their own thoughts about purpose, audience, genre, vocabulary choice, and spelling as they write demonstrations in class. Teachers model their revising and editing processes by rereading and evaluating out loud what they have written. The ELLs may simply observe and listen or the teacher may engage the students as participants by asking for help or opinions (Yedlin, 2003).

Another tested strategy to assist ELLs with composing, rereading, and revising is for teachers to reference and graphically display the structural features in writing samples. For example, they could focus on the beginning, middle, and end features of the passage, or discuss setting and character, or explain cause and effect. In these situations, the teachers use and explicitly explain the language markers that signal what follows in the text, such as: *Once upon a time, but, since, because,* and *for example.* Gradually, teachers involve students in interactive and shared writing activities where students gain increasing independence in writing (Carasquillo, Kucer, & Abrams, 2004).

Teachers can support ELLs' writing by simplifying complex tasks into steps and stages that the students can manage. Giving a variety of assignments, such as writing reports, essays, and letters or journal entries by a historical figure, encourages academic writing. ELLs can be highly motivated by opportunities to do authentic writing assignments (e.g., invitations, letters, recipes, and simple books for younger children), or to write on culturally relevant topics in formats such as oral histories, country reports, and biographies of their native heroes and celebrities. Although writing is the most challenging of the literacy domains, well-planned assignments in a rich and responsive environment can help ELLs become successful writers. See **Teaching Tip 4.5** for specific suggestions on how to help ELLs improve their writing.

WHAT'S COMING

Among the greatest challenges most ELLs face in school is trying to understand academic vocabulary in the content areas. Specialized vocabulary in science and other subjects can make reading texts a very frustrating experience for ELLs. The few things that content-area teachers can do to help ELLs succeed in mastering the subject-area vocabulary in social studies, mathematics, language arts, and science are explained in the following chapter.

Teaching Tip 4.1: Getting
Background Information on ELLs

Many ELLs come to school with the ability to think, speak, read, and write in their native language. Their L1 proficiency, however, may vary due to disrupted schooling, the use of several languages spoken in the home, or to limited exposure to the literature in the first language. Teaching your ELLs to read and write English can be more successful as well as more interesting when you are aware of the ELL's background and prior knowledge. ELLs are usually pleased when teachers want to know more about their background and demonstrate interest in their culture and language. Dong (2009) recommends that teachers ask their ELL students the following questions in order to get a more complete picture of their language experiences:

- What is your native language?
- When and how did you learn your native language?
- Which writing assignment or book that you have read do you remember the most? Why do you remember it?
- How did your teacher in your home country teach you to read and write your language?
- Are you still reading and writing in your native language? If so, what are you reading and writing about?
- What are the similarities and differences between our schools and those in your native country?

ELLs who have difficulty writing in English can write their answers in their native language. Either a bilingual teacher or a native language peer can translate the ELL's answers into English. Share this information with the ELL's other teachers so they can use the student's prior knowledge when designing their own lesson activities.

Teaching Tip 4.2: Helping ELLs
With Reading Comprehension

Because many ELLs will have difficulty comprehending English texts, there are several steps that teachers can take to help these students understand what they are reading. Here are some suggestions that can be modified according to the age and English proficiency of the learner.

- Teach the alphabet when necessary. The ELLs' schooling and literacy skills can vary dramatically. Preliterate students and literate ELLs who speak a language that does not use the Roman alphabet will need direct instruction in letter recognition and formation as well as beginning phonics.

- Identify information that is prerequisite for understanding the text, assess the students' prior knowledge of these prerequisites, and fill any gaps that are found. The most effective kinds of activities for building background knowledge are those that get students involved in manipulating language and concepts, rather than just receiving information from the teacher. These include experiential activities such as role playing, science experiments, classification activities, previewing a reading and generating questions about it, and sharing predictions about the answers to those questions.

- Modify reading comprehension instruction for ELLs to address their needs. Asking ELLs to read the same texts and do the same activities as non-ELLs will only result in frustration for you and potential failure for students. This is not a matter of lowering or applying different standards. Rather, it is a matter of implementing the curriculum at a language level that makes it accessible to ELLs, while working to develop their oral language so they will be able to comprehend reading at higher levels of vocabulary and grammar.

- Use as much nonverbal support for reading comprehension as possible. This can include pictures, diagrams, manipulatives, gestures, acting, and technology. Also, teach students to use graphic organizers, such as story maps, while they read. Visual depictions of information allow ELLs to better understand the material while learning important vocabulary. Use the support both for helping students understand a reading passage and for assessment, so students can show what they have understood in ways that are not entirely dependent on verbal ability.

- When you read to beginning-level ELLs, look for ways to help support their comprehension of new vocabulary and the story. Read sentences at a slow-to-normal speed, using an expressive tone. Allow time after each sentence or paragraph for students to assimilate the material.

- Point to the words in the text as you read them. This is particularly useful for students (such as native speakers of Hebrew and Arabic) who need to learn and adjust to the left-to-right flow of English text.

- Point to the corresponding pictures as you read the text. Verify comprehension of the story by asking students to point to items in the illustrations. Check comprehension with yes/no and either/or questions at first, and then move to fill-in-the-blank or to the who, what, when, where, and why questions when students are more comfortable.

- Read the same story on successive days. Pause at strategic points and ask students to supply the words or phrases they know. When students are familiar with the story, ask them to read along with you as you point to the words. If appropriate for younger students, use Big Books, as both text and illustrations can be easily seen.

- Avoid giving reading assignments that include too many pages to be read at one time. ELLs who are beginning readers may get intimidated when facing too many reading challenges and just give up. In this instance, less is more. Reading just a few pages with solid understanding of the vocabulary words and good comprehension is more effective than trying to read a lot of pages with frustration.

- Consider focusing on a single theme, author, or type of literature. This narrow reading builds the student's background knowledge and vocabulary. Furthermore, with a narrow focus, the reading puts new vocabulary words in context, thereby increasing comprehension and interest. Themes can include environmental concerns (e.g., weather, energy production, air and water pollution), music, and the various cultures of the ELLs in the class. Check with colleagues to determine if some of the themes may be appropriate to study across several of the ELLs' subject areas, thereby allowing them to transfer knowledge and see relationships between concepts.

- Teach comprehension strategies explicitly, such as reader-generated questions, summarizing, and monitoring comprehension. After teaching the strategies, ask students to practice them with texts that are available at their level of language proficiency. If students do not quickly experience successful application of the strategies, they will not even try to use them with other texts.

- Test the students' ability informally to place material from a story in proper sequence. For example, print sentences from a section of the story on paper strips, mix the strips, and ask the students to put them in order according to the story line.

- Plan interactive activities around reading and interpreting texts. Sharing ideas, comparing perspectives, and coming to agreement are all ways that students use the language of the text in meaningful ways, and thereby progress to higher levels of language proficiency and reading comprehension.

- Establish an age-appropriate ELL center in the classroom and fill it with items that may include the following: a picture dictionary, copies of appropriate activity pages, labels for classroom objects, a picture file, well-illustrated magazines for cutting out pictures, blank 3" × 5" index cards for flash cards, nonfiction picture books from the library that cover the same content material you are currently teaching, beginning phonics books with tapes, taped music in both English and ELLs' native language, picture books and well-illustrated beginning-to-read books with tapes, tape recorder and earphones, simple games (word searches, concentration games, sequencing activities, and jigsaw puzzles), and a box containing small manipulative objects for beginning vocabulary or phonics learning.

Teaching Tip: 4.3: Using Cooperative Learning Strategies to Teach Reading to ELLs

The Bilingual Cooperative Integrated Reading and Composition model has shown success teaching reading to ELLs in the elementary grades. However, some of the activities can be adapted for use with older ELLs. The model uses cooperative learning techniques and includes the following 15 activities:

- **Building background and vocabulary.** Select vocabulary that might be particularly difficult, strange, or important. Write the words on chart paper and develop semantic maps with the students. The maps are displayed on a wall and are used later during reading, discussion, and writing activities.

- **Making predictions.** Model how to make and confirm predictions. Students work in their teams with the title and illustrations of a story and then with the elements of that story to explain why they made their predictions.

- **Reading a selection.** Students track as you read aloud the first part of a story. During the second part, the students are encouraged to read in a whisper along with you.

- **Partner reading and silent reading.** For partner reading, the students sit in pairs and take turns reading alternate paragraphs aloud. They assist each other in pronouncing and decoding the meaning of words. Then each student reads the assigned text silently. Consider using some type of brief oral follow-up assessment to ensure that the silent reading took place.

- **Treasure hunting.** The focus here is on comprehending the story. After partner reading, pairs discuss the answers to questions about key elements of a narrative, such as characters, setting, problems, and problem solutions. Working together, students help each other to understand the questions, to look up the answers, to look for clues to support their answers, to make inferences, and to reach consensus.

- **Mapping the story.** After the treasure hunts, each team reviews a variety of graphic organizers and chooses one to map the story. This visual aid helps to organize the story elements. After discussing story elements, such as character names, the setting, the main idea, major events of the story, and problems the characters encountered, the team members represent these creatively in the story map. They can use the maps later to provide visual clues for retelling the story and for story-related writing later in the cycle.

- **Retelling the story.** Students use the maps to retell the stories to the partners within their teams and evaluate their partners' verbal summaries. Afterward, the students discuss with their partners what they liked about the story.

- **Story-related writing.** In this part of the lesson cycle, students engage in a variety of writing activities that are related to the selection they have been reading all week. For the students who are acquiring English, model the writing process extensively each time. Then, with a partner or in teams of four, students write in various genres. During this time, the students help each other to develop story lines and characters, to sequence events, and to give each other feedback. They are also learning to engage in a process of drafting, revising, rewriting, editing, and publishing.

- **Saying words aloud and spelling.** Words from the story become the word bank to be used throughout the week. Students say the words aloud to ultimately master their meaning, pronunciation, and spelling. This activity includes 10 to 12 words from the story that students must be able to read fluently, spell, and use correctly in meaningful sentences.

- **Checking the partner.** When students complete the activities listed above, their partners initial a student assessment form indicating that they have completed and achieved the task. Give the student teams the daily expectations about the number of activities to be completed. However, the teams can proceed at their own rate and complete the activities earlier if they wish, creating additional time for writing and for independent reading of other books on the same theme. Because the scores of individual students also become the team's score, the partners have a vested interest in making sure that all students correctly finish their work.

- **Making meaningful sentences.** The students carefully select five or more words from the story. They discuss their meanings and use these words to write meaningful sentences that denote the definitions and give a clear picture of the word's meaning.

- **Taking tests.** After three class periods, give the students a comprehension test on the story. The test should ask them to write meaningful sentences for each vocabulary word and to read the word list aloud to you. Students are not allowed to help one another on these tests because the test scores and evaluations of the story-related writing are the major components of students' weekly team scores. These weekly tests provide you and your colleagues a progressive view of the students' listening, speaking, reading, and writing performance. They can help you determine whether any additional activities are needed to help the student progress satisfactorily.

- **Direct instruction in reading comprehension.** Throughout the lesson cycle, provide direct instruction in reading comprehension skills such as identifying main ideas, drawing conclusions, and comparing and contrasting. The students practice these skills in their teams and take quizzes on them individually (without the help of their teammates) to contribute to their team scores.

- **Writing workshops.** These workshops consist of a series of mini-lessons on the writing process. First, give step-by-step explanations and ideas for completing a writing assignment. Then the students work closely with their peers (and with your help) through the phases of prewriting, writing, revising, and editing.

- **Independent reading.** Ask students to read a book of their choice for at least 20 minutes each evening. Talk with their parents and encourage them to discuss the reading with their children, and to initial the forms indicating that the children have read for the minimum time. The students will earn points for their team if they submit a completed form to you each week. Additional points can be earned by completing a book report every two weeks.

Teaching Tip 4.4: How English Teachers Can Support ELLs in Learning to Read

English teachers can work with teachers of ELLs and support their efforts to develop literacy and reading comprehension by considering the following (NCTE, 2006):

- Introduce classroom reading materials that are culturally relevant to the ELLs.
- Connect the readings with the ELL students' background knowledge and experiences.
- Encourage students to discuss their readings, including the cultural dimensions of the text.
- Ask students to read a more accessible text on the topic before reading the assigned text.
- Ask families of ELLs to read with students a version in their native language.
- Replace repetitive skill exercises and monotonous drills with many opportunities to read.
- Provide opportunities for silent reading in either the students' first language or in English.
- Read aloud frequently to allow students to become familiar with and appreciate the sounds and structures of the English language.
- Read aloud while students see the text and can connect what they hear to what is written.
- Stimulate the students' content knowledge of the text before introducing the text.
- Teach language components explicitly, such as text structure, vocabulary, and text- and sentence-level grammar to facilitate comprehension of the text.
- Recognize that both first- and second-language growth increases with abundant reading and writing.
- Relate the topic to the cultural experiences of the students.
- Walk through the text or a preview of the main ideas, and other strategies that prepare students for the topic of the text.
- Do prereading activities that elicit discussion of the topic.
- Teach key vocabulary words that are essential to comprehend the topic.
- Recognize that experiences in writing can be used to clarify understanding of reading.

Teaching Tip 4.5: Helping ELLs Improve Their Writing

A variety of research sources point to the following specific strategies that are effective in helping ELLs learn to develop writing skills in English (Carasquillo et al., 2004; Samway, 2006).

- **Demonstrate how reading and writing are connected.**
  - Increase the ELLs' exposure to a variety of texts by arranging for volunteers, aides, librarians, and older students to read to and with them. Choose two different books to compare their genres. For example, they could look at the topic of animal behavior in fiction and nonfiction books. Follow up a week of reading books on animals with a group analysis of the types of information these books include, such as habitats, food, species, breeds, and caring for young. Students can compare different books using focusing questions and Venn diagrams (diagrams that use intersecting circles to show relationships among sets of objects).
  - Consider including the home connection. Establish a flow of books to and from home. ELLs can read at home with English-speaking older siblings and family members. Parents who speak little or no English are often proud to have their own children read to them in English. Appropriate children's books in Spanish and other languages may be read aloud in school by bilingual adults or older students, and the books may be sent home for families to enjoy together.

- **Demonstrate how reading and writing are tools for thinking and learning.** At the beginning, ELLs need to write frequently and become accustomed to the idea that writing is a recursive process involving revision and editing. With skillful teacher modeling and a sequence of manageable steps to follow, ELLs can use writing and reading as tools for thinking and learning.
  - Demonstrate how writers read their writing and get more ideas about what else to write, and model some of the questions that writers ask themselves to evaluate what they have written.
  - Show students how to use graphic organizers such as timelines, Venn diagrams, semantic webs, and lists of pros and cons for decision making.
  - Demonstrate how you evaluate your own writing and prompt students to do the same. They can ask questions such as: Does my title fit my story? Did I introduce my main character, and did I tell where and when my story happens?
  - Encourage the ELLs to review their writing portfolios and to think and talk about what they have learned. Ask them to select a paper from the portfolio to revise and edit once they have learned more.

- **Model exemplary writing practices and demonstrate how writers write about topics that are meaningful to them.** ELLs are often unfamiliar with the kinds of writing used in our society and practiced in our schools and thus may not know what to write about. Teacher modeling can be a big help here.

  o Model how to write for a purpose and for a specific audience. By inviting students to observe and participate in your own writing process, ELLs can better understand ways to approach the task of writing.

  o Talk with the students about selecting their writing topic. Then share the various decisions you make in your own writing process. This approach provides ELLs practice in the tasks of a writer and a glimpse into the decision-making process.

- **Explicitly demonstrate how brainstorming, drafting, revising, and editing are recursive processes.**

  o Encourage ELLs to revise and edit by asking for more information or clarification. These prompts for revision can come from both teachers and students when students read to their classmates from the author's chair or during a writing workshop.

  o Structure writing projects in deliberate and distinct stages that require multiple rereadings and rewritings. You could ask students to write their stories in stages: beginning, middle, and end. After each section is completed, ask the writer to read it aloud to classmates and to makes revisions based on their responses. When completed, each student reads aloud as you type the text into the class computer, asking questions or making suggestions for revision. The final printed pages can then be illustrated, bound, and read to classroom visitors, families, and friends.

- **Provide varied and increasingly challenging writing experiences for students at all grade levels.** ELLs may need to gain experience in basic genres typically learned in earlier grades. Those who are beyond the beginner stage can write in more challenging genres, such as informational reports, short skits, and fictional narratives.

  o Assign writing projects such as journals, narratives, letters, plays, poems, reports, instructions, lab reports, book reports, persuasive essays, and other genres that students will practice again in the grades to come.

  o Add new and challenging writing tasks, while revisiting writing genres that their students may or may not have experienced or mastered previously, such as letter names and sounds, sentence punctuation and capitalization, and possessives and apostrophes.

- **Teach grammar in the context of actual writing.** ELLs learn many structural patterns of English unconsciously through listening and then using them in their speech. But in writing, they may convey a message even though the sentence is not grammatically correct (e.g., *Want* *paper, Him taking mine book*). Young ELLs may not have a sense of what sounds right in English, but that will come with time and experience as long as they have good models, guided practice, and clear explanations of what is grammatically correct.

o As you model your own writing process, use the opportunity to present mini-lessons in grammar. For example, if you write the sentences: *We talked in class yesterday. I answered a question.* You could then ask, *Why did I put the* -ed *after the verbs* talk *and* answer*?* Pronounce the verbs again so they hear the final phoneme. Ask, *What sound do you hear at the end? What does that sound tell you?*

o Use the students' writing as an opportunity to focus on form. When you find grammatical errors, discuss them with the student and explicitly model the correct form. If you see consistent error patterns among students, design guided writing practice activities to focus on grammatical features that need attention. For example, tell students you would like them to write three sentences about something that they did over the weekend with a friend or relative. Ask them to first create a list of past tense verbs that they can use. Call on students for their suggestions. Write their words on the board or chart paper, dividing the words into two columns to show the difference between irregular past forms, such as *went, saw, had, ate, bought, made,* and regular verbs, such as *talked, fished, played, cooked, visited.* When a student contributes a verb without using the past tense, like *listen,* the teacher prompts the student to say the past form, *listened.* After they finish their compositions, the students read them aloud, and their classmates point out any edits that are needed.

- **Develop a list of core words for the students to use in their writing.** The success of a piece of writing depends largely on the writer's vocabulary choices. To communicate effectively, writers need to know many words and their meanings. This means knowing how to use the word grammatically, knowing the words it typically occurs with, and knowing its level of politeness or formality. Acquiring this knowledge requires time and multiple exposures to each word in a variety of contexts, so ELLs need a great deal of work in vocabulary in order to read and write like their English-proficient peers.

o Augment the core word list for the grade level by including words that were taught in previous grades.

o Define words that students have asked for in their writing. Be sure to include content-area and thematic words by connecting with the science, math, and social studies curricula as well as to cross-curricular themes.

o In classrooms where many ELLs can already read Spanish, make a list of Spanish-English cognates (e.g., *telephono/telephone, sal/salt, estudiar/study*) and post them on the wall for Spanish-speaking students' reference.

- **Integrate spelling into reading and writing instruction.** Sounding out words and inventing spelling may be difficult for ELLs as they often have inaccurate impressions of how some words are pronounced. They may be unclear about how particular sounds are represented in English. Some ELLs come from language backgrounds where sound-letter relationships are more constant (e.g., Spanish, Italian) or from backgrounds that disapprove of unconventional spelling. To learn to spell, ELLs need explicit instruction in the conventions of English spelling in the context of actual reading and writing.

o Direct students' attention to the spellings of words encountered while reading.

o Point out common spelling patterns and ask students to think of other words that follow the pattern (e.g., *bark, dark, lark, mark*) as well as derivational patterns (*truth/truthful*).

o Note spelling oddities (e.g., the */f/* sounds in *phone* and *photograph* or the rhyming words *good* and *could*).

o When writing with students, demonstrate how to segment words into phonemes and how to represent the phonemes with letters. Use spelling terminology, such as *silent e* or *double letter.*

o Reference rules as you write (e.g., *I am going to write about our parties. How do you spell* party*? When we write the plural of* parties*, I change this* -y *to* -i *and add* -es. *Do you know any other words like that? How about* puppy *and* bunny*?*).

o To avoid errors, some ELLs use only words they have memorized or can copy from the classroom print environment. Encourage ELLs to figure out the spellings of new and different words that express their thoughts. View unconventional spelling as progress when the spelling reflects a student's willingness to experiment with sound-letter relationships and a desire to say interesting things. But to cultivate accurate spelling, design manipulative spelling activities in which students arrange, combine, match, and sort cards containing words, letters, syllables, prefixes, and suffixes.

CHAPTER 4

Key Points to Ponder

Jot down on this page key points, ideas, strategies, and resources you want to consider later. This sheet is your personal journal summary and will help to jog your memory.

_____

_____

_____

_____

_____

_____

_____

_____

_____

_____

_____

_____

_____

_____

_____

_____

Chapter 5

Teaching Language Arts and Social Studies

ELLs tend to acquire social (or conversational) English much more readily than the academic English needed to succeed in content-area classrooms. Generally, ELLs take about two to three years to be on grade level in social English. They are motivated to learn this type of English so they can be accepted and socialize with their peers. Furthermore, social English is easier to learn because it is usually accompanied by inflection, facial expressions, intonation, and gestures that help the ELLs comprehend the conversation. Academic English refers to the more challenging, abstract, and complex language that allows ELLs to participate successfully in mainstream classroom instruction. Academic English is sometimes described as the "content" language, that is, the language unique to a particular field of study. But it really encompasses more than that. It refers also to groups of words, phrases, or grammatical constructions such as, *which of the following, if . . . then, if . . . always then . . . always.*

Academic English involves being able to read texts written in a decontextualized discourse style. Decontextualized texts have few context clues and an expository writing style that even native English-speaking students find difficult. Knowing academic English means being able to relate events to others who were not present, to make comparisons between reasonable alternatives and justify a choice, knowing the appropriate use for different words and their forms, and, above all, possessing and using content-specific vocabulary in the different academic disciplines such as mathematics, social studies, and science. It takes ELLs about five to seven years to reach grade-level proficiency in academic English.

ELLs who do not have a good command of academic English are very likely to fall behind their classmates, make poorer grades, get discouraged, and face fewer educational and vocational options in their future. Because acquiring academic English is such a challenge, ELLs as a group tend to lag behind their peers in achievement. Recent National Assessment of Educational Progress (NAEP) results indicate that a large majority of ELLs scored below the basic level in almost all categories of achievement, including reading, writing, social studies, science, and mathematics. Moreover, they did so at all grades tested—4th, 8th, and 12th (Rampey, Dion, & Donahue, 2009). The causes of academic failure or stress are several, ranging from practices such as academic tracking to the students' level of native language literacy to poverty (Callahan, 2005). One critical issue, however, is that content-area teachers are often not trained to work with nonnative English speakers. Moreover, although the number of teacher education programs that require preparation for mainstream teachers to work with ELLs is growing, it is not enough to keep up with the burgeoning ELL enrollment in public schools. Some general strategies for working with ELLs in the content areas can be found in **Teaching Tip 5.1.**

THE LANGUAGE COMPONENTS OF LEARNING CONTENT IN ENGLISH

For content-area teachers to be successful in teaching ELLs, they should have a good understanding of the degree and scope of the cognitive challenges involved in this task. Figure 5.1 illustrates the components involved when ELLs are attempting to acquire subject-matter content in English-language classrooms. Here are the considerations involved:

- The ELLs' brain is processing two mental lexicons, one for their native language and one for English.
- Depending on the ELLs' age and English language exposure, their social lexicon is likely to be larger than the academic lexicon.

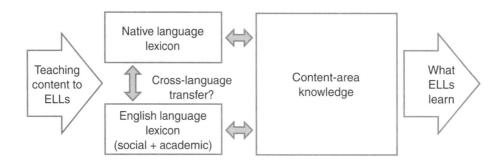

Figure 5.1   This diagram illustrates the components involved as ELLs try to learn subject-matter content in English language classes. Cross-language transfer between the native and English language lexicons may or may not exist, and it could either help or interfere with comprehension. The task is for ELLs to translate and comprehend in English the content knowledge that they already know in their native language along with the new content they acquire.

- The amount of cross-language transfer depends mainly on the degree of similarity between the writing system and grammar of the ELLs' native language and English.
- The ELLs must acquire and comprehend the academic English they need to (1) translate the content knowledge that they already possess in their native language and (2) acquire new content information so that all of it can be expressed in English.

Thus, teachers in the various curriculum areas are faced with the task of helping their ELL students acquire and understand the academic English that will help them learn the content of the particular subject. This task is particularly challenging for the content-area teachers because they are likely to have ELLs at different levels of English proficiency and from different language and cultural backgrounds. Nonetheless, there are some important steps that content-area teachers can take to help their ELLs learn the necessary academic English, and these are shown in **Teaching Tip 5.2.**

Content-Area Reading

General Guidelines

Imagine if you were asked to read and learn something of great importance related to your job. How well you learned it would decide your success or failure. But there is one catch: What you need to read and learn is in a language that you have little or no knowledge of. Sound daunting or intimidating?

One of the most difficult challenges for ELLs is reading in the content areas. Specialized vocabulary and language constructions pose potential barriers to comprehension. Some ELLs know very little English, but have a rich content background from their primary language. Other ELLs may have acquired intermediate or advanced English skills, but still have gaps in their content knowledge. In order for ELLs to become successful overall students, they need to learn both English and grade-level content. Teachers of the content areas have to make grade-level academic content accessible to ELLs without watering it down. This does not have to be an overwhelming task. If ELLs get a good understanding of the lesson, especially the content in the reading materials that support a lesson, then they are likely to retain the new content in English. Content-area teachers do not have to be reading specialists to help their ELLs achieve in their subject. Just by following a few guidelines, content-area teachers can boost their ELLs' confidence and also their subject-matter comprehension. Perhaps the first step is to assess the English language skills of the ELLs and how much they already know about the content area. Figure 5.2 illustrates the four major categories that the ELLs will fall into as a result of that assessment. Knowing the level of these proficiencies for each ELL can help teachers determine what instructional strategies to select. See **Teaching Tip 5.3** for some suggested guidelines for working with these ELLs.

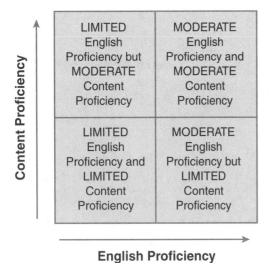

Figure 5.2 The diagram shows the different populations of ELLs depending on their levels of English and content proficiency.

Teaching Comprehension Strategies

Teaching ELLs reading comprehension strategies will help them in all their content-area classes. Skills such as making inferences, summarizing, drawing conclusions, and problem solving are of special importance when trying to comprehend the basic information presented in expository reading. Of course, they will still need vocabulary development to deal with words and terms unique to the content area. This development of vocabulary and comprehension strategies should continue even if the ELLs have been mainstreamed after some bilingual instruction or have been assessed as English proficient but you know that they still need additional help with language, reading, and writing in the content areas. See **Teaching Tip 4.4** for steps for explicitly teaching comprehension strategies.

It is only in recent years that research has looked at what might be effective methods for teaching ELLs in the content areas, especially in the subjects of social studies, language arts, mathematics, and science. These represent the four major areas of the core curriculum (and often high-stakes testing) and the subjects in which ELLs have the greatest difficulty because the areas are so heavily language dependent. The research is sparse and, frankly, the suggestions that have come forth would be effective for *all* learners. Nonetheless, researchers are still trying to parse out those strategies that appear to be particularly effective for helping ELL students to excel.

One set of strategies that can help make content accessible and comprehensible to ELLs is often referred to as *sheltered instruction* (SI). In sheltered instruction, the content is determined by standards developed in curriculum areas such as English language arts, social studies, mathematics, and science. However, teachers make modifications in their instruction and materials (e.g., using socialization practices or multiple intelligences activities) based on the students' level of English proficiency so that the ELLs can understand the academic content. Instead of providing watered-down curriculum for ELL students, sheltered instruction allows for the academic content to be equal to that of native English speakers while improving their grasp of the English language. For example, ninth-grade ELLs receiving sheltered instruction in American history are expected to learn ninth-grade-level American history. However, the instruction is "sheltered" so that the students who are less than proficient in English can comprehend the content even though the content itself (e.g., facts, concepts, and theories) remains at the ninth-grade level. Typical components of sheltered instruction include:

- **Preparation:** Each lesson should have clear, separate language and academic content objectives that are linked to the curriculum or standards and that are taught systematically. Content concepts should be appropriate for the grade and developmental level of the students. High school ELL students should not, for instance, use elementary-level materials to study ancient Egypt even though the language complexity of the materials might fit the students' English proficiency levels. Lessons include meaningful activities that integrate concepts with language practice along with supplementary materials that support the academic text. Supplementary materials can be particularly useful in a classroom of students with varying levels of English proficiency. Some students in a mixed class may be able to use the regular grade-level textbook whereas others might need adapted text.

- **Building Background Knowledge:** ELL students frequently have gaps in their knowledge base, even if they are well schooled, because other countries may emphasize different topics in their curriculum. In SI, teachers make connections between new concepts and the students' past learning and their personal experiences. These connections promote transfer and help students organize new information as part of their cognitive processing. In addition, teachers should explicitly teach and emphasize the key academic vocabulary of the concepts and provide opportunities for ELLs to use this vocabulary in meaningful ways.

- **Comprehensible Instruction:** SI teachers are cognizant of the English-proficiency level of their ELL students and modulate their rate of speech, their choice of words, and the complexity of their sentence structure accordingly. They make the academic content comprehensible by using techniques such as visual aids, graphic organizers, vocabulary previews, demonstrations, predictions, tutoring, cooperative learning, and peer and native language support. SI teachers explain academic tasks clearly, both orally and in writing, providing models and examples wherever possible.

- **Student Interaction:** SI classes provide many opportunities for interaction and discussion between teacher and students, and among students. Sometimes, teachers of ELLs monopolize class discussions because their students have weak English skills. But it is through discussion with classmates and with the teacher that ELL students practice important skills like acquiring meaning, clarifying and confirming information, elaborating on ideas, persuading others, disagreeing, and evaluating options.

- **Practice and Application:** SI lessons include activities that encourage students to practice and apply the language skills they are learning. These activities are most effective when they include visual, hands-on, and other kinesthetic tasks.

- **Review and Assessment:** SI lessons should include a review at the end of the learning episode as well as frequent feedback from teacher to students and informal assessment of student learning throughout the lesson. Depending on the students' English proficiency levels, SI teachers offer students numerous pathways to demonstrate their understanding of the academic content. These may include hands-on or performance-based assessments for individual students, group tasks or projects, informal class discussions, oral reports, written assignments, portfolio assessments, and the occasional paper-and-pencil tests and quizzes to check on student comprehension of the academic subject matter and growth in the English language.

Scaffolding strategies can also be effective. Some secondary-level content-area teachers use scaffolding strategies during their instruction. But recent studies have shown that these teachers are not familiar with how to use these strategies with ELLs (Pawan, 2008). There are professional development opportunities available for those interested in how to successfully use scaffolding strategies for ELLs in the content areas. These strategies include verbal prompting (e.g., asking students to elaborate on a response) and instructional tools (e.g., an outline of major topics in a chapter). Teachers highlight study skills and learning strategies for students and create tasks and ask higher-order questions that require students to use the strategies and talk about them.

Let's look at what research is revealing about each of the four major content areas. This chapter will focus on language arts and social studies; the next chapter, on mathematics and science. Research on the difficulties of teaching curriculum content to ELLs generally centers around three major areas:

- Language issues associated with the challenges of reading content-area texts and learning the content material
- Social issues related to the mainstream classroom setting
- General suggestions for instruction in the content areas

TEACHING ENGLISH LANGUAGE ARTS TO ELLs

Although it may seem somewhat confusing at first glance, this section deals with the content area of English language arts rather than the disciplinary area of teaching English as a second language, which was the subject of Chapter 3. Granted, both areas emphasize the development of literacy skills, and English teaching is more likely than other content areas to address linguistic topics such as grammar or vocabulary knowledge. Although some ELL students may learn about acquiring the English language in sheltered classes, the teaching of English language arts or literature in English typically occurs in classrooms that serve native English speakers as well as language minority learners.

Language Issues

Research on successful strategies for teaching ELLs in English language arts classes is limited, but some findings do suggest alternative linguistic approaches. One study investigated the value of vocabulary teaching with fifth-grade monolingual and bilingual children in mainstream and bilingual classrooms (Carlo et al., 2004). Over a period of 15 weeks, the intervention students were taught 10 to 12 new vocabulary words each week, encountering these words in the context of a thematic unit.

Teachers used a variety of activities to promote student engagement with the target words, including word association tasks, analysis of word roots, and cloze. (Note: A cloze test is one where students have to provide words that have been omitted from sentences using context clues, thereby demonstrating their knowledge and comprehension of the text.) The students were given a number of pretests and posttests that measured vocabulary knowledge and reading comprehension. The researchers found positive change over time in both vocabulary and reading. They noted that the specific techniques used had previously been found effective either with native English speakers or with ELLs, but that this study demonstrated effectiveness with both groups and in a mixed classroom.

One factor that may ease instruction in language arts classes that include both English learners and native English speakers is that there are a significant number of cognates between English and the Romance languages among commonly used literary terms. Here, for example, are some language arts terms and their cognates in Spanish: *anecdote/anécdota, autobiography/autobiografía, antagonist/antagonista, protagonist/protagonista, comedy/comedia, fiction/ficción, hyperbole/hipérbola, irony/ironía, metaphor/metáfora,* and *theme/el tema.*

Cognitive and Metacognitive Issues

Several studies describe short-term interventions conducted with Spanish-speaking middle school students in which they were taught how to deal with unknown vocabulary, to recognize Spanish cognates in English, to use their background knowledge, and to ask questions (Jiménez, 1997; Jiménez & Gaméz, 1996). Results indicated that students developed more awareness of their own cognitive behavior as well as a more positive attitude toward reading, both of which are characteristics of skilled readers. Another study involved high school students who were taught several strategies including inferencing, previewing, and guessing the meaning of unknown words (Wright, 1997). The students showed improvement from pretests to posttests of reading comprehension and were more positive and confident in their outlook on reading.

These approaches can be extended into metacognition—thinking about one's thinking. Instead of having students memorize information, teachers can model and explicitly teach the metacognitive skills needed to learn new concepts. Research studies show that metacognition is a critical skill for learning another language and a skill used by highly proficient readers of any language (Wang, Spencer, & Xing, 2009). Metacognitive skills include prereading, prewriting, word analysis, and methods for ELLs to monitor their reading comprehension.

Sociocultural Issues

A study of sociocultural issues examined a class of native Spanish ELLs who were paired with a class of academically at-risk, native English speakers (DeStigter, Aranda, & Eddy, 1997). For a period of 10 weeks, the students completed several tasks in which they shared information about themselves and their families, read and discussed short stories, and shared their experiences. The study focused on the struggles that all the students faced in maintaining a positive social identity. Various activities in the project gave the nonnative English speakers the opportunity to assert a uniquely Latino identity. The researchers suggested that projects of this sort can be beneficial for all concerned—English learners, native English speakers, and teachers—in developing understanding of the students' potential and of each other.

Pedagogical Issues

Some studies exist that offer instructional recommendations in the content area of English language arts. Two studies used a quasi-experimental research design to examine a short-term (over a few days) and a long-term (over a few years) intervention for ELLs in Grades 2 to 5 (Saunders, 1999; Saunders & Goldenberg, 1999). In these projects, the authors investigated an extensive program designed to teach literature in upper-elementary classrooms serving both ELLs and native English speakers. This program relied essentially on *instructional conversations* and *literature logs.* In instructional conversations, the teacher's goal in the interaction is not really to transmit knowledge or a particular interpretation, but rather to assist students in arriving at a complex level of understanding of a given text.

Literature logs ask students to make different sorts of written responses to a specifically designated section of expository text as, for example, analyzing it or connecting it to their own experiences. These responses are then shared with a partner or in a small group. The researchers compared students assigned to one of four categories: (1) literature logs, (2) instructional conversations, (3) literature logs and instructional conversations, and (4) a control group. Although the essays and posttests of reading comprehension showed some significant results for all the intervention groups, the combination of instructional conversations and literature logs seemed to be most effective for improving the ELLs' reading achievement and language development. These techniques have also been successful with secondary school students where they can promote higher cognitive abilities, such as critical thinking, reflection, and analysis (Jacobs, 2001).

These findings suggest that ELLs who are moving into the mainstreamed classroom can participate successfully in a grade-appropriate language arts curriculum when they are given the kind of support provided by these two techniques—instructional conversations and literature logs—when used in combination. It is no surprise that these techniques increase language and content comprehension. When used together, they allow the brain to rehearse the English language in the context of a relevant idea, thereby increasing both the acquisition and meaning of English vocabulary words not found in casual peer-to-peer conversations. Furthermore, the act of writing their responses to questions about the text adds another modality to the learning process while allowing for practice in physically writing English and mentally rehearsing meaning. See **Teaching Tip 5.5** for suggestions on using instructional conversations and literature logs with ELL students.

Other studies show the value of graphic organizers to assist student understanding of vocabulary and story organization; explicit instruction in difficult vocabulary; finding ways to value students' language, cultures, and opinions; and requiring students to elaborate on their responses (Cruz, 2004; Ernst-Slavit, Moore, & Maloney, 2002). Reciprocal teaching and targeted questioning are also effective strategies that lead to increased reading comprehension and English language development (Calderón, 2007). Reciprocal teaching is an effective technique because students assume a dominant role in their own learning. Teachers and students become partners in improving the students' understanding of the story and the ability to monitor their own comprehension. Although the technique was developed more than 20 years ago, it is still not a common practice for secondary-level content-area teachers. When it is used, however, research studies at the elementary level (Pilonieta & Medina, 2009) and secondary level (Alfassi, 2004; Slater & Horstman, 2002) have demonstrated that students increased their group participation and use of the strategies taught, learned from the passages studies, and increased their learning when reading independently. See **Teaching Tip 5.10** for suggestions on using reciprocal teaching and questioning techniques.

> *Reciprocal teaching and targeted questioning are effective strategies for increasing reading comprehension.*

TEACHING SOCIAL STUDIES TO ELLs

In a recent study, more than 30 social studies teachers with ELLs in their classroom were asked to identify the three greatest challenges they face (Coop & Reich, 2008). Their responses were as follows:

Challenge	% of Respondents
ELLs lack of knowledge of content area	70.6
Language barriers between you and ELLs	58.8
Lack of time and resources to devote to ELLs	41.2
Lack of guidance and support systems at school levels	35.3

Apart from the need for additional time, resources, and support for these teachers, clearly background knowledge and language barriers are the areas of greatest concern.

Language Issues

ELLs can have language issues with both the teacher and the textbook. Some ELLs who were taught English in countries other than the United States or Canada may find it difficult to understand the teachers' accents and pronunciations. Other ELLs may have lived in North America too short a time to develop a sufficient listening vocabulary or listening skills. These students may be proficient in comprehending written English but unprepared to comprehend the teacher's spoken English.

Textbooks are another challenge. In social studies texts, facts and details are usually condensed, and authors often omit the types of concrete or anecdotal detail that can help ELLs relate unfamiliar concepts to their own experiences. Social studies textbooks tend to have what is called *high lexical density,* that is, a high number of content words per sentence. Vocabulary words are highly abstract and subject to culturally embedded meanings, so a simple explanation or demonstration becomes a considerable challenge. This makes it difficult for ELLs to find meaning in their reading. Researchers suggest that social studies teachers explicitly teach their ELL students the grammatical features of social studies language to develop their proficiency in reading and writing. For instance, students could be taught to identify different types of verbs while reading textbook passages (Schleppegrell & Achugar, 2003). Further, the researchers connect this type of analysis to critical questions that teachers and students investigate in social studies classes, such as *Whose opinions are presented in the text? What are those opinions? Do the opinions agree with each other or not?*

> *Social studies textbooks have a high number of content words per sentence.*

Another facet of language and social studies teaching was highlighted in a study that investigated interactions in sheltered social studies classes at the middle school level (Short, 2002). Researchers found that teachers were much more likely to discuss content and tasks rather than language—with language defined as instruction that helps students acquire semantic and syntactic knowledge of English, as well as pragmatic knowledge about how English is used. As a result, the researchers suggested that content-area teachers of ELLs include explicit instruction in the four language skills of listening, speaking, reading, and writing as well as developing the acquisition of vocabulary and grammar.

One long-term school-university project that was successful in enabling middle school ELL students to participate in classes with their native English-speaking peers included coordination between the content and ELL teachers to create curriculum that developed the students' use of academic language (Bunch, Abram, Lotan, & Valdés, 2001). Another successful approach included word walls that focused on different types of language and hand motions and chants to consolidate the students' memory of specific vocabulary. As a result, the students used academic language that they had encountered in class when writing their final class reports (Zwiers, 2006).

Sociocultural Issues

Students whose native culture is very different from that of an American, Canadian, or other English-speaking culture can find learning social studies to be a difficult task. Concepts that the U.S.-born student knows through enculturation may be completely foreign to the ELL student.

Some ELLs may, for instance, have a very different concept of government. The difficulty arises because students learn new concepts by fitting them into their preexisting mental schemas—those networks or frameworks of knowledge that they have built through experience. Consequently, the less experience a student has with a subject, the more difficult it is for the student to learn that subject because there are few opportunities for transfer to occur. Furthermore, cultural differences may inhibit the ELLs from asking questions of their teacher because in some cultures, it is impolite for students to speak to a teacher unless the teacher speaks to them first.

Teachers sometimes make assumptions that overestimate their ELLs' background knowledge about important events in American history or the structure of its government. It should be remembered, however, that even though ELLs are challenged by language difficulties and lack of background knowledge, they can bring diverse perspectives and knowledge that is not familiar to American students and can—when handled appropriately—enrich the classroom experiences of the native speakers.

> *ELLs often bring diverse perspectives and knowledge that can enrich the classroom experiences of the native speakers.*

A few studies have looked in depth at the social and cultural issues facing ELLs in the classroom and school. One major study conducted by Duff (2001) investigated the experiences of ELLs in two mainstream 10th-grade classes in Canada. Most prominent among the findings was that the information and skills needed for students to be successful went beyond their knowledge of language and social studies to include factors such as familiarity with popular culture, confidence, and the ability to participate in quick-paced classroom interactions. The ELLs in the study were generally very quiet in class discussions. They also expressed the fear of being ridiculed by native English speakers, who saw them as a silent, undifferentiated mass, ignoring their different backgrounds and personalities. The author suggested that language be taught explicitly in terms of text structure and vocabulary, and that more attention be paid to the students' social-psychological needs by teachers.

Pedagogical Issues

Most articles that examine teaching strategies for ELLs in social studies center around recognizing cognates or word roots when reading, and fostering active processing of content such as using guiding questions and brainstorming. Also recommended are projects that connect to the ELL students' home languages and cultures; use of photographs, children's literature, or texts written at lower grade levels; graphic organizers; and group work. More recent studies focus on using technology, such as word processing or other software programs, to engage students with course content, as well as using storytelling and personal narrative (Janzen, 2008).

Some suggestions for working with ELLs in social studies classes are found in **Teaching Tip 5.6.**

WHAT'S COMING

We continue to look at how to help ELLs in the content areas. We move on now to the subjects of mathematics and science. Will mathematics come easier to ELLs because it is a universal language? How do we help ELLs tackle word problems that even native speakers of English find difficult? Are there ways to make scientific vocabulary easier to learn and understand? These and other related questions will be addressed in the next chapter.

Teaching Tip 5.1: General Strategies for Working With ELLs in the Content Areas

ELLs in all content areas will have varying degrees of difficulty depending on their proficiency level in English. The following are some general guidelines that teachers in all content areas can find useful in helping their ELLs achieve success.

Classroom Environment

- Develop trusting relationships with ELLs through informal conversations and by maintaining a culturally rich classroom.
- Schedule ELLs into the content-area class that has students who have some proficiency in both languages. Work with counselors and others to ensure that this happens.
- Before asking ELLs to speak on a content-area topic or problem in class, give them sufficient time to practice what they will say with a peer tutor or partner. Otherwise, ELLs may resort to just saying "I don't know" when asked a question in order to avoid possible embarrassment over their language deficiencies.
- Use examples that are relevant to the lives of ELLs because they are helpful in motivating students and in promoting their engagement with the academic content.

Instructional Considerations

- Include English language objectives in content lessons for ELLs when appropriate.
- Present new concepts first in a concrete manner, followed by a semiconcrete manner, and finally an abstract manner.
- Model the expected task and use visual representations to reinforce concepts and steps in the problem-solving process. Critical content-area concepts should be clearly emphasized and repeated.
- Provide for hands-on activities because they involve multiple learning modalities and do not require the students to rely solely upon their ability to understand verbal instructions.
- Allow ELLs to use or develop learning aids that show content-area vocabulary in both English and their native language and permit them to use this tool when working on assignments. Student-made glossaries, word walls, and compare-and-contrast charts may help ELLs learn content-area vocabulary more effectively.
- Give ELLs numerous opportunities to write about the content-area concepts they are learning. Journal entries, for example, provide opportunities for the students to consolidate their thinking

about concepts and for you to check for understanding. Allow ELLs with limited English language skills to write in their first language initially without penalties for spelling or grammar errors. Journals are also useful as closure devices at the end of a lesson. To be effective, ask the ELLs (and all students) to answer these three questions in their journals in complete English sentences:

- ○ *What did I learn today?* (This helps the students make sense of what they learned.)
- ○ *How does what I learned connect to what I already know?* (This helps build long-term memory networks.)
- ○ *How will I be able to use this in the future?* (This helps establish meaning.)

- Make a special effort during instruction to assist, reexplain, and demonstrate again, if necessary, and use encouragement and reinforcement frequently.

- Support ELLs who need extra time for dialogue by providing opportunities to work in groups. Pair each ELL, when possible, with another student who has some fluency in the ELL's dominant language and who can function as a peer tutor.

- Ensure, when forming groups, that ELLs are assigned with a peer tutor, that ELLS are distributed among groups, and that no group is predominantly comprised of ELLs.

- Provide ELLs with shortened assignments or, when appropriate, extra time to complete assignments as they may work at a slower pace than other students because of limited English language skills.

- Give homework assignments that reinforce the ELLs' understanding of the instructional objectives. Appropriate homework can enhance communication with parents, but such homework should not be dependent upon the parents' skills in the content area.

- Offer tutoring as frequently as possible and encourage ELLs to come in for extra assistance. If possible, arrange for an aide or parent volunteer who speaks the ELL's native language to help with translation during the tutoring period.

- Ensure that grading policies are flexible enough to provide ELLs with multiple opportunities to demonstrate mastery without severe grade penalties.

Teaching Tip 5.2: Helping ELLs With Academic English

As with learning anything new, exposure to excellent models is a valuable experience. One of the ways that ELLs learn academic English is to participate in carefully designed lessons that expose them to the vocabulary they will need to achieve the content-area learning objective. The following suggestions offered by Himmele and Himmele (2009) are effective instructional strategies that would also benefit native English speakers:

- **Mind-Set.** Develop a mind-set in which you see almost any verbal interaction with ELLs as an opportunity for developing their academic language proficiency. Make an intentional effort to speak using academic language within a context that makes your meaning clear to the students.

- **Synonymous Tags.** Use academic language, such as non-content-specific words, and follow them with a synonymous tag that makes the meaning of the words clear to students. For example, say, "What are some ideas for categorizing your words? How can you make categories, or different groups?"

- **Meaningful Contexts.** Use academic language in a manner whereby the meaning of your words is obvious to ELLs because of the context, as in, "I'm sorry that you injured your elbow. Let me get you a bandage."

- **Visual Cues.** When reading a passage to ELLs, select certain words that are important for them to know in order to comprehend the passage. Write these words on strips of chart paper before reading each section and introduce them to the class by first reading the sentence in which they appear. Ask students to use the words when they refer to the story. Post on a wall or board the academic words that the students will need for their lesson and rehearse them frequently. Seeing the words repeatedly adds visual information in addition to saying them aloud.

- **Emotions.** Create language-rich lessons in which ELLs hear the language in contexts that are comprehensible and that engage their emotions through activities that are relevant and authentic. This leads to an excitement among the students, who then want to write and use the language in a way that allows them to express and celebrate their emotional attachment to the learning.

Teaching Tip 5.3: Guidelines for Supporting ELLs in Content-Area Reading

Content-area teachers may feel somewhat daunted by the task of trying to teach language in addition to content. But just a few simple language-related steps could make the difference between success and failure for the ELLs in your class. Moreover, there is a good chance that other students in the class will benefit from better comprehension and increased retention of the subject matter. Here are a few guidelines (Kauffmann, 2007).

Prereading: Setting Language Objectives

- After you identify lesson objectives and related readings, read through the materials and create language objectives as well.
- Share the language objectives and purpose of the reading with the students to focus your teaching and their learning. Language objectives should include all four parts of language: listening, speaking, reading, and writing. For example, your language objectives for a particular lesson might be the following:
    - Students will be able to **listen** to and discuss the activity with peers.
    - Students will be able to **verbally explain** the three types of rocks (igneous, metamorphic, and sedimentary), using three new vocabulary words.
    - Students will be able to **recognize** metaphors in text.
    - After the lesson, students will be able to answer comprehension questions **in writing**, using complete sentences and proper punctuation.

- Prior to meeting with students, read through the materials associated with the new content of the lesson and identify all new or difficult vocabulary words. Consider printing out pictures to accompany the vocabulary (*Google Images* is a handy resource for photos). Before students start their reading in class, review the images and new terms, post them on a word wall, or have students create their own graphic organizers that define and depict the new words, which they can keep as a reference during the reading.
- To support the ELL students' attainment of language objectives, consider scanning the text for words with multiple meanings, metaphors, idioms, or any other language that a language learner could misinterpret. For example, when students see a phrase like, "The darker the rock . . . ," they may think the passage is about a "darker" and not a rock. Prior to reading, extract instances of complicated usage from the text and discuss them with students. Ask students to write down in their own words and drawings the meanings of these grammatical structures and to refer to them while they read. ELLs can also put the information in their personal word walls or dictionaries.

During Reading: Graphic Organizers and Modeling

- Ask the students to make whole-class or personal predictions about the lesson objective, which they will check after the reading is complete. ELLs can also complete a KWHL chart before the reading, thinking about what they know (K), what they want to learn or wonder about (W), how they will find it out (H), and what they learned from the reading (L).

- Make graphic organizers more accessible by thinking about the kinds of language students will need to complete them, and add a column or a word box with these words and phrases. For instance, in a comparing and contrasting activity, include prompts such as *similar, alike, both, however, although,* and *in contrast* so that students feel prepared and confident.

- Use modeling whenever possible. A strategy called "think-alouds" will help not only language learners, but also the rest of the class. Give the class clear examples of how you process the language or content. Answer a sample question on the board, large chart paper, or projector, talking out everything you are doing. When you have modeled how to answer a question, ask for volunteers to model the next question. Student models raise student engagement and confidence, and help you identify any areas needing clarification. Check for understanding frequently and be prepared to rephrase concepts so that they are clear to students.

Postreading: Checking for Comprehension

- After reading, ask students to complete the "Learned" portion of their KWHL charts or graphic organizers. Integrate some type of writing activity, which helps you check for comprehension and the students' achievement of lesson goals and gives the ELLs practice writing in complete sentences, writing a summary, or learning the academic language of synthesizing information.

- In groups or individually, encourage students to use text and images to compare and contrast characters or concepts in their reading, create a sequential flowchart of processes or events, explore cause-and-effect relationships, or summarize what they have read.

Teaching Tip 5.4: Steps for Explicitly Teaching Comprehension Strategies

Because comprehending content-area material can be so difficult for ELLs, consider taking the time to help these students learn and use reading comprehension strategies. The following steps for explicitly teaching comprehension skills are useful for all students. However, these need to be complemented with the additional steps below to ensure comprehension for ELLs (Calderón, 2007).

Steps for All Students

- Introduce the comprehension strategy or skill. Examples of such strategies are:
  - Sequencing
  - Making inferences
  - Comparing and contrasting
  - Relating background knowledge
  - Distinguishing between fact and opinion
  - Finding the main idea, important facts, and supporting details
  - Problem solving
  - Self-questioning
  - Summarizing
  - Drawing conclusions
- Discuss how, when, where, and why the particular strategy or skills are used. Give clear and specific examples, such as contrasting the main idea with details, fact with opinion, or good summaries with poor summaries. Have students volunteer additional examples to contrast and discuss.
- Label, define, model, and explain the strategy or skill. For example, after listing four facts about the U.S. Constitution and four opinions about what is good government, label one list as facts and the other list as opinions. Give students opportunities to practice using the strategy with a peer as they apply it to a short, simple paragraph from a social studies text or any expository text.
- Debrief with the whole class and ask students to share how they applied the strategy or skill, and what other ways they think it would be useful.

Additional Steps for ELLs

- Identify vocabulary words that you think might be difficult for ELL students to understand when they read the assigned passages from the text. Write ELL-friendly definitions for each word—that is, simple, brief definitions that ELLs can easily understand.

- Model think-alouds as they help students understand your thought processes. For example, you can mention a confusing point in the text or show how you use a strategy to comprehend something. You might say, *This sounds very confusing to me. I better read this sentence again.*

- Demonstrate strategies to help clarify text. Say, for example, *I need to think more about this. Let me rethink what was happening. I had better reread this section. I am going to read ahead for a moment and maybe that will help.*

- Partner ELLs with more dominant English speakers and ask each student to take a turn reading and thinking aloud with short passages.

- After working with their partners successfully, ask ELLs to practice independently by using a checklist, such as the following. Be sure to explain all the terms and model each. Include in the list those strategies that are most appropriate for the particular student.

While I was reading, how did I do?

Strategy	Not much	A little bit	Much of the time	All of the time
Finding the meaning of a new vocabulary word				
Rethinking a section				
Rereading				
Reading ahead				
Summarizing				
[Add strategies as needed]				

Steps for Advanced ELLs

The following steps will be helpful for ELLs whose English proficiency and basic reading skills have increased. Once again, these steps can benefit all students.

- In pairs, ask students to review the text and use an idea map to record the main idea and the supporting details.
- Ask partners to read the text as well.
- Ask the partners to restate the main idea and the supporting details. At this point, the partners can add to their idea map or make necessary corrections.

- Then ask the students to reread the text and to either develop their own questions (pretending to prepare a test for their partner) or to write a short summary of what they just read.
- After that step, ask the partners to check each other's work.
- Finally, the partners can share their questions or summaries with other teams or the whole class.

In all comprehension activities, ask students to use the following strategies to summarize (orally or in writing):

- Retell what you read, but keep it short.
- Include only important information.
- Leave out less important details.
- Use key words from the text.

Questioning ELLs After Reading

After the ELLs and/or whole class have completed the reading comprehension activities above, assess their comprehension with carefully worded questions, taking care to use simple sentences and key vocabulary from the text they just read. Examples of such questions are the following:

- Why is it important to have protein in your diet? (Literal level)
- Why do you think so many people are overweight? (Interpretive level)
- What foods will you select for your meals? Why?

Teaching Tip 5.5: Using Instructional Conversations and Literature Logs in English Language Arts Classes

When used together, instructional conversations and literature logs have been particularly effective with culturally and linguistically diverse learners. With this combined technique, ELLs (and other students) talk and write about ideas rather than answering test questions. The following are typical features of this approach:

- It centers around an idea or a concept that has meaning for students.
- It has to be a topic that is interesting and engaging.
- There is a high level of participation, but with no one individual dominating the conversation, particularly the teacher.
- Students engage in extended, language-rich discussions with the teacher and among themselves.
- The focus of the conversation may shift as the discussion evolves, but it remains discernible throughout.

Procedure

These procedures can be adjusted for the ELLs' age and level of English competency. For the instructional conversation lessons:

- Ask students to read a passage from or an entire story.
- Facilitate discussions with the ELLs in small groups about the content of the story. These discussions can occur for approximately 45 minutes per week, longer for older students.
- Assess the ELLs' comprehension and assist in broadening their understanding of the story content and themes.

For the literature logs lessons:

- Assign entries for different segments of the readings discussed during the conversations.
- Ask ELLs to write about personal experiences relevant to a character in the story, provide a detailed description of an event that occurred in the story, and evaluate a theme from the story.
- The students should write in their logs independently in English and then participate in a discussion led by the teacher comparing their own personal experiences to those of the character in the story.

Teaching Tip 5.6: Instructional Strategies to Help ELLs in English Language Arts Classes

With modifications, the following strategies can be used at most grade levels. Although they are particularly effective with ELLs, all students can benefit from them.

Reciprocal Teaching and Questioning

Guidelines: The teacher explains the four supporting strategies used in this technique:

- *Questioning* focuses the students' attention on main ideas and provides a means for checking their understanding of what they are reading.
- *Clarifying* requires students to work on understanding confusing and ambiguous sections of text.
- *Summarizing* requires students to determine what is important in the text and what is not.
- *Predicting* requires students to rehearse what they have learned and to begin the next section of text with some expectation of what is to come.

The teacher models the sequence of strategies. Eventually, the teacher increasingly hands over responsibility to the students who now assume leadership roles in the discussion. The teacher monitors the group to keep students on task and to facilitate the discussion. Although the questions here relate to language arts classes, they can be easily adapted to any content-area instruction. (Adapted from Cibrowski, 1993; Slater & Horstman, 2002).

Specific Steps:

1. The student leader reads aloud a short segment of text.

2. Questioning: The leader or other group members generate several questions related to the passage just read, and group members answer the questions, keeping in mind the level of English competency of the ELLs. Examples:

What was the problem here?
What was the cause?
What was the solution?
What was the chain of events?

3. Clarifying: The leader and group members clarify any problems or misunderstandings. Examples:

   What does the word _____ *mean?*

   What did the author mean when he said _____ *?*

4. Summarizing: After all problems have been clarified, the leader and group members summarize the text segment.

5. Predicting: Based on the discussion and the reading thus far, the leader and group members make predictions about the contents of the upcoming text.

6. This sequence is repeated with subsequent sections of the text. With daily practice, struggling readers will master the four supporting strategies and will use them for all their independent reading in other content-area courses.

7. Some cautions:

   Start with simple questions at the beginning. But as the ELL students gain more practice and better competency in English, model open-ended questions that are thought-provoking:

   Explain why _____ .

   Explain how _____ .

   What is a new example of _____ ?

   What conclusions can you draw from _____ ?

   What do you think causes _____ *? Why?* _____

   What evidence do you have to support your answer? _____

   What are the strengths and weaknesses of _____ ?

   Compare _____ *and* _____ *with regard to* _____ .

Do not hesitate to provide more modeling and direct explanation, when needed, throughout the reciprocal teaching process.

Working in Small Groups

ELL students working with native English speakers in small groups can discuss and learn about various aspects of a story they have read. Cooperative learning groups can tackle problem solving, creative projects, investigations, and explorations. When forming these groups, consider the following:

- Group size should be between three and five, with four being the ideal number.
- Avoid putting two ELLs with the same native language in a group, otherwise they will talk to each other in their native language thus defeating one of the purposes of the activity—English language development.

- Ensure that the group's goal is clear. Ask each student to tell you what the group is expected to accomplish by the end of the activity.
- Set a time limit depending on the complexity of the objective and remind students periodically of the time they have left to finish the task.
- When appropriate, use the jigsaw format explained in **Teaching Tip 5.5.**
- Group assignments can involve covering the elements of the story, such as prior events that occurred (*What happened before this story began that is important to know?*), descriptions of the characters (*Which character is the protagonist, antagonist, static, dynamic?*), description and importance of the setting (*Does the setting matter or is it just a backdrop?*), conflict (*What conflict exists and what problems can it cause for the characters?*), and plot (*What type of plot is this story?*).
- Assignments for the group can also focus on the author's style, such as imagery, figurative language, point of view, and the author's intent in writing this story.

Debriefing for Language Development

One of the most effective ways for the learner's brain to remember what it has just learned is allowing it to rehearse the new information very soon after being exposed to it. This process allows the learner to attach sense and meaning to the new learning—two requirements needed for most information to be encoded into long-term memory (Sousa, 2006). Take just a few minutes before the end of class and ask students to answer the following questions that can be done orally or in writing (Calderón, 2007):

- *What did you learn in this activity?* Be sure to say "learn" and not "do," as younger children may then focus on the mechanics of the activity (*We sat in a group, chairs in a circle . . .* , etc.) rather than on the content of the learning.
- *What made your learning easier?*
- *What made it difficult?*
- *How can you improve your learning?*
- *How can your team improve for the next time?*
- *What new words did you learn in this activity and what do they mean?*

Teaching Tip 5.7: Suggestions
for Teaching Social Studies to ELLs

Here are some strategies to consider for helping ELLs learn social studies. Adjust the strategies as needed for the students' age level and degree of competency in English.

- **Preteach Reading Assignments.** Discuss a reading assignment with ELL students before they read it. Model how they can use features of the textbook such as chapter overviews and summaries to preview the chapter content, to determine the learning goals, and to generate questions to self-monitor comprehension. Be sure to preteach unfamiliar vocabulary and help students activate prior knowledge through the use of KWL (Know/Want to Know/Have Learned) activities.
- **Use Role Plays.** Role plays help to make abstract concepts more concrete. For example, if ELLs are unfamiliar with the concept of negotiation, you could create a role play in which family members work together to resolve a dispute. If the ELLs lack the language skills to participate in a role play, other students can play the roles. The ELLs will still benefit from watching and listening.
- **Create Analogies.** Create analogies to help students link the unfamiliar with the familiar, especially for ELLs coming from a culture that is very different from that of the United States. For example, you might help the ELLs understand the concept of the U.S. president's cabinet by comparing it to a school in which each teacher has responsibility for a particular subject and group of students but reports to the principal. Be sure to point out differences as well as similarities to avoid oversimplifying or inadvertently misleading students.
- **Be a Considerate Lecturer.** To help struggling ELL listeners, distribute fill-in-the-blank lecture guides or graphic organizers before you lecture. As you lecture, tell students when to fill in each blank. Speak slowly and distinctly, and write key concepts and vocabulary on the board or on a flip chart. Use simple, familiar language whenever possible, avoid idiomatic expressions, and pause frequently to ask and answer questions.
- **Use Jigsaw Groups.** This form of collaborative learning provides support in reading and study. Divide a subject or a textbook chapter into five or six logical parts and assign each student to be responsible for learning and then teaching one of those parts. For example, if you want the students to learn about John F. Kennedy, you might divide a short biography of him into stand-alone segments on: (1) his childhood, (2) his family life with his parents and siblings, (3) his military service, (4) his major accomplishments as president, and (5) his tragic death and the aftermath.

To create jigsaw groups, assign each student a number from 1 to 5 or 6, then assign all the number 1 students the first part of the chapter, all the number 2 students the second part, and so on.

Then form temporary expert learning groups by putting all students with the same number in the same group (see diagram below). In this way, native speakers and ELLs work together to understand their section of the chapter, and ELLs are not overwhelmed by a long assignment.

After expert learning groups have finished reading and discussing their portions of the chapter, reorganize the class into teaching groups, each group containing one number 1 student, one number 2 student, and so on. Ask students to present their segment to the group. Encourage others in the group to ask questions for clarification. Move from group to group, observing the process. If any group is having trouble (e.g., a member is dominating or disruptive), make an appropriate intervention. At the end of the session, give some sort of assessment on the material so that students quickly come to realize that these sessions are not just fun and games but really count.

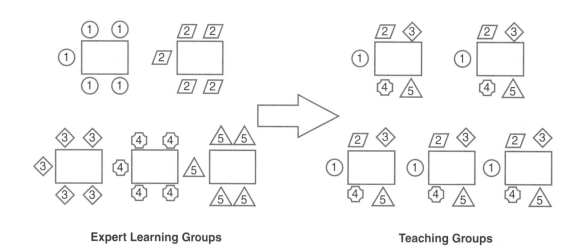

Expert Learning Groups   **Teaching Groups**

CHAPTER 5

Key Points to Ponder

Jot down on this page key points, ideas, strategies, and resources you want to consider later. This sheet is your personal journal summary and will help to jog your memory.

_____

_____

_____

_____

_____

_____

_____

_____

_____

_____

_____

_____

_____

_____

_____

Chapter 6

Teaching Mathematics and Science

TEACHING MATHEMATICS TO ELLs

Along with their ELL peers, even native English-speaking students have difficulty with learning mathematics, as evidenced by the poor performance of U.S. students on international standardized mathematics exams. For example, in the 2007 Trends in International Mathematics and Science Study (TIMSS) test for fourth grade, U.S. students stood in 11th place among the 36 nations whose students took the exam; in the eighth-grade test, U.S. students stood ninth among the 48 nations involved. The good news is that the U.S. scores have improved during the last 12 years that these tests have been given (IEA, 2007). On national tests, 39 percent of all fourth graders score at or above the proficient level on a national assessment of mathematics, whereas only 12 percent of ELLs score at or above the proficient level (NCES, 2009a). Clearly, there is a significant achievement gap that educators need to address. But of all the major content areas, research on teaching mathematics to ELLs is the sparsest. This may be due to the misguided belief that mathematics is less difficult for ELLs to learn because it is based on a more universally understood language: numbers, rather than English.

Just as we are born with an innate ability to acquire spoken language, we are also born with a number sense that allows us to assess how many objects are in a small collection. This capability, called *numerosity,* is not limited to humans; it exists in other animals as well. The logical extension of numerosity is the ability to learn the symbols and words that express larger numbers. Despite these inborn predispositions, we often hear students say, *I can't do math!*, but we never hear them say, *I can't do spoken language!* (Sousa, 2008). This lack of recognition that both the linguistic and number sense skills are innate has been the cause of wonder and frustration among neuroscientists who explore how the brain does arithmetic processing.

Some of the confusion occurs because many people, including educators, believe that mathematics is a nonverbal discipline. But recent research in how the brain learns mathematics contradicts this belief. Brain imaging studies show that language processing regions in the brain are activated along with the areas responsible for computation and symbolic representations (Dehaene et al., 2004; Siegler & Opfer, 2003). This alone is reasonable support for allowing ELLs, whenever possible, to master basic mathematics concepts in their primary language before tackling learning mathematics in English (Gutiérrez, 2002).

Figure 6.1 illustrates the three systems that researchers believe are involved when dealing with quantities and arithmetic computation. The visual processing system records the set of objects, the language processing area selects the appropriate word from the learner's mental lexicon, and the symbol representation area identifies the appropriate symbol for the number of objects. These systems are continually interacting with each other to provide a

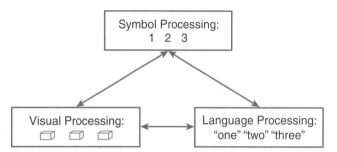

Figure 6.1 The diagram illustrates the three interactive cerebral systems involved in processing quantities. The visual system records the set of objects, the language processing area finds the word representation for their number ("three"), and the symbol representation system identifies the appropriate symbol (3).

response. Although ELL students may be able to mentally picture and even write down the correct symbol for a computation problem, the ability to say the answer in English relies on learning the words for number and mathematical operations. See **Teaching Tip 6.1** for general strategies that can help ELLs learn mathematics.

Language Issues

Language is a critical issue in mathematics teaching because most of the content is conveyed through oral language: Teachers tend to do the majority of the talking in mathematics class. ELL students do not derive a significant portion of their learning from reading mathematics textbooks. To understand mathematics, students need to be able to read, solve problems, and communicate using technical language in a specialized context—and to properly discuss and explain mathematics content, teachers must use technical language. Lower achievement in mathematics for ELLs is often the result of the high neural demand for English language processing. As Figure 6.2 illustrates, if significant working memory capacity must be devoted to language processing, then it follows that fewer cognitive resources are available to allocate to higher-order problem-solving activities, such as setting up the problem appropriately, identifying needed information, and checking progress toward the solution.

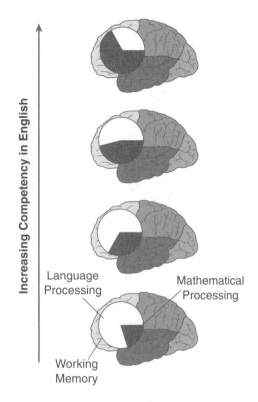

Increasing Competency in English

Language Processing

Mathematical Processing

Working Memory

Figure 6.2 As an ELL's competency in English increases, the amount of working memory resources (circle) devoted to language processing (white area in circle) decreases. Consequently, more resources can shift to mathematical processing and problem solving (dark area in circle).

Thus, the lack of proficiency in the English language and the specialized language of mathematics leads to frustration on the part of teachers who are faced with more and more ELL students in their mathematics classroom. When planning a lesson, teachers need to decide on a language objective in addition to the mathematics content objective. While the language objective includes those English mathematical terms and expressions that describe the problem and the operations, the content objective demonstrates the steps involved in solving it.

No doubt the language of mathematics presents an array of challenges to ELLs. Features such as symbolic notation, graphs, technical vocabulary, and complex grammatical phrases all pose substantial barriers. For instance, *5 multiplied by 10* is very different from *5 increased by 10. Divided by* and *divided into* will produce vastly different results. Number notation can even pose problems. For example, some countries use a comma to separate whole units from decimals instead of the period commonly used in North America, and a period to separate thousands (e.g., one million dollars in Europe is written as $1.000.000,00). The difficulty of learning the already-foreign language of mathematics is compounded when the instruction is also in a nonnative language.

Words and Symbols of Mathematics

The multiple meanings of words and the rules of English syntax allow us to interchange numerous terms or expressions to identify one mathematical concept. Teachers of mathematics are so accustomed to the content vocabulary that they are often not aware of the multiple terms used to describe the same operation. Addition, for example, uses *plus, total, add, combine, sum, put together, altogether, increase by, more than,* and *in all* to indicate its operation. Subtraction has its own list: *less, take away, difference, subtract, decrease by, minus, fewer than, are left, take from,* and *remain.* Thus, an ELL who has learned only the words *add* and *subtract* will be confused most of the time whenever a teacher uses other words to describe those operations. For instance, in a simple addition problem where two sets of apples are being combined into one, the teacher could say any of the following:

- *How many do we have in all?*
- *How many apples if we combine them?*
- *If we put together the first group of apples with the second group, what is the total?*
- *How many apples do we have altogether?*
- *The first group of apples plus the second group is how many?*

Spanish-speaking students might recognize *sum* and *total* as the Spanish cognates *suma* and *total*. But the other expressions would not be readily understood. Here is another example:

Johnny bought four bags of apples with six apples in each bag.

How many apples did he buy?

In this simple word problem we have both the past and present tense of the irregular verb *to buy* which could cause confusion for an ELL student with limited proficiency in English.

Although the language of mathematics and the language of everyday life can overlap, mathematics language in the classroom is often used to express concepts that are not necessary or important in everyday usage. Words such as *regroup, hypotenuse, coefficient,* and *exponent,* or the more complex terms such as *least common denominator, greatest common factor,* and *rational function,* are common in mathematics class but not in the students' social environs. On the other hand, many mathematical terms, such as *product, chance, table, scale,* and *value,* are deceptively familiar. Thus ELLs may believe that they comprehend the concepts that these terms represent long before they really do. Furthermore, the language of mathematics involves not only the language of specific terms but also the language of symbols such as $>$, $<$, $\sim$, $\div$, and x. Students need to know the words to understand the big concepts in mathematics and they need to know the symbols to engage in mathematical problem solving.

Consequently, one of the major challenges for ELLs in learning mathematical language is that most of it can be acquired only in the classroom and not through casual conversation. Mathematics teachers who have English learners in their classroom need to bridge this gap. For example, they might derive word problems from their students' personal narratives, thus helping students to comprehend the language of mathematics by placing it in the context of everyday experience. Teachers could also use familiar language to understand new concepts and find ways to use language cognates where appropriate, thereby promoting mathematical thinking.

Algebra, of course, poses its own set of linguistic challenges. One study of more than 220 middle school students, including both native speakers and English learners, compared the correctness of their answers to algebra problems to other data, including terms they indicated as being confusing (Lager, 2006). The study found that some of the words causing problems were not those generally considered to be part of the mathematics register, such as *extension* and *previous.* Rather, the more conceptually abstract terms were more difficult. Algebra teachers should be aware that language issues are fundamental to effective teaching of ELLs. Consider the linguistic challenge an ELL might have to face with the following problem:

Louis gave a total of 16 treats to his dogs. He gave his large dog two more treats than he gave his small dog. How many treats did he give to each dog?

In this problem, the ELL students need to understand the meaning of words such as *total* and *treats*. In addition, they must also comprehend the grammatical construction that conveys a mathematical relationship such as *more . . . than.* They also have to infer that Louis has just two dogs.

The structure and standard format for word problems can create difficulties not only for ELLs, but for native English speakers as well. This is because word problems often pose the following obstacles:

- The language used in the problem is more complex than it needs to be in order to do the mathematics. For example, *Three times a number is 2 more than 2 times the number. Number* refers to the same number in both cases.
- The language of the problem is tight and lacks redundancy. There are no repetitions or expansions, both of which help ELLs construct and validate meaning. The two most common ways to make the language tight are to leave out words, called an *ellipsis,* and to use pronouns and articles. Both of these linguistic features can lead ELLs to misinterpret a word problem.

Here are two ellipsis examples: (1) *All numbers greater than six . . .* is short for *All numbers (that are) greater than six . . .* (2) *John earns twice as much money as Robert* is short for *John earns twice as much money as Robert (earns).*

Here is an example using pronouns: *Juan has 16 action figures. He gave 9 of them away. How many action figures does he have now?* If the ELL students cannot figure out what the pronouns refer back to, they miss out on how the sentences relate to each other. The students may know all the words, yet not comprehend the meaning.

- The problem is either set in an artificial context or lacks context altogether, which can create confusion. For example, *Where in a tunnel would you see two trains pass each other if one train is traveling south toward it at . . . ?* The student wonders why anyone would be in that train tunnel in the first place.
- There is a lack of one-to-one correspondence between the words used in the problem and the mathematical symbols to express it. For example, if the expression *twelve divided by three* is written in this order, the resulting expression would be $12 \div 3 = ?$. English learners will tend to duplicate this sequence when constructing the mathematical expression from the order of words in a problem. Thus, for the statement, *The number* a *is six less than the number* b, they are likely to write $a = 6 - b$ instead of $a = b - 6$. And for the statement, *There are six times as many students in the mathematics department as teachers,* they may write $6s = t$, instead of the correct equation $6t = s$.
- The illustrations accompanying word problems often do not help in understanding the problem.

One approach to helping ELL students with word problems is to find out what strategies they use when they solve word problems and then to design instruction to build on successful strategies and eliminate unsuccessful ones. For example, one study used think-alouds to find out how Spanish-speaking ELLs in Grades 6 to 8 approached word problems (Celedón-Pattichis, 2003). Among the successful strategies the students used were reading the problem twice, translating the problem into Spanish, inferring meaning, using symbols to help understand the mathematics, and ignoring irrelevant words. Problems arose through misinterpreting words that students incorrectly assumed were homophones (such as *many* and *money,* or *than* and *then*), and misinterpreting mathematical symbols (such as reading 3 1/2 as "thirty-one slash two"). The students were also confused by mathematics language being used in a nonmathematical context (for example, a "2 1/2 can" to describe a large can in a problem about food containers of different sizes). Despite these problems, the think-alouds were helpful.

See **Teaching Tip 6.2** for suggestions on how to help ELLs with word problems and **Teaching Tip 6.3** for practice in rewriting word problems.

Cognitive Issues

Because cognitive processing is so closely tied to language processing, mathematics teachers of ELLs are faced with trying to assess whether the students have mastered a concept even if they have difficulty expressing their understanding in English. One method that has shown to be effective in dealing with this issue and assisting students in solving mathematics problems is *reciprocal teaching.* In reciprocal teaching, students read in small groups using cognitive strategies to comprehend the text. One study taught ELLs how to use four cognitive strategies to help them deal with the language challenge. The strategies were: (1) clarifying the meaning of words and phrases, (2) questioning to identify the key elements of the problem, (3) summarizing the purpose of the problem, and (4) coming up with a plan to solve it (van Garderen, 2004).

Sociocultural Issues

Culture is now defined at a level that emphasizes the beliefs and values that are often deeply rooted in a group's history and traditions. Many of the studies that examine sociocultural issues in mathematics address the teaching of native Spanish speakers. As is often the case, the studies show that teachers' beliefs and attitudes toward ELLs have a significant impact on the success of ELLs in learning mathematics. One extended study looked at a high school mathematics department in which the teachers had been consistently successful in convincing their students to take mathematics classes beyond what was required for high school graduation (Gutiérrez, 2002). Using observations and interviews of teachers and students, the study describes the attitudes and classroom techniques that characterized three particular mathematics teachers. These teachers possessed the following three characteristics that made them effective when working with ELLs:

- They were careful observers of their students and could identify their needs and backgrounds without relying on stereotypes.
- They did not require their students to speak in English at all times, thereby demonstrating that they valued their students' first language and culture. This was true even for those teachers who were not Spanish speakers.
- They asked their students to work in cooperative groups, giving the learners regular opportunities for exploring ideas through discussion with their peers.

Another study of successful interventions examined an urban school in which all the students were recent immigrants from Puerto Rico or Mexico (Daisey & José-Kampfner, 2002). Mathematics and language arts teachers collaborated on a project combining mathematics instruction, writing, and storytelling. The ultimate objective of the project was to help ELL students build their self-esteem through studying relevant role models. Through storytelling, the teachers spoke of successful Latina mathematicians and engineers, and followed that up with discussions to assess their students' prior knowledge. After one year, many more students produced drawings of Latinas at work, thereby displaying their newly discovered awareness of professional and technical careers for women.

One mathematics project with students from Mexico drew on their traditions by incorporating the contributions to mathematics made by the Mayans (Reyes & Fletcher, 2003). Teachers gave examples of using the Mayan calendar and Mayan mathematics. This culturally relevant approach is sometimes referred to as *ethno-mathematics.*

Pedagogical Issues

Successful mathematics teachers of ELLs believe that their students can achieve and value connections between their students' native cultures and the course curriculum. Because the English language can often be a barrier to ELLs trying to deal with mathematical language, these teachers pay close attention to classroom interactions and help ELLs talk their way through problems and give verbal explanations of their reasoning. By using oral language more than written, students can discover different approaches to problem solving while teachers get a better grasp on their ELLs' depth of understanding. Other successful instructional strategies include connecting the mathematics curriculum to ELL students' interests and to other curriculum content areas. Cooperative learning and other grouping strategies are also particularly effective because native English speakers in the group can help English learners get past any language difficulties and focus on learning and solving the problem at hand (Lee & Jung, 2004; Torres-Velasquez & Lobo, 2004/2005).

ELL students will have an easier time connecting mathematical concepts to their meaning in English through the use of manipulatives. Examples of manipulatives include calculators, rulers, compasses, scales, number lines, Cuisenaire rods, timekeepers of any type, and geometric objects. Use the manipulatives that are appropriate for the students' age and the lesson objective. The visual, tactile, and spatial components of using manipulatives to carry out mathematical operations can be a great help in overcoming the inherent difficulties of language comprehension. Different technological tools

> *ELLs have an easier time connecting mathematical concepts to their meaning in English through the use of manipulatives.*

can also aid ELLs. One study found that using interactive whiteboards with students in Grades 3 to 5 helped close the mathematics achievement gap between ELLs and students who were native English speakers (Lopéz, 2010).

Beal and her colleagues (2010) conducted a study to investigate the relationship of English language proficiency to mathematics problem solving and mathematics motivation in adolescent ELLs. Their sample included nearly 450 ninth-grade students enrolled in Algebra 1, roughly half of whom were English learners and half whose primary language was English. The researchers had available to them multiple measures of mathematics problem solving, including state achievement test scores, software pre- and posttest scores, and correct solutions to word problems recorded as students worked with an online tutorial software for prealgebra review. Also, the students completed a survey of their mathematics self-concept and the perceived value of mathematics in their lives.

The researchers found that many of these students were struggling with basic mathematics, and the teachers rated almost half of their students as failing or at risk of failing their algebra class. Although overall mathematics performance was poor, there were significant variations related to English proficiency. Not surprisingly, the ELL students scored lower than the students who spoke English as their primary language. The students' reading skills in English were significantly related to mathematics performance, whereas measures of English conversational proficiency (speaking and listening) were not. Perhaps more surprisingly, reading proficiency also predicted the ELL students' self-concept in mathematics. Thus, the ability to read English seems critical for success in mathematics for adolescent ELLs.

TEACHING SCIENCE TO ELLs

Studying science appeals to the curiosity in every child. Science is an uplifting subject. It is full of wonder. Albert Einstein said, "The most beautiful thing we can experience is the mysterious. It is the source of all true art and science." Because of its natural appeal and attention to everyday phenomena, science can be one of the content areas where ELLs feel most comfortable at first. They can touch rocks and minerals, grow and tend to plants and animals, and perform experiments to test ideas. But science has developed its own specialized vocabulary (often based in Latin and Greek words) so that scientists around the world can communicate. Native English speakers and ELL students alike need to learn this vocabulary in order to read science textbooks. An exciting and inquiry-based science program, however, may make it easier for the ELLs (and other students) to do so.

Language Issues

The reality of preparing ELLs for high-stakes testing presents a significant challenge for science teachers. Not only do ELL students vary greatly in their science knowledge and backgrounds, but they are often placed in science classes with native English speakers long before they are fluent in English. To make matters more challenging, ELLs are often required to pass a state science exam in order to receive a high school diploma. These realizations have prompted researchers to explore the classroom dynamics that occur when ELLs from different cultures interact with science teachers and science curriculum.

> *Studies reveal that ELLs learn specialized science vocabulary better when they are actually doing science.*

One group of Canadian studies examined classes of mixed ELLs at the secondary level and investigated how students' knowledge of science content and language developed in a classroom setting (Huang, 2004; Huang & Morgan, 2003). Students were taught about the structure of classification, read a text on the forms of matter that utilized the classification structure, and used a graphic organizer that represented the ideas found in the text. They were given examples of several linguistic features used in classifications such as how subcategories were named. Finally, the students wrote multiple drafts of a classification text, also on the topic of matter. The researchers analyzed the drafts and found that the ELLs showed a good command of science content knowledge, and used scientific terms and examples correctly.

Two studies looked at elementary-level science classes and found that ELL students' understanding of science improved when teachers used experimentation and writing in their instruction (Merino & Hammond, 2002). One study examined the language characteristics of different sections of lab reports written by students in a fifth-grade class. The other investigated the various ways that teachers structured and presented science writing assignments. For example, the teacher asked students to conduct an experiment and discuss the results with the class, generating a set of lab notes that the students then copied. These findings reinforce how important it is for ELLs to learn specialized vocabulary in the context of *doing* science. This approach allows the brain's mental lexicon to link unusual words with visual representations and physical actions.

Technical Vocabulary

Of all the content areas, the specialized and complex vocabulary of science probably poses the greatest language challenge to ELLs. Nonetheless, because many words used in science come from Latin roots, there are numerous cognates with similar words in the Romance languages. Here are some English/Spanish cognates of scientific words:

classification/clasificación

experiment/experimento

hypothesis/hipótesis

inference/inferencia

investigation/investigación

observation/observación

prediction/predicción

process/proceso

It should also be noted that some words in science are also used in mathematics but have different technical meanings. Examples of these words include *degree, density, experiment, image, radian, radical, simulation,* and *solution.*

ELLs need to acquire scientific vocabulary so that they can comprehend scientific discourse patterns. These patterns help ELLs recognize and understand the differences between expository and narrative text. Students read and process fiction and nonfiction differently. ELLs need to have practice reading, listening to the material, and using the common discourse patterns of science, such as *if_____, then_____.* One way to introduce the patterns of language used in talking and writing about science is to use children's books on scientific topics such as weather, environmental concerns, or the water cycle. Following small-group reading and discussion of parts of the book, students are asked to restate the information in the form of a science discourse pattern. Each pattern represents a different function of language within the science classroom. See **Teaching Tip 6.4** for some sample science discourse patterns that help ELLs understand the language of science.

Sociocultural Issues

Social and cultural connections can be easily overlooked in the fast-paced, curriculum-driven classroom. However, studies appear to show an improvement in ELLs' motivation and success in science when teachers design their instruction with an awareness of students' cultural backgrounds.

One major study investigated elementary science instruction carried out with students from differing cultural backgrounds (Lee, 2005). Among the objectives of the study was to determine how teacher–student discourse might differ among cultural groups, specifically monolingual English speakers, bilingual Spanish speakers, and bilingual Haitian Creole speakers. The researchers placed a teacher of one language background with a pair of students from the same background and asked them to complete three tasks found in their elementary science curriculum. The researchers found different patterns of interaction and task engagement among the three language groups. For example, the bilingual Spanish speakers often talked simultaneously, whereas both the Haitian Creole speakers and the monolingual English speakers used linear turn-taking. The Haitian Creole speakers, however, also had pauses and wait times in their interactions that the English speakers did not. Apparently, the style exhibited by the English-speaking groups was most compatible with the discourses of science, at least as practiced in a U.S. classroom. The Haitian students, for instance, seemed to rely heavily on the authority of the teacher, whereas the Spanish speakers' use of multiple turn-taking did not reflect the linear and sequential communication on a single topic that is favored in science discussion.

> *ELLs learn better in classrooms where the teacher incorporates instructional congruence.*

Teaching students of differing cultural backgrounds in ways that are familiar to them is called *cultural congruence,* but some suggest it should really be called *instructional congruence.* In instructional congruence, ELLs are expected to achieve and succeed according to the same standards of the science discipline as their native English-speaking peers. But for learning to take place, teachers need to make meaningful connections to the knowledge, perspectives, and behavior English learners bring to their classroom. These researchers give the example of how instructional congruence is realized with Latino students when their teachers talk at the same time as their students, use Spanish in the classroom, or use examples of science content familiar to these students.

Achieving instructional congruence is not easy because it is affected by several factors, including the cultural backgrounds of teachers and students, the content of the science teaching standards, and the depth of understanding teachers have of instructional approaches like inquiry learning that are currently favored when teaching science. Nonetheless, the researchers claim that when teachers are trained in instructional congruence in elementary school classrooms, it has a positive effect on student performance.

Researchers investigating sociocultural issues are concerned with providing ELLs with opportunities to succeed in science learning by doing science, rather than simply learning facts. Science discussions should open up a whole new range of ideas and investigations rather than lead students into an already-defined formulation of scientific definitions. One finding is clear across grade levels: It is recommended that teachers view their ELL students' perspectives as valuable intellectual resources that are complementary to scientific discourse.

Pedagogical Issues

Two studies investigated the effectiveness of an inquiry-based science curriculum with ELLs, based on the National Science Education Standards (Amaral, Garrison, & Klentschy, 2002;

Hampton & Rodriguez, 2001). With this approach, students learn scientific behaviors such as asking questions, gathering data, and considering evidence through hands-on activities. In these studies, some of the instruction was provided to elementary school students in English as well as in Spanish, and the authors found evidence of increasing academic success over time. In addition, the teachers believed that inquiry-based instruction increased the ELLs' language skills in both languages as well as their knowledge of the science content. A project in an urban setting helped teachers teach science through inquiry to third-grade students from a variety of language backgrounds (Lee et al., 2008). Researchers found that students in the inquiry classrooms scored higher on both science and mathematics achievement tests than students in comparison classrooms. Moreover, the achievement gap between ELLs and non-ELLs disappeared. These studies demonstrate that all students benefit when they have opportunities to interact with and talk about phenomena in science class. They also address the use of the ELLs' first language in content teaching, and it is worth noting that the teachers perceived the use of the first language as being beneficial.

Despite the numerous studies on ELLs in the science classroom, there is no research consensus on the best instructional approaches for ELLs. However, those strategies that show promise— instructional congruence, incorporation of student modes of discourse into classroom interaction, and explicit teaching of the discourses of science—do require that teachers understand these approaches. To be successful with ELLs, science teachers must be familiar not only with science content, but also the ways of knowing embraced by the ELLs' culture and must demonstrate their respect for them within the classroom. Ultimately, the best approach for all students is to effectively engage them in practicing what scientists do (rather than simply memorizing facts) through classroom activities that are student centered, exploratory, and meaningful.

Edmonds (2009) suggests that teachers must recognize the five primary challenges ELLs face when learning science content in their classrooms. Some are related to their cultural perceptions of science while others stem from their language and writing skills. These challenges include:

- **Relating to How American/Western Culture Perceives the Sciences.** Culture plays an important role in our understanding of science, and in North America, it is very much linked to the worldviews held by Western societies. Western scientists have laid the foundation for the perception that we live in a linear-progressive world. When viewed through a linear-progressive lens, the world is seen as a place that is continually improving. But many cultures that are not part of Western society see the world through a cyclical lens. They believe that the world is at its best when the wisdom and traditions of the ancestors are revered, and see the condition of the environment as evidence that we are straying from ancient wisdom. From their worldview, industrialization and globalization may look more like destruction than progress. ELLs who have cultural beliefs that are not consistent with Western science should be taught in a way that allows them to cross cultural borders between the two domains.
- **Understanding the Science Content Being Taught.** If the instruction is basically through lecture, ELLs can easily become lost. Although they may have interest in the science content,

their inability to persevere with the lecture format will raise their anxiety and cause them to give up out of frustration.

- **Using Academic Language to Discuss Scientific Concepts.** ELLs who demonstrate some fluency in English may struggle with the type of English used in science class. Science language is different from conversational English, and even seemingly fluent speakers of English need to develop discourse specific to science in order to accurately conceptualize the science they are being taught.
- **Participating in Class Discussions.** ELLs are often reluctant to participate in class discussion because of their limited proficiency in English and for fear of making grammatical and content-related mistakes. Yet discussion is an important part of discourse in science to review experimental results and their implications and to propose further investigations.
- **Writing Appropriate Scientific Academic Texts.** Some ELLs can speak English well but write poorly. Standards for scientific writing vary among cultures. Although the writing of some ELL students may appear disorganized to us, it may be well-constructed according to the writing norms of their native culture.

See **Teaching Tip 6.5** for suggestions on how to help ELLs with these five challenges in their science classes.

Focus on the Scientific Method

Among the most important tools that the ELLs learn in science classes is the scientific model. Consisting of seven steps, it is a universal model that will help ELLs solve problems in other content areas outside science. The scientific method is the basis for the inquiry approach to teaching science. Rather than teaching inert facts, the inquiry approach poses scientific questions and problems for students to explore. It offers ELLs opportunities to participate in and develop the language of school science. As ELLs read scientific texts and laboratory manuals, science teachers should use clear and simple language to help the ELLs recognize the following steps in the inquiry model.

- **Statement of the Problem.** What does the scientist want to know?
- **Information Needed.** What information does the scientist already have about the problem?
- **Hypothesis.** What would be an educated guess about the answer to the problem?
- **Method.** What carefully followed procedure (experiment) will the scientist use to test the hypothesis?
- **Data.** What information was collected during the experiment?
- **Observations.** What was noticed during the experiment?
- **Conclusion.** Based on the data and observations, was the hypothesis correct or incorrect?

See **Teaching Tip 6.6** for suggestions on helping ELLs learn and use the scientific method.

Science teachers of ELLs have the opportunity to use strategies that help their students not only to understand science concepts but also to develop English listening, speaking, reading, and writing skills. These strategies include modifying teacher talk, promoting collaboration among ELL and non-ELL students, making science relevant to the students' everyday lives, adapting existing science textbooks, and using language-teaching techniques when presenting science concepts. By doing so, science teachers can demonstrate to ELL students the preparation they need to succeed in understanding the language and nature of science while improving their English language skills as well.

WHAT'S COMING

As in all student populations, some portion of ELL students will have learning disabilities. But recognizing whether a student is struggling because of language acquisition or a learning problem is not easy. Consequently, some ELLs may be misidentified as needing special services while others who do have a disability may be overlooked. So how do we get it right? The next chapter offers suggestions on how to assess the nature of a struggling ELL student's learning problems and how to address them.

Teaching Tip 6.1: General Strategies for Helping ELLs Learn Mathematics

Many mathematics teachers often have a wide range of language levels in their classrooms, from beginning ELLs to fully proficient native English speakers. Determining how to meet all their needs in one mathematics lesson can seem overwhelming. Nonetheless, the dual challenges of learning the language of English and the language of mathematics simultaneously pose significant barriers to ELLs. Although their motivation to learn mathematics plays a key role, their success will also depend largely on their learning environment and the strategies their teachers select for instruction and assessment. Here are some suggested strategies culled from numerous sources. They fall into five categories: auditory (oral), visual, instructional, scaffolding, and assessment. As you review them, write in those strategies that you are currently using or would like to try.

Auditory/Oral Strategies

ELLs who have difficulty reading their mathematics text in English will rely heavily on your oral presentations in class, so you may wish to consider the following strategies.

- Use simple sentence structures in your speech, and provide direct instructions.
- Avoid jargon, idiomatic speech, and figurative language, and explain the meaning when you do use it.
- Provide opportunities for ELLs to practice their mathematics vocabulary using a variety of strategies, such as think-alouds and grouping. Research studies show that ELLs succeed more in mathematics when they become part of an oral discourse where they can communicate mathematical thinking, make sense of mathematical tasks, and exchange and debate mathematical ideas (Hufferd-Ackles, Fuson, & Sherin, 2004).
- Clearly model the language and vocabulary that you expect the ELL students to use.
- Explain any homophones that are used in the mathematics assignments as, for example, *cosine/cosign, dual/duel, graph/graft, pi/pie, plane/plain, rows/rose, sine/sign, sum/some,* and *whole/hole.*
- For native Spanish speakers, there are some cognates that will help them with mathematical terms. Here are some English/Spanish cognates: *algebra/algebra, complement/ complementar, equation/ecuación, factor/factor, graph/graf, perpendicular/perpendicular, sum/suma.*
- Provide alternatives to oral presentations, such as using presentation software.

Visual Strategies

The ELL's mental lexicon has the task of connecting English phonemes to the letters that represent them. By providing opportunities for ELLs to make these auditory-visual connections in English, teachers support the growth of that lexicon and help motivate ELLs.

- Write key mathematical words on an overhead projector, chalkboard, interactive board, or on a flip chart whenever you are discussing them. Pronounce them slowly and clearly so ELLs can connect the sounds they hear to the letters they see.
- Identify language that might confuse ELLs because the words mean one thing in everyday conversation and another in mathematics as, for example, *create a table* and *determine the volume*, and review those terms prior to teaching the lesson.
- Connect verbal, written, and pictorial or symbolic representations of the same word or expression.
- Explain any structural patterns that are found in expository text as, for example, a sequence or a series of steps to solve particular types of problems.
- Make available any type of visual vocabulary and language supports that make use of the ELLs' first language such as charts, dictionaries, and word walls that the students can use when translating is needed.
- Guide students through the text before they begin reading and have them focus on headings, subheadings, charts, graphs, visuals, and symbols.
- Point out contextual clues that help with meaning, especially with words such as *table* and *operation* that have a different meaning from everyday language.
- Ask ELLs to keep a personal word study notebook or journal that includes key words from each mathematics lesson. Drawings, symbols, and words in their first language are appropriate additions to the vocabulary list.

Instructional Strategies

All instruction needs to take place in a classroom climate that welcomes and supports English language learners. Start by encouraging ELLs with sufficient oral language skills to share how classrooms and expectations differ in their home countries. Realize that some students may not have been attending school in their home countries. If possible, pair each English learner with a first-language peer who also speaks English.

- Teach key vocabulary explicitly and reinforce it on an ongoing basis.
- Whenever possible, post mathematical symbols with word definitions and examples to clarify meaning.

- Explain the strategies and steps necessary to complete instructional tasks and check for student understanding before students start the task independently. Present numerous examples of the concepts being taught.
- Reinforce mathematical concepts and vocabulary by
  - incorporating the systematic use of visuals and graphic organizers, such as T-charts and Venn diagrams for relationships.
  - moving from concrete (manipulatives) to visual (charts and graphs) to abstract (concepts) representations when teaching and when asking students to present their solutions.

- Make strategic use of the ELL's first language, whenever possible, to set the context for introducing new concepts. Provide access to materials written in the ELLs' first language to support their literacy and cognitive development.
- Consider using a word generation chart to help ELLs with mathematical and English language acquisition. Here is an example of one possible format:

Word Generation Chart for Lesson(s) on _____					
Word	Mathematics language meaning	Everyday language meaning	Other forms of the word	Cognates in ELLs' first language	Example of how word was used in lesson

Scaffolding Strategies

Scaffolds are incremental learning steps that expand on previous knowledge and skills and build toward an instructional goal. For ELL students, scaffolds help support English language development as well as the development of mathematical skills and concepts.

- Ask students to restate other students' comments, ask a question, or add their own ideas. This technique allows for rehearsal of both the languages of English and mathematics.
- When showing the steps of problem solving, explain your thought process by using vocabulary that English learners will understand.
- Provide sentence prompts for ELLs to use as they learn new academic language in mathematics, such as "Another way of saying this is. . . ."

- Use questions that help ELLs sort out what they understand and what they need to learn next, such as "What do you already know that can help you solve this problem?" and "What else do you need to know?" This sets the stage for the next scaffolding activity.
- Help students use manipulatives, interactive games, and technology as thinking tools.
- Encourage ELLs to use graphic organizers, diagrams, gestures, and sketches to aid in thinking and in communicating with others.
- Correct errors and give positive feedback using prompts, gestures, encouragement, and praise. ELLs from various cultures may react quite differently to criticism.
- Provide handouts that help students structure, organize, and guide their work, such as skeleton notes, summaries of past concepts, and outlines of future topics to be covered.

Assessment Strategies

Assessment in mathematics can be challenging because it may be difficult to determine whether ELL students' errors are due to lack of competency in English, mathematics, or both. Formative assessments can be very useful tools in distinguishing between language and content knowledge.

- Gather as much data as possible about your ELLs' prior knowledge and experiences to help them make connections to new learning.
- Check for accuracy of the ELLs' prior knowledge.
- Design assessments to uncover specific gaps that might exist in the ELLs' mathematical knowledge and experience.
- Realize that mathematical concepts or ideas learned in any language can be transferred to English.
- Prepare students for assessment by incorporating strategies that activate any prior knowledge. These include brainstorming, providing analogies, and using organizers such as KWL charts, T-charts, Venn diagrams, and flowcharts.
- Help students use mathematical tools with which they might be unfamiliar, such as calculators, rulers, and computer software programs.
- Check for understanding by also observing students' body language and facial expressions.
- Use assessment practices that are good for all students, and that can be adjusted for ELLs.
- Avoid relying on just one type of assessment by incorporating a wide variety of assessment strategies, such as performance tasks and conferences, that allow students to demonstrate their understanding in ways other than through reading and writing.
- Observe and assess students as they work in groups and provide encouragement for interaction and contribution. Ask questions to check for understanding and to maintain accountability.

- Guide students in acquiring self-monitoring skills that help them identify difficulties they have in understanding what they know, need to know, and do.
- Conduct frequent briefing sessions with ELLs to discuss difficulties resulting from a lack of understanding of the language.
- Provide timely and frequent feedback on their growth in English language acquisition, especially academic language.
- Teach self-evaluation strategies, and involve the students in self-monitoring their learning.
- Differentiate assessment by adjusting the assessment tools and strategies to meet the needs of ELLs.
- Provide bilingual dictionaries (first language/English), or allow ELLs to use their personal word study notebook, when taking tests.
- Use assessment information to guide further instruction to help the ELLs acquire the language skills needed to understand the mathematics.

Debriefing Strategies

Whenever possible after an activity, debrief the ELLs (and other students) on their learning. This rehearsal helps students reflect on the content they learned during the activity as well as any problem-solving strategies that were successful. It reinforces positive behaviors, gets them talking about mathematics, and increases the likelihood that what they learned will be placed in long-term memory for future recall. The debriefing includes questions such as the following:

- *What mathematics did you learn today?*
- *What strategies did you try and why?*
- *How did you solve the problem?*
- *Are there other solutions that could work?*
- *What difficulties did you have? Were you able to solve them?*

The debriefing takes only a few minutes, but it can be a valuable investment in time because of the increased possibility that the learner will retain the content and skills that were part of the learning objective.

Teaching Tip 6.2: Suggestions for Helping ELLs With Word Problems in Mathematics

Word problems can pose a significant language challenge for ELL students. Recall that the more resources working memory must use to process language, the fewer resources are available for mathematical processing. Thus, the easier you can make it for ELLs to get past the language hurdles and understand what one is looking for to solve a word problem, the more successful they are likely to be. Here are some suggested strategies for dealing with the language component of word problems.

- **Be alert for words in problems that are the cause of comprehension difficulties.** The words in English that cause particular difficulties for ELLs are usually those that (1) express quantitative relationships and (2) link phrases and sentences to express a logical relationship. See the following.

    Quantitative relationships: *hardly, higher, last, least, less, longer, many, most, next, older, rarely, scarcely,* and *younger.*

    Logical relationships: *alike, almost, always, because, different from, exactly, if, never, not quite, opposite of, probably, same, since, unless,* and *whether.*

    Explain these words using visual aids and manipulatives whenever possible.

- **Rewrite the problem and put the question first.** When and where appropriate, rewrite the problem so that it is clear what is being sought. Remove unnecessary words, phrases, and complicated syntax, and replace complex words with simpler synonyms. Most importantly, put the problem's question *first*. This alerts the ELL's brain at the very beginning as to what it must solve, thus enabling it to select the information it needs from the remaining text to perform the needed mathematical operations. Here is a simple example:

    (Original problem):   *If Peter can type one page of his homework report on his computer in 17 minutes, how much time will it take him to type three pages?*

    (Rewritten problem):   *How much time will it take Peter to type three pages? He can type one page in 17 minutes.*

The rewritten problem is easier for ELLs (and non-ELLs, too) because it removes extraneous words, places the question up front, and avoids the difficult *If . . . then* logical connector. Try your hand at rewriting some typical word problems in **Teaching Tip 6.3.**

- **Explain difficult vocabulary and syntax.** Understanding a word problem is more difficult when the concept relies on the relationship between two words. For example:
    o Billy is *as* old *as* Jane
    o Jane is 6 years *older* than Robert

○ All numbers *greater/less* than *x*

○ *By what percent is* 12 *increased to make* 18?

○ *Divided by* versus *divided into*

○ Bart earns 5 times *as much as* Homer

○ When 8 *is added* (passive voice) to *x*

- **Use think-alouds.** Use this technique to review the problem and to narrate the problem-solving process, including any needed algorithms. Some ELLs may be accustomed to algorithms that are different from traditional algorithms taught in your curriculum. Allow students the opportunity to share their algorithms, and use this discussion as a learning opportunity by comparing algorithms and analyzing their similarities and differences.

- **Teach meaning of common terms.** When reviewing the problem, clarify any terms that have other definitions outside of mathematics and explain their meaning in a mathematical context. Such words include, *prime, term, root, table, mean,* and *face.*

- **Use informal language.** To increase understanding, use informal language as you demonstrate the various thought processes and steps to follow in solving a problem. Explain when you are using a simpler word or words to replace a technical one as, for example, *We want to find the distance around the circle, that is, we want to find the circumference.* Now the ELL's mental lexicon can associate the word *circumference* as meaning the *distance around the circle.*

- **Check for understanding.** Check for understanding of the task at hand and the processes involved before the ELLs get started working on the assignment. ELL students often do not seek clarification for fear of calling attention to themselves.

- **Use real-world situations and context.** Use (or rewrite) word problems so that they involve applications to real-world and contextualized situations such as those involving entertainment, sports, and games. These problems should also encourage critical thinking and mathematical reasoning. Engaging ELLs in this way makes learning relevant to the real-life experiences of your students.

- **Include relevant diagrams and graphs.** Use a diagram, graph, and other visual aids to help ELLs understand what mathematical processing they need to solve the problem. For example, you can use diagrams to help ELLs understand the various ways to approach solving word problems by building a chart, such as the one on the next page.

- **Provide for student discussions.** After working on the word problem, ask students to reveal where they may have had problems, such as what words or expressions were difficult to understand. During the discussion, focus on reasoning and decrease the focus on language. This emphasis encourages ELLs to expand their mathematical abilities without getting bogged down with issues related to language acquisition.

Strategies for Problem Solving in Mathematics		
Draw a Picture Create a Model	Use Simpler Numbers 1, 5, 20 ~~100, 500, 20, 000~~	Write an Equation $a^2 + b^2 = c^2$
Look for a Pattern	Make a Chart, List, or Table	Work Backwards

- **Maintain word-problem journals.** Use journals to practice and strengthen new language skills and to include any new mathematical terms the ELLs learned when solving the word problem. Journals help students develop language skills in a nonthreatening manner. Some ELLs may feel more comfortable using their native language in their journals as a way to help solidify their understanding of mathematical concepts, but it is important that they practice the associated English translation as well.

Teaching Tip 6.3: Rewriting
Word Problems in Mathematics

Simply rewriting a word problem for language clarity can help ELLs be successful at solving them. When rewriting, consider the following:

- Deleting irrelevant information
- Replacing complex phrases with simpler ones, using present tense and active voice
- Where possible, reordering words so the syntax has a one-to-one correspondence to the appropriate mathematical expression
- Putting the question first, using high-frequency words

Here are some typical word problems similar to those found on state tests. Rewrite the problem in a way you think will make the problem more understandable for ELLs. Share your rewrites with colleagues and discuss other rewriting possibilities. Finally, consider what you might do as a result of this activity. (Note: This activity presumes that the ELLs have knowledge of the U.S. Customary System of measurements and the Fahrenheit scale.)

- Cathy drove her new hybrid car an average of 40 miles per day for the first 4 days of her work week. What would her daily average be for her five-day work week if she drove 35 miles on the fifth day?

_____

_____

_____

- George spent 1 hour and 30 minutes raking the yard in the morning and 1 hour and 45 minutes in the afternoon. How long did he rake altogether?

_____

_____

_____

- In a football game, a team gained 3 yards, then another 11 yards, was penalized and lost 15 yards and gained 6 yards. What was the net gain of their three successive plays?

_____

_____

_____

- At 8:00 a.m., John's thermometer registered 5° F. By 5:00 p.m., the temperature had dropped 18 F degrees. What was the temperature at 5:00 p.m.?

  _____

  _____

  _____

- A jacket in the department store was regularly priced at $63. The jacket went on special sale at $1/3$ off the regular price. How much was saved?

  _____

  _____

  _____

- The plan for a new country house is drawn to the scale of $1/4$ inch = 4 feet. What is the length of the house if it measures 3 $1/2$ inches on the floor plan?

  _____

  _____

  _____

- A sewing machine can sew a set of curtains in $3/4$ of an hour. It takes a person 6 $1/2$ hours to do this same job by hand. How much less time is required to do the job by machine?

  _____

  _____

  _____

Reflection:

As I reflect on this activity, I will consider doing the following:

_____

_____

_____

_____

_____

Teaching Tip 6.4: Sample
Science Discourse Patterns for ELLs

To succeed in science courses, ELLs will not only need to learn the vocabulary of scientific language but also understand how science is spoken and written—what is called the discourse of science. An effective method for helping ELLs gain an understanding of scientific discourse is to have them read a simple book on some scientific concept such as weather, dinosaurs, or environmental pollution. After reading the book, the ELLs discuss what they learned by trying to fit their statements into the appropriate science discourse pattern. For example, after reading a book on dinosaurs, a student may use the Cite Information discourse and say, *Here we see that the birds of today are related to the ancient dinosaurs.* With practice and corrective feedback, the ELLs will become accustomed to phrasing their statements in science class in scientific discourse language.

Here are some language functions and their related scientific discourse patterns:

- **Cause and Effect**

  The _____ had _____ so _____.

- **Cite Information**

  Here we see that _____.

- **Compare**

  This _____ is similar to that _____ because both _____.

- **Construct Charts, Tables, and Graphs**

  Plot _____ and _____.

  Plot _____ as _____.

  Graph the independent variable _____ as a function of _____.

- **Contrast**

  This _____ is different from that _____ because one has _____ and the other doesn't _____.

- **Describe**

  The _____ has _____, _____, and _____.

- **Disagree**

  I don't think the evidence supports _____ because _____.

  I don't agree with that statement because _____.

- **Distinguish Fact From Opinion**

  Although you say _____, the table/graph says _____.

- **Draw Conclusions**

  The _____ is _____ because _____.

- **Estimate**

  Looking at the _____, I think there are _____.

- **Give and Support Opinions**

  I think_____is_____because_____.

- **Hypothesize**

  If _____had_____, then_____would have_____.

- **Identify Relationships**

  This_____is necessary for_____because of_____.

- **Make Predictions**

  I think_____will_____.

- **Measure**

  A _____is _____cm. long, _____cm. wide, and _____cm. tall.

  This_____holds a volume of_____ml.

- **Persuade**

  As we just saw in the experiment,_____does_____due to_____.

- **Retell**

  First_____, next_____, and then_____.

- **Sequence**

  We saw that first_____, then_____and at the end_____.

- **Summarize**

  The main idea from this observation is that_____.

Teaching Tip 6.5: Instructional Strategies to Help ELLs in Science Classes

Here are five major challenges that ELLs face in science classes and some suggestions on how to address them (Edmonds, 2009).

- **Relating to How American/Western Culture Perceives the Sciences**
  Using ELL students' native culture to build on Western science concepts can be done in several ways.

  o Draw on the students' background knowledge from their native cultures at the beginning of each lesson by activating prior knowledge. This positive transfer also helps you assess what students know and whether or not they are connecting with the topic.

  o Access the ELLs' store of knowledge by asking them to speak with older relatives to get cultural information about a science topic being introduced in class. For example, in a lesson on managing waterways, the teacher could ask students to interview an older relative about how they (in their native cultures) took care of the waterways where they lived. This information that students bring back to class serves as the beginning of a list of things we could do to improve our waterways.

  o Establish a word wall. Post new vocabulary terms on the wall in an organized, grouped manner. For example, you may wish to post new biology terms in columns according to the level of organization (cell, tissue, organ, etc.). Scientific terms in the ELLs' native language can be placed alongside the English terms.

- **Understanding the Science Content Being Taught**
  Students who are not native speakers of English can easily get lost during a lecture, so you want to prevent this from happening.

  o Ensure that the lesson is clearly spelled out on the board and through discussion at the beginning of the class.

  o Provide students with markers to help them get back on track if they get lost. Markers are like street signs on the road map to scientific understanding. When students realize they are lost, they can look for a marker to figure out what is taking place in class. Markers are provided through a simple numbered outline, and each number represents an objective. As you progress through the lesson, state (and point out on the overhead or board) the number. This way, if students are struggling with listening comprehension, they can use the written language as a guide.

  o Make concepts highly visible. Lessons should always begin with a visual aid that will assist ELLs with understanding the concept being taught. Visual aids include a photograph, graph, cartoon, demonstration, or any other creative visual aid.

- **Using Academic Language to Discuss Scientific Concepts**

  ELLs are likely to have difficulty with the specialized vocabulary of science.

  o Model the language and thought process for ELLs with think-alouds and other metacognitive techniques for understanding.

  o Ask the students to explain a concept first. Then repeat the concept, model the scientific language, and write the new terms on the board. Use these terms frequently and ask students to use them as well. This technique ensures that students notice this new language while making connections between the words and the concept in their mental lexicon.

  o Consider using language-based science games such as Science Bingo, and concepts with Science Pictionary. These games require minimal spoken language and provide an excellent review of science vocabulary.

  o Develop a picture-based glossary. One of the best ways to learn the vocabulary of a new language is with pictorial flash cards. A picture of the concept is on one side while the English term is on the reverse. The student learns to correlate concepts directly with words, eliminating the need for translation.

  o Identify cognates. Many science terms are used internationally. Identify such terms and ask your students to notify you whenever they recognize a new term that is pronounced or written similarly in their first language. This helps build your knowledge of cognates so you can help future learners master science vocabulary.

- **Participating in Class Discussions**

  In a class with ELLs, teachers often encounter the problem of having some students who do not verbally participate and some who may participate too much. Try these techniques to achieve a more balanced level of participation from students.

  o At the beginning of the school year, explain what it means to take part in discussions and to allow others to talk as well. Tell them that students are expected to talk and participate in class by answering questions or sharing a thought or idea. They should also respectfully listen to other classmates sharing their answers or ideas and allow some moments of silence so that students can gather their thoughts and courage.

  o Model talking and yielding to another student so that they understand how to do both. With a few gentle reminders to the most talkative students, the quieter students soon get the courage to participate.

  o Help students demonstrate what they understand without having to rely fully on their ability to articulate their knowledge. For example, you could provide a visual module for a concept you are teaching and ask ELLs to explain the process. As students demonstrated their knowledge, supplement their verbal explanation and allow them to rephrase it themselves after providing the missing vocabulary they need. If their verbal explanation still lacks fluency or competence, give them credit for correctly demonstrating their knowledge, but then repeat the correct verbal form of the response to model the English for them.

o Group students together to work collaboratively toward a clear learning objective. One option is for them to first work in pairs and then for two pairs to work as one group of four. Starting with pairs and gradually building to larger groups allows students who are not used to participating in classroom discussions to slowly build confidence.

- **Writing Appropriate Scientific Academic Texts**

  It is important to help ELLs notice the difference between their native writing norms and those of native English speakers in science.

  o Model a writing sample for each formal assignment. Explain specifically what makes the sample a good model of formal scientific writing.

  o After the ELLs have written their first draft, meet with them individually and explain one or two of the biggest difficulties with their formal writing. This helps ELLs notice the gaps between their formal writing and the model.

Remind ELLs that science is not about specific terminology or content. Rather, it is an approach to problem solving that involves questioning, gathering and analyzing data, and communicating results to others. As the English proficiency of ELLs grows, so will their confidence in mastering the language of science.

Teaching Tip 6.6: Strategies to Help
ELLs Learn and Use the Scientific Method

The scientific method is one of the most valuable tools that all students learn in science. But the science classroom is often a frustrating place for ELLs. Science has a complex vocabulary that is difficult even for native English speakers to learn. Nonetheless, difficulty in learning English should not be confused with an inability to think scientifically. Many of the following strategies that are useful for ELLs are also effective for differentiating instruction for other students. Use a variety of techniques to determine which ones work best with your teaching style and students.

- **Preparing for a Scientific Investigation (What do you want to find out?)**
  - Discover what your students already know about the given topic and relate the investigation to their background knowledge of science concepts.
  - Use analogies to relate new concepts to previously learned concepts.
  - Review the experimental procedure. Speak slowly, distinctly, and write down key terms so students can see them and connect them to the spoken word.
  - Find a video that explains the problem under investigation, but does not give away the conclusion. Most science videos have closed captioning. Turn on the closed captioning so students can see what narrators and actors are saying. This helps the ELLs correlate written and spoken English, and helps them see spelling and sentence construction.

- **Collecting Information (What will you examine?)**
  - Introduce visual aids whenever possible as they often help ELL students transcend the scientific language barriers.
  - Use graphic organizers as a means of introducing an experimental problem and assessing concepts in a manner that encourages meaningful learning. Because graphic organizers show the relationship between new and existing concepts, they facilitate the integration of new and familiar ideas. They require minimal language and are therefore helpful tools when teaching science to ELLs. Conceptual grids, Venn diagrams, flowcharts, mind maps, and concept maps are some of the more common graphic organizers.

- **Formulating a Hypothesis (What do you think will happen?)**
  - Use earlier projects and cooperative learning to provide opportunities for students to exchange, write, and present ideas when formulating a hypothesis. Projects require a variety of skills that work together to increase understanding and retention of learning.
  - Show a science video that introduces the new terms and concepts related to the experiment. Pause the video to discuss key concepts. Use the bookmark and video clip features to return to precise sequences for review after the experiment.
  - Partner ELLs with strong English speakers or with bilingual students who can translate laboratory and activity procedures.

- **Testing the Hypothesis: Procedure/Method (What procedure will you follow to find your answer?)**

  o Ensure that the ELL students are fully aware of and understand the laboratory safety procedures before they begin work.

  o Recognize that the science laboratory can be a confusing and potentially dangerous setting for ELLs. Present procedures clearly using flowcharts, pictures, and outlines.

  o Provide a visual reference to glassware and other materials used in experiments and activities. Review safety symbols and post them in the room and in the lab handout.

  o Model laboratory activities, if needed, in front of the class to ensure that ELL students can see the procedures before engaging in an activity.

- **Collecting Data (What information do you need to answer the question?)**

  o Provide an outline of a chart or other type of organizer that ELL students can use to record their data without having to rely on complex scientific vocabulary.

- **Making and Reporting Observations (What did you find out and what does the information tell you?)**

  o Show students how using scatter and line graphs, column and bar charts, pie and area graphs, and high-low, combination, and log plots to present their data can communicate their findings with minimal use of spoken or written language.

  o Encourage ELL students to report their experimental findings to a group or to the class. Remember that many ELLs come from countries in which student participation is not encouraged. They may be reluctant to speak, not only because of their lack of proficiency in English, but also because they are uncomfortable sharing their ideas. Sometimes, requiring ELLs to speak in front of the class may be counterproductive and cause great anxiety. Encourage them to express themselves, but do not force them to participate prematurely.

  o For ELL students who are eager to share their ideas, the think/pair/share strategy is a particularly effective way of encouraging them to express science concepts in English. This technique is a cooperative discussion strategy whereby the teacher provokes students' thinking with a question or prompt or observation. The students take a few moments to think about the question and then pair up to talk about the answer that each came up with. They compare and identify the answers they think are best, most convincing, or most unique. The teacher calls for pairs to share their thinking with the rest of the class.

- **Reporting the Conclusion (Based on the information you collected, what is the answer to your question?)**

  o Ask ELLs to report their findings to a group or to the class, using any charts, graphs, or visual aids that will reduce their dependence on spoken and written language.

  o Consider requiring ELLs to keep science journals in which they write the results of their experiments, lecture notes, and new terms. Students become better writers by writing.

CHAPTER 6

Key Points to Ponder

Jot down on this page key points, ideas, strategies, and resources you want to consider later. This sheet is your personal journal summary and will help to jog your memory.

_____

_____

_____

_____

_____

_____

_____

_____

_____

_____

_____

_____

_____

_____

_____

Chapter 7

Recognizing and Addressing Problems in Learning English

LEARNING PROBLEM OR LEARNING DISABILITY?

Juan was having a difficult time learning English. He had been living in New Jersey for more than four years. He was in the fourth grade and his teachers could hardly understand him when he spoke or read in English. His parents were from Venezuela, but they often spoke English at home to help and encourage their children to learn the language. Juan's two younger siblings were making exceptional progress in developing their English language skills. Why not Juan? His classroom teacher had worked with other Spanish-speaking students over the years. But Juan's progress in English was just too slow and she suspected a language-learning disability. She referred Juan to a Child Study Team (a special education prereferral panel). A battery of tests and subsequent visits to medical specialists revealed that Juan had developmental dyslexia. Fortunately, in Juan's case, a perceptive teacher who had experience teaching many ELLs decided Juan's progress was not typical and got him the help he needed. But there are other ELLs like Juan who continue to struggle with no supplemental assistance.

One of the most difficult challenges facing teachers who work with ELLs is determining whether their lack of progress in learning English is due to insufficient practice or to a learning disability related to language acquisition. The first question that arises is: How can we tell the difference? And the second question is: If we find that an ELL student's poor performance in acquiring English is the result of a learning disability, what do we do about it? Most curriculum in our schools is written for middle-class native English speakers. The assumptions that the writers make about the cultural and social background of these students influence the organization, content, and activities that the curriculum encompasses. Yet the curriculum may have little in common with the wide variety of backgrounds that ELLs represent in our schools today. Consequently, students struggle not only with the language challenges but also with the social and cultural components of curriculum that may seem very foreign to them. This struggle may result in greater difficulty in learning to speak, read, and write English and may be misinterpreted as a learning disability.

Dilemmas in Identifying ELLs With Disabilities

Just how difficult the identification of ELLs with disabilities can be was apparent in a recent study of three school districts in New York State (Sánchez, Parker, Akbayin, & McTigue, 2010). Total enrollment in the districts ranged from 6,000 to 10,000 students, and their ELL populations ranged from 13 to 28 percent. An analysis of district and school interviews revealed the following challenges in the process of identifying learning disabilities among students who are English language learners:

- Difficulties with policy guidelines
- Different stakeholder views about timing for referral of students who are English language learners
- Insufficient knowledge among personnel involved in identification
- Difficulties providing consistent, adequate services to students who are English language learners
- Lack of collaborative structures in prereferral
- Lack of access to assessments that differentiate between second-language development and learning disabilities
- Lack of consistent monitoring for struggling students who are English language learners
- Difficulty obtaining students' previous school records

These challenges reflect the difficulties school districts face in complying with the Individuals with Disabilities Education Act of 2004. The IDEA requires evidence that learning difficulties for students who are ELLs are not due primarily to a lack of appropriate instruction or to the student's lack of proficiency in English before the student can be identified as having a learning disability. As a result of the study, five interrelated elements were identified as important for avoiding misidentification of learning disabilities among students who are English learners:

- **Adequate Professional Knowledge.** Having access to professional expertise about cultural differences, language development, learning disabilities, and their convergence among classroom teachers, specialists, and administrators

- **Effective Instructional Practices.** Providing effective instruction to students who are ELLs before and during prereferral

- **Effective and Valid Assessments and Interventions.** Providing valid assessments and effective intervention strategies

- **Collaboration Among Departments.** Establishing structures for collaboration between the ELLs and special education departments, as well as opportunities for teachers to collaborate and problem solve in schools

- **Clear Policy Guidelines.** Providing streamlined and clear policy guidelines on procedures to follow and criteria to use in identifying learning disabilities among students who are ELLs

A language difference is not a learning disability. As well-intentioned as teachers of ELLs may be, they often need specific training to recognize the differences between problems with English language acquisition and problems due to a learning disability. Layton and Lock (2002) suggest that teachers without specific training may mistake the following six characteristics of English language learning as indicators of a learning disability:

> *A language difference is not a learning disability.*

1. *A lower rate of learning* may appear as an intrinsic processing disorder because of the uneven development in academic areas. The rate of learning in ELLs may actually be negatively affected by the rate at which the student is acquiring English.

2. *A low-level competence in communication* may seem to indicate an intrinsic processing disorder when in fact the complexity of English language acquisition may be the real issue.

3. *Problem behaviors* may arise. Difficulty in following directions, poor eye contact, inattention, and daydreaming are behaviors that may be apparent in students who are English learners as well as those with learning disabilities.

4. *Reading skill difficulties* are sometimes manifested in the ELL students' inability to identify sounds, analyze and synthesize sound sequences, and break words into phonetic units when reading texts in English.

5. *Poor expressive language skills* may be evident when students use conceptual language, including temporal and spatial terminology, and can be characteristic both of students who are English learners and those with learning disabilities.

6. *Limited proficiency in the literacy-related aspects of language* such as narrative skills, story-retelling skills, and the ability to use language abstractly may be found both in students who are English learners and students with diagnosed learning disabilities.

Thus, the teacher's ability to distinguish between language development in English and intrinsic processing difficulties can have a significant impact on their referral of ELL students to special education. The degree of sensitivity that teachers have to the issues associated with English language acquisition is critical to the development of skills necessary for instruction and for the evaluation of ELLs. Sometimes, teachers are unable to cope with or understand the demands placed on an English learner and will look to special education for assistance. But specialized training can improve these teachers' sensitivity to the challenges facing ELLs.

One study provided teachers of ELLs with training in topics that included understanding and respect for the students' differences in culture, environment, expectations, values, and relationships with peers, families, schools, and communities (Layton & Lock, 2002). It also included information on typical language development, the impact on learning of nondisabled and disabled language acquisition, and information about how language development affects assessment and instruction. A survey after the training showed increased sensitivity amongst the trained teachers compared to those without training, regarding the specific evaluation procedures necessary to accurately differentiate between ELLs with learning disabilities and ELLs without them.

But even with training, identification of ELLs with a learning disability is not easy. The problem is compounded by the lack of appropriate and reliable assessment tools for culturally and linguistically diverse learners. Many schools do not have staff who are familiar with different languages and cultures, nor is there adequate communication among the bilingual education, ELL, and special education programs. ELL students are often assessed with tests in English, making evaluations difficult. Even when bilingual assessment personnel are available, many of them have little or no training in assessing ELLs, and instruments in languages other than English may not have acceptable validity and reliability.

What Current Research Says

Despite some recent research, the ability of educators to determine with certainty whether an ELL's academic difficulties stem from learning the English language, the presence of a disability, or some combination of the two is limited. Surveys of school districts reveal both an over- and an underrepresentation of ELLs with special education designations. Although there is no scientific evidence to suggest that disabilities should occur more frequently in some subgroups than in the larger population, researchers have found that minorities have been disproportionately represented in special education, particularly in high-incidence disability categories such as learning disabilities or speech and language impairment. At the same time, minorities do not appear to be over-represented in low-incidence, medically diagnosed disability categories such as visual or hearing impairment (Bedore & Peña, 2008).

Although ELLs' overall representation in disability categories compares to that of the general student population, separating the data by grade level reveals a different pattern. A look at the

U.S. Department of Education's Early Childhood Longitudinal Study (n.d.) indicates that ELLs are underrepresented in special education in kindergarten and first grade as compared to all students. However, by Grade 3 ELLs are overrepresented in special education. Furthermore, ELLs with genuine special education needs appear to be identified for services later than their native English-speaking peers. One study found an increase in the identification of ELLs with learning disabilities in Grades 4 through 6, about two or three years later than the grades in which native English speakers were identified (McCardle, Mele-McCarthy, Cutting, Leos, & D'Emilio, 2005).

ELLs may be inappropriately placed in special education due to their limited English proficiency and resulting low academic achievement. These students may be getting services and using resources they do not really need. At the same time, ELL students with special needs may be overlooked for services on the assumption that their difficulties are related exclusively to a lack of full proficiency in English. These students are not getting the services and resources they need to address their learning disability. In both cases, the determinations have a negative effect on the progress that ELLs must make in order to catch up to their native English-speaking peers.

The difficulties facing the assessment of culturally and linguistically diverse students with learning disabilities can be summarized as follows (Barrera, 2008):

- **Cultural:**

  Diagnostic: A bias between the instrument validation and specific experiences of the test taker

  Instructional: A bias in the expectations of the teacher with regard to differences in the ELL's motivation and exposure to curriculum

  Outcomes: Divergence between the curriculum or program and the content used in testing; a divergence between the outcome being tested and the real needs of the ELL

- **Linguistic:**

  Diagnostic: Lack of appropriately validated assessments in the ELL's primary language; a divergence between expected linguistic competency of the test and the ELL's observed linguistic competency

  Instructional: Lack of research-supported methods for curriculum-based assessments or for instructional approaches when language is a challenge; lack of training for teachers in how to assess or teach linguistically diverse ELLs

  Outcomes: Assessment of outcomes may be testing linguistic competency rather than mastery of content; use of language proficiency testing to determine the ELL's competency on graduation (or other outcome-based) standards

Problems Developing Oral Language Proficiency

Many schools and districts use literacy programs that place a heavy emphasis on developing the ELLs' reading and writing skills in English and less on developing oral language proficiency. But recall from Chapter 2 that one of the main predictors of how well and how fast an individual will learn to read a language is the size of the individual's mental vocabulary in that language. Thus, when teachers work to enhance their ELLs' oral proficiency in English, they are expanding that mental lexicon and increasing the likelihood that the ELLs' reading comprehension and fluency will also improve. More effective literacy programs, then, would also emphasize the explicit teaching of speech as well as reading and writing text.

Such oral language development focuses on helping ELLs detect and understand key vocabulary words, explaining English grammatical structures and literary forms, and strengthening their narrating and retelling skills. It is important to observe how struggling ELL students progress in English language proficiency and determine what additional instruction they might need. More structured talk in the classroom provides additional opportunities to assess the oral language proficiency of ELL students in different contexts.

At the same time, the students can monitor and observe their progress in their own language development. With guidance, students can use learning logs that allow them to keep ongoing records of their progress. They might write a short one- or two-sentence response every day, to keep track of the books they are reading, or to map out their work in progress. Teachers can also provide a variety of individual worksheets to focus the students on the self-observation process. This self-observation of their progress can increase the ELLs' motivation to learn. No one doubts that motivation is a basic ingredient for successful teaching and learning. Sometimes, ELLs who are unmotivated may appear to teachers as lazy or unwilling to learn. Before reaching this conclusion, however, teachers should ensure that the instruction is relevant to the students, that it is at an appropriate level of difficulty, that the students understand the learning objective, and that they have the resources to accomplish it. How well ELLs respond to sustained explicit instruction and practice in oral language development in a motivating classroom environment is one of the important criteria that determine if an ELL's lack of progress in English language proficiency could be due to a learning disability.

Problems With Reading in English

In Chapter 3, we saw how the brain learns to tackle the enormous challenge of matching the sounds of language to written symbols in order to learn to read. We noted that beginning readers of English must develop these five important skills to manage the neural systems needed to learn to read English successfully: phonemic awareness, the alphabetic principle, vocabulary acquisition, comprehension, and fluency (National Reading Panel, 2000). Of course, these skills, with modifications, are required to read in *any* language. The skills are needed for all beginning readers regardless of whether English is their first or second language. But the National Literacy Panel on Language Minority Children and Youth recommended that instruction in these five skills be modified in ways that can be beneficial to ELLs learning to read English (August & Shanahan, 2006). Without modifications, ELL students may struggle and seem confused, which in turn can lead to misdiagnoses of learning disabilities.

Here are some of the problem areas that could arise as teachers provide instruction in the five skills (Klingner & Geisler, 2008):

1. **Phonemic Awareness**
   - If the ELL's first language does not include English phonemes, then the student is not accustomed to hearing those sounds, making it difficult to distinguish between or pronounce the new sounds. Consequently, any phonological task will pose a challenge.

2. **Alphabetic Principle**
   - Many languages are written differently from English. Even languages written similarly to English, such as Spanish, can pose problems because letters may look the same but represent different sounds. Unfamiliar English sounds and their various spellings can make decoding difficult, and learning these letters and sounds may seem very abstract.

3. **Vocabulary Acquisition**
   - ELLs may pronounce the words but not understand what they are reading.
   - Students may be confused by common words such as prepositions (*on, above*), pronouns (*she, they*), linking words (*however, therefore*), words with multiple meanings, figurative language such as similes and metaphors, and idioms.
   - False cognates can be vexing.

4. **Reading Comprehension**
   - Many factors affect comprehension including oral language proficiency, vocabulary, word recognition skills, interest, and cultural differences.
   - To assess comprehension, provide ELLs with alternative ways to show understanding as, for example, using diagrams or explaining in their first language.

5. **Fluency**
   - ELLs usually have fewer opportunities to read aloud in English than their English-speaking peers.
   - ELLs may read more slowly and with less comprehension.
   - ELLs can have an accent but still read fluently.

See **Teaching Tip 7.1** for suggestions on how to adapt instruction in the five skills of learning to read for ELLs to reduce reading difficulties.

Monitoring Reading Progress

As ELLs learn to read English, their schools should continually monitor their progress through an established program that includes the following important components:

➡ **Identify or develop valid assessments and develop a plan for administering them.** Schools select the reading assessments and plan a flexible schedule of administration that is aligned with the sequence of instruction in the core reading program. Consistent use of reading assessments leads to more effective decision making about interventions. ELLs at higher risk for reading failure will require more frequent assessments.

➡ **Use the data from these assessments to make decisions about extra support and interventions.** ELL teachers and reading specialists interpret data from the assessments for individuals and groups of students. Systematic examination of results will help determine which groups of students should receive what types of interventions. This information will also determine which teachers may require additional support.

➡ **Determine if teachers need professional development and other support to help interpret and take action on assessment results.** Many teachers were not trained in the systematic analysis of assessment data. With appropriate support, teachers can better utilize assessment results to find students with skill deficits, group students with similar needs, and organize particular types of interventions.

Even in a program that provides explicit instruction in oral language proficiency, a motivating classroom environment, and recommended adaptations for teaching reading, there may still be ELL students who struggle with reading and writing English. What if some of the ELLs do have a learning disability? At what point does the teacher decide that further intervention is necessary? These are not easy questions to answer. But there are some basic steps that teachers of ELLs can follow to help them decide if they have done all they can to adapt their instructional strategies for their ELL students. See **Teaching Tip 7.2** for questions to help teachers reflect on their instructional strategies with ELLs.

Signs of a Reading Disability

Some ELLs may actually have a reading disability that affects their ability to read in their native language as well as in English. Reading disabilities run the gamut in terms of severity. The more severe forms are grouped under the general heading of *dyslexia.*

Dyslexia. There are at least a dozen linguistic and nonlinguistic causes of dyslexia, and some children may suffer from more than one cause, adding to the severity of the disorder. Imaging technologies have compared the brain structure of individuals with dyslexia to typical readers and have found some interesting differences. These differences were more evident in individuals with dyslexia who had early spoken-language problems than in those with dyslexia whose speech progressed normally. The regions of the brain that showed structural variations were consistent across multiple MRI studies and were closely associated with those neural areas involved in spoken language processing (Broca's and Wernicke's areas—see Chapter 1). The implication here is that an individual with atypical brain structures that hamper speech is likely to have difficulties in learning to read as well (Leonard, 2001).

Dyslexia appears in all languages, including those that are read from right to left, such as Hebrew and Arabic. People with dyslexia who speak highly phonetic languages, such as Spanish and Finnish, are identified with the disorder later than those who speak deep morphological languages such as English, where the linguistic demands of the language are more challenging. The key seems to be the degree to which there is a one-to-one correspondence between letters and sounds. Italians with dyslexia, for example, have an easier time because, as we noted in Chapter 3, there are only 25 letters or combination of letters to represent Italian's 33 phonemes. French speakers with dyslexia have more difficulty because the 32 phonemes in French can be represented by about 250 letter combinations. But English has over 1,100 ways to spell its 44+ phonemes and English speakers experience this complex phonetic structure early on in their schooling (Paulesu et al., 2001).

Readers can also experience difficulties in logographic languages, such as Chinese and Japanese, which use complex symbols to represent words. Brain imaging studies seem to indicate that readers of logographic languages use different neural regions to decode the meaning of symbols because of the added visual processing involved compared to alphabet-based languages. Deficits in these brain areas lead to visual confusion, probably due to poor visual-spatial memory. Chinese individuals with dyslexia, thus, have difficulty converting symbols into meanings, not letters into sounds. These findings imply that dyslexia may not have a universal origin in all humans, but that the biological abnormality of impaired reading is dependent on culture (Siok et al., 2008). Dehaene (2009), on the other hand, suggests that reading does rely on globally similar cerebral pathways in all cultures. The impairments in those with dyslexia who are taught in an alphabetic writing system may be phonological (i.e., sound related) while those with dyslexia taught in a logographic system may have impairments in remembering and re-creating the vast number of characters.

Symptoms. ELLs who are struggling readers in both English and in their native language should be observed to determine if they display any of the following indicators for an extended period of time (few individuals exhibit all symptoms):

- Difficulty recognizing written words
- Difficulty rhyming or sequencing syllables
- Difficulty determining the meaning or main idea of a simple sentence
- Difficulty encoding words—spelling
- Poor sequencing of letters or numbers
- Delayed spoken language
- Difficulty separating the sounds in spoken words
- Difficulty in expressing thoughts verbally
- Confusion about right- or left-handedness
- Difficulty with handwriting
- Possible family history of dyslexia

Remember that all ELL children make errors in spoken language and while reading. But the number of errors should decrease with time, and there should be clear evidence of growth in vocabulary and reading comprehension in both the native and English languages. Determining whether a child has consistent problems with reading requires careful and long-term observation of the child's fluency in speaking and reading. Most children display obvious improvements in their speaking and reading skills over time. Researchers, clinicians, and educators who study dyslexia and who work with poor readers look for certain clues that will show whether a child's reading ability is progressing normally.

Using Valid Assessment Instruments

The evaluation and assessment process for identifying ELLs with a learning disability must be done with great care to avoid inequalities. A study by Figueroa and Newsome (2006) clearly demonstrated how the writers of psychological tests often fail to use current legal or professional guidelines for making nondiscriminatory assessment practices. The practice of assessing ELLs in English rather than in their native language is of dubious validity in that the students may not fully understand the task instructions even though they have the competence to perform the task in English. Thus, ELLs must be evaluated and assessed with nonbiased procedures that do not cover up the skills and content knowledge they bring to school. Otherwise, ELLs face the risk of being placed in special education because of their culturally and linguistically diverse backgrounds rather than because of cognitive or physical disabilities.

> *ELLs must be evaluated with nonbiased procedures that do not cover up the skills and content knowledge they bring to school.*

Hoover and Barletta (2008) warn about concerns over the validity of the instruments used to assess and classify ELLs for special education. They suggest that when assessing ELLs for a learning disability, it is important to take into account the following characteristics that ELLs display during testing:

- ELLs generally perform lower than their non-ELL peers on tests in the content areas even though they might know the material equally well.
- The ELLs' level of proficiency in English affects their response to instructions and assessments.
- How well ELLs perform on content-based assessments may be confounded by their language background.
- Assessments for ELLs have lower validity and reliability, especially for those with lower levels of English proficiency.
- Language factors may well be the source of measurement error, thereby affecting the instrument's reliability and validity.

Of particular concern, too, in ELL testing are *linguistic features, dialect,* and *register.* Variations in linguistic features can affect an ELL's results on an assessment. These features include compare/contrast ideas, concrete/abstract examples, long noun or question phrases, prepositional phrases, passive/active voices, sentence length, subordinate clauses, and word length and familiarity. Test administrators should determine the extent to which each of these features appears in the assessment. The more extensively these features are used in the instrument, the less likely it will produce a valid test score for the ELL.

Dialect is a variation of language that reflects the social structure of the speakers. Every language has different dialects distinguished from others of the same language through vocabulary, grammar, pronunciation, and the rules of discourse. An automobile, for example, can be called *car, wheels, ride,* or *auto.* Register refers to language used for a specific situation or context. For example, each of the words *bag, bat, plate,* and *strike* can have various meanings in different contexts, but take on specific meanings when used to discuss baseball. These words and their specific meanings are part of baseball's language register. Assessments used for ELLs need to be linguistically appropriate. Otherwise, they may have what is called *linguistic misalignment.* This represents the mismatch between the linguistic features, dialect, and register used in the test and those of the ELL students being tested for language proficiency and learning problems. See **Teaching Tip 7.3** for a list of questions that should be asked to determine the linguistic appropriateness of an assessment.

Other researchers believe that insufficient consideration is given to the procedures used to test ELLs for their native and English language proficiencies and for a learning disability. Solano-Flores (2008), for instance, contends that current testing practices are limited in their effectiveness because they are based on erroneous assumptions about the ability of the assessments to communicate with ELL students. These practices include:

- Classifying ELLs into a few categories of language proficiency
- Assigning them to treatment conditions as if they were linguistically homogeneous
- Looking for the form of testing accommodation that works for all ELLs
- Assessing language development without considering proficiency in the students' first language
- Assuming that all schools are equally capable of implementing testing accommodations properly

The suggestion here is that social and linguistic groups are dynamic, not static, and that too many variables are present that are beyond the control of simple testing procedures. For example, different first languages, different migration histories, different kinds of exposure to formal instruction both in L1 and in the English language, and dialect variation within both L1 and English are among the numerous factors that make ELL populations considerably heterogeneous, even within a given classroom. In addition, different tests used by states and provinces to measure English proficiency, different criteria used for defining ELLs, and different capabilities of schools to adequately provide testing accommodations for these students are just some of the many factors that limit the ability to make valid interpretations of the ELLs' test scores.

Deciding if an ELL has a learning disability can be done with greater confidence when there are multiple sources of information indicating that a learning problem exists. Wilkinson and her colleagues (2006) studied a large school district with a substantial Spanish-speaking student population. Reviewing the procedures for evaluating ELLs' language proficiency and learning progress led to the development of a series of questions that can be used to guide data gathering and deliberations related to early intervention, referral, assessment, and eligibility determinations for ELLs. See **Teaching Tip 7.4** for the types of questions that should be asked and answered when evaluating an ELL student for a learning disability.

HELPING ELLs WITH LEARNING DISABILITIES

Teacher Preparation

How teachers use their knowledge, training, and skills can have a tremendous impact on the success of their students. It is not uncommon to find well-intentioned and hardworking teachers who are frustrated because they have been placed in an instructional environment for which they do not have an adequate knowledge base or appropriate skill set. Teachers educating ELLs with a learning disability are likely to be successful if they know how to recognize and use the linguistic and cultural diversity of their students to develop their native language skills while promoting English language acquisition.

ELLs with learning disabilities are often uncomfortable outside their culture and reluctant to mix with their native English-speaking peers who often shun them due to differences in appearance, dress, and manner. They may fear a loss of their own cultural identity. Successful teachers educating ELLs with disabilities integrate multiculturalism into the curriculum to engage, affirm, and accept diversity within

> *Successful teachers educating ELLs with disabilities integrate multiculturalism into the curriculum to engage, affirm, and accept diversity.*

the classroom and school environment. They also have a deep understanding of how their students differ in terms of language proficiency, culture, learning, and cognitive styles. Drawing on this knowledge can help these students ease their way into a new language and culture, while still retaining their own cultural identity. Recall the power of transfer we discussed in Chapter 2. The idea here is to connect aspects of the ELLs' language and culture to the curriculum components designed to help them acquire English.

Just how well teachers affirm, respect, and promote multiculturalism in the educational settings depends largely on their knowledge, training, and experience. Banks (2006) believes that for ELLs with learning disabilities to make academic achievements, teachers have to understand, comprehend, and learn the following six stages of cultural identity.

Stage 1: **Cultural psychological captivity:** Students take in negative beliefs and stereotypes of their own culture.

Stage 2: **Cultural encapsulation:** Students believe that their culture is superior.

Stage 3: **Cultural identity clarification:** Students clarify their attitudes and identity perceptions to reduce conflicts within themselves.

Stage 4: **Biculturalism:** Students have a sense of cultural identity and are able to participate in both worlds, their own culture and the second acquired culture.

Stage 5: **Multiculturalism and reflective nationalism:** Students reflect positively on both cultures.

Stage 6: **Globalism and global competency:** Students have an understanding of global identity issues and can function within various cultural groups.

Any group of ELLs will be at various stages of their cultural identity. Determining where they are and how that affects their intellectual, academic, and social growth requires sensitivity to the students' culture and linguistic heritage. Villegas and Lucas (2002) suggest that for many teachers of ELLs with disabilities to succeed, knowledge of the following can help them with this challenge:

- Gaining sociocultural consciousness
- Developing and affirming a positive attitude toward students from culturally and linguistically diverse backgrounds
- Developing and acting as agents of change
- Understanding the constructivist foundations of culturally responsive teaching
- Learning about their students and communities
- Cultivating culturally responsive teaching practices

With this knowledge of culture and linguistic diversity in their ELLs, teachers can then focus on helping students with specific learning problems.

Response to Intervention (RTI)

In recent years, one method of determining whether students have learning difficulties is assessing if their responses to the methods, strategies, curriculum, and interventions they encounter lead to increased learning and appropriate progress. This concept forms the basis of the approach known as *response to intervention* (RTI), and it was addressed in the Individuals with Disabilities Education Improvement Act of 2004 (IDEA, 2004). Let's first describe the basic components of RTI and then take a look at whether its application to students with culturally and linguistically diverse backgrounds can be successful.

Key Elements of RTI

Early Intervention. A key element of a response to intervention (RTI) approach is to provide early intervention when students first experience academic difficulties, with the goal of improving the achievement of all students, including those who may have learning disabilities. In addition to the preventive and remedial services this approach provides at-risk students, it shows promise for contributing data useful for accurately identifying learning disabilities. Thus, a student exhibiting significantly low achievement and insufficient RTI may be viewed as being at risk for learning disability and possibly in need of special education services. The assumption behind this model, referred to as a dual discrepancy, is that when provided with quality instruction and remedial services, a student without disabilities will make satisfactory progress.

A Problem-Solving Approach Using Data. Another key element of RTI is that it uses a systematic problem-solving process involving the following steps:

1. Identifying and analyzing the problem, including collection of baseline data

2. Generating possible scientific, research-based strategies or interventions

3. Implementing an intervention plan

4. Monitoring student progress to determine the student's response to these interventions

5. Using the RTI data to review and revise plans as needed

The data used in the RTI process should include the following (NJCLD, 2005).

- High-quality, research-based instruction and behavioral supports in general education
- Scientific, research-based interventions focused specifically on individual student difficulties and delivered with appropriate intensity
- Use of a collaborative approach by school staff for development, implementation, and monitoring of the intervention process
- Data-based documentation reflecting continuous monitoring of student performance and progress during interventions
- Documentation of parent involvement throughout the process
- Documentation that the timelines described in the federal regulations are followed unless extended by mutual written agreement of the child's parents and a team of qualified professionals as described in these regulations
- Systematic assessment and documentation that the interventions used were implemented with fidelity

Multiple Tiered Model. Although there is no universal RTI model, it is generally viewed as having three tiers consisting of the following (NJCLD, 2005):

Tier 1. High-quality instructional and behavioral supports are provided for all students in general education.

- School personnel conduct universal screening of literacy skills, academics, and behavior.
- Teachers implement a variety of research-supported teaching strategies and approaches.
- Ongoing, curriculum-based assessment and continuous progress monitoring are used to guide high-quality instruction.
- Students receive differentiated instruction based on data from ongoing assessments.

Tier 2. Students whose performance and rate of progress lag behind those of peers in their classroom, school, or district receive more specialized prevention or remediation within general education.

- Curriculum-based measures are used to identify which students continue to need assistance, and with what specific kinds of skills.
- Collaborative problem solving is used to design and implement instructional support for students that may consist of a standard protocol or more individualized strategies and interventions.
- Identified students receive more intensive scientific, research-based instruction targeted to their individual needs.
- Student progress is monitored frequently to determine intervention effectiveness and needed modifications.
- Systematic assessment is conducted to determine the fidelity or integrity with which instruction and interventions are implemented.
- Parents are informed and included in the planning and monitoring of their child's progress in the Tier 2 specialized interventions.
- General education teachers receive support (e.g., training, consultation, direct services for students), as needed, from other qualified educators in implementing interventions and monitoring student progress.

Tier 3. Comprehensive evaluation is conducted by a multidisciplinary team to determine eligibility for special education and related services.

- Parents and caregivers are informed of their due process rights and consent is obtained for the comprehensive evaluation needed to determine whether the student has a disability and is eligible for special education and related services.

- Evaluation consists of multiple sources of assessment data, which may include data from standardized and norm-referenced measures; observations made by parents, students, and teachers; and data collected in Tiers 1 and 2.
- Intensive, systematic, specialized instruction is provided and additional RTI data are collected, as needed, in accordance with special education timelines and other mandates.
- Procedural safeguards on evaluations and eligibility apply, as required by the IDEA 2004 mandates.

Variations on this basic framework may occur. For example, Tier 2 might consist of two hierarchical steps, or subtiers (e.g., a teacher first collaborates with a single colleague, then works on problem solving with a multidisciplinary team, creating in effect a four-tiered model). Another possibility is that more than one type of intervention might be provided within Tier 2 (e.g., both a standard protocol and individualized planning, based on the student's apparent needs).

Potential Benefits of RTI

Proponents of RTI cite the following potential benefits:

- Earlier identification of students with learning disabilities using a problem-solving approach rather than an ability–achievement discrepancy formula, thus minimizing the "wait to fail" approach
- Reduction in the number of students referred for special education
- Reduction in the overidentification of minority students
- Data that have the maximum relevancy to instruction
- Focus on student outcomes with increased accountability
- Promotion of shared responsibility and collaboration

RTI and ELLs

Although the research base on using interventions with ELLs is not as extensive as on non-ELLs, there have been studies looking at the effectiveness of reading interventions with ELLs with reading difficulties. One study investigated the effect of two comprehensive reading interventions on the reading progress outcomes of Hispanic ELLs in kindergarten through third grade (Gunn et al., 2000). The intervention provided students with a reading program based on direct instruction in English for 25 to 30 minutes per day for 5 months to 2 years. ELLs in first or second grade who were beginning readers either received an intervention that focused on phonemic awareness, letter-to-sound correspondence, phonics, and practice reading of decodable text or were assigned to a control group. Students in third and fourth grade received instruction in phonics and structural analysis, decoding, comprehension, and fluency or were assigned to a control group. The results revealed significant differences between the ELLs in the intervention and control groups only in oral reading fluency and marginal though not significant differences in favor of the intervention group on word attack, letter–word identification, vocabulary, and passage comprehension.

Another study examined the effects of two reading interventions (22 sessions each) on the English reading outcomes of ELLs in Grades 2 through 5 who were enrolled in bilingual programs (Denton et al., 2004). Students were assigned to one of two groups based on the severity of their delay in learning to read. Those with significant reading problems received a systematic decoding, fluency, and comprehension intervention, whereas better readers were provided with a fluency program. The ELLs in each group were then randomly assigned to either an intervention program or a control situation. The researchers found that the students who received systematic phonics instruction made significant progress in word identification but not in word attack or comprehension of passages.

The results of these two studies are promising but cautionary. Their limited success may be the result of making assumptions about the effectiveness of RTI when applied to ELLs and other culturally and linguistically diverse students. Klingner, Barletta, and Hoover (2008) suggest that practitioners understand the following three misguided assumptions about using RTI with ELLs so that they can make the best instructional choice for them:

- **Evidence-based instruction is good for everyone, including ELLs.** Many of the evidence-based instructional approaches recommended by RTI have not been tried out with ELLs.
- **Learning to read in English is similar to learning to read in one's native language.** There are developmental similarities to be sure, but there are also important differences. As we noted earlier, ELLs benefit from additional oral language instruction.
- **Students who fail to respond to RTI have a learning disability.** ELLs may not respond to an approach because it is not effective for them, the level of instruction might not be a good match, or the environment might not be conducive to learning.

This is not to say that RTI approaches cannot be successful with ELLs who have learning difficulties. It just means one cannot assume that instructional strategies that work with non-ELLs will automatically work with struggling ELLs. Careful assessments and appropriate choices need to be made. For example, Linan-Thompson and her colleagues used the RTI of ELLs identified as at risk for reading difficulties in the fall of first grade (Linan-Thompson, Vaughn, Prater, & Cirino, 2006). The students at risk for reading problems were randomly assigned to intervention or control groups. Intervention students received supplemental reading intervention daily for 50 minutes in small groups from October to April. Students in the control groups received the school's existing instructional program for struggling readers. Criteria were established

> *One cannot assume that instructional strategies that work with non-ELLs will automatically work with struggling ELLs.*

to determine adequate RTI at the end of first grade and at the end of second grade. The results showed that more students who participated in the first-grade intervention in either Spanish or English met the established RTI standards than students who did not, and this finding was maintained through the end of second grade.

Overcoming Reading Problems

Several successful interventions have been used to help ELLs at the primary grades improve their reading skills when learning disabilities that affect reading have been identified. For example, one large study worked with 166 Canadian ELL children all of whom had demonstrated severe underachievement on multiple measures of word identification and word attack (Lovett et al., 2008). These struggling readers had incomplete letter-to-sound knowledge and limited decoding skills.

The intervention provided 105 hours of remedial reading instruction. It included an emphasis on phonologically based word attack and word identification training. It also focused on teaching basic word identification and decoding skills, using material ranging in complexity from one-syllable, high-frequency words to low-frequency words of five or more syllables. Reading materials were graduated in difficulty, permitting individualization of instruction according to student needs and progress. On almost all outcome measures, the ELL children who had received the research intervention outperformed their peers who received an equivalent amount of special education reading remediation. Furthermore, the ELL children in the study demonstrated greater rates of growth over time in their reading and reading-related skills. These effects were substantial and significant for all experimental measures of learning and transfer of learning.

One interesting study asked both teachers and Hmong ELL students with learning disabilities in Grades 5 through 7 which strategies they thought best improved their reading skills (Shyyan, Thurlow, & Liu, 2008). The five following strategies ranked high with both groups:

- *Fluency Building:* Helping students to build fluency in frequently occurring words through short assessments and exercises that give increased exposure to high-frequency words
- *Direct Teaching of Vocabulary:* Teaching vocabulary directly through listening, speaking, reading, and writing in short time segments; students are exposed to vocabulary in different ways, and movement during activities helps hold attention
- *Relating Reading to Student Experiences:* Having students talk in large or small groups about connections in the reading to their own experiences
- *Chunking and Questioning Aloud:* Reading a story aloud to a group of students and stopping after certain blocks of text to ask the students specific questions about their comprehension of the story and some key features of the text
- *Practicing Paraphrasing and Retelling:* Working on specific skills to retell orally or summarize in writing what happened in a story

This study suggested that the teacher and student perceptions of effective instructional strategies for ELLs with disabilities have the ultimate potential of enhancing the achievement of these students. By allowing the voices of ELL students with disabilities to be heard, it provided an opportunity for these students to express their perceptions about the effectiveness of instructional strategies. ELL student input is especially important in the upper grades where they face the increasing demands of the complex learning material in the content areas.

See **Teaching Tip 7.5** for suggested strategies for teaching ELLs with reading difficulties.

Overcoming Problems in Mathematics and Science

We discussed in Chapter 5 the limits of working (temporary) memory. It is not unusual for students with learning disabilities to have reduced working memory capacity and slower processing. If much of these students' working memory is devoted to English language processing, then there are even fewer cognitive resources available—compared to ELLs without a learning disability—to allocate to processing and remembering higher-order problem-solving activities in, say, mathematics and science. Consequently, the ELL with a learning disability must devote greater mental effort to forming an appropriate representation of a problem, identifying the needed information, and checking progress toward the solution.

One approach to this situation is to use simplified English text on the ELLs' high-stakes tests. Although the evidence is somewhat mixed, the general finding is that ELLs are more likely to solve mathematics problems correctly when the demands of understanding the problem are reduced by accommodations such as simplified English and definitions for any unfamiliar vocabulary (Abedi & Lord, 2001; Abella, Urrutia, & Shneyderman, 2005). In other words, when ELLs do not have to devote cognitive resources to English comprehension, their performance in mathematics improves. Thus, ELLs with a learning disability need additional help when trying to conquer material in the content areas. Again, research in this area is limited. However, several studies—mainly in the areas of mathematics and science—indicate that teachers and students have found some successful strategies.

Dyscalculia: Because of the challenge of learning English while trying to learn mathematics, it is often difficult to detect when a true mathematics disability exists in ELLs. But with careful observation and an accurate assessment of an ELL's English proficiency, it is possible to determine if the student has a mathematics disability. A condition that causes persistent problems with numerical calculations is called *dyscalculia.* Dyscalculia is a difficulty in conceptualizing numbers, number relationships, outcomes of numerical operations, and estimation, that is, what to expect as an outcome of an operation. Dyscalculia manifests in a person as having difficulty doing the following:

- Mastering arithmetic facts by the traditional methods of teaching, particularly the methods involving counting
- Learning abstract concepts of time and direction, telling and keeping track of time, and the sequence of past and future events

- Acquiring spatial orientation and space organization, including left/right orientation, trouble reading maps, and grappling with mechanical processes
- Following directions in sports that demand sequencing or rules, and keeping track of scores and players during games such as cards and board games
- Following sequential directions and sequencing (including reading numbers out of sequence, substitutions, reversals, omissions, and doing operations backwards), organizing detailed information, remembering specific facts and formulas for completing their mathematical calculations

Dyscalculia can be (1) quantitative, which is a difficulty in counting and calculating, (2) qualitative, which is a difficulty in the conceptualizing of mathematics processes and spatial sense, or (3) mixed, which is the inability to integrate quantity and space. Some of these difficulties in ELLs can be the result of poor English proficiency. If so, the difficulties are likely to decrease as the student's language proficiency improves. However, true mathematics disabilities exist when ELLs show little or no sign of improvement even as they become more competent in their English language skills.

Effective Instructional Strategies in Mathematics: Apart from the Beal et al. (2010) study we cited in the previous chapter, only a few other studies look into how limited English proficiency in students with learning disabilities affects their ability to learn mathematics. In the Shyyan et al. (2008) study noted earlier, ELL students with learning disabilities said that the following strategies seemed to help them the most when learning mathematics:

- problem-solving instruction and task analysis
- reciprocal peer teaching
- model-lead-test strategy instruction
- explicit vocabulary building and random, recurrent assessments
- monitoring of progress through charts
- teacher think-alouds
- student think-alouds

When the teachers in this study were asked which strategies they thought were most effective with the ELLs, they gave less weight to the reciprocal peer tutoring and the monitoring of progress through charts. Furthermore, they indicated that the following two strategies were particularly effective even though the students gave them less weight:

- tactile, concrete experiences of mathematics
- daily relooping of previously learned material

See **Teaching Tip 7.6** for a fuller explanation of these and other suggested strategies to use with ELLs who have mathematics difficulties.

Effective Instructional Strategies in Science: Referring once again to the very helpful study by Shyyan et al. (2008), teachers and ELLs with learning disabilities were asked which strategies seemed to be most effective when learning science. Both teachers and students were in close agreement that the following strategies worked well:

- hands-on, active participation
- using visuals
- using pictures to demonstrate steps
- modeling or teacher demonstration
- using prereading strategies
- preteaching vocabulary
- teaching how to pick out the main idea and justify it
- KWL chart
- peer tutoring

See **Teaching Tip 7.7** for suggested strategies to use in science with ELLs who have learning difficulties.

Overcoming Writing Problems

Dysgraphia. Once the enormous task of learning a new language is undertaken, the ELL's brain is faced with the daunting task of learning to draw the abstract symbols that represent the sounds of the English language. As discussed in Chapter 4, just how similar the ELL's native writing system is to English will determine the degree of difficulty in learning to write English. Typically, ELL students will eventually learn to write in English, and their handwriting will improve with practice as their brain permanently encodes the fine muscle movements needed for this task. But some ELL students will display persistent problems with writing. In this instance, the first question to ask is: Does this student also have difficulty when writing the native language? If the answer is no, then the student very likely needs more concentrated practice in forming English words on paper. But if the answer is yes, then this may be an indication that the student is not able to put thoughts into writing or accomplish other parts of the writing process such as letter formation. This condition is known as *dysgraphia.*

Dysgraphia (also known as *agraphia*) is a spectrum disorder describing major difficulties in mastering the sequence of movements necessary to write letters and numbers. The disorder exists in varying degrees and is seldom found in isolation without symptoms of other learning problems. Many ELLs as well as non-ELLs have difficulty with writing as they progress through the upper-elementary grades. But those with dysgraphia are inefficient at handwriting more than anything else, and this inefficiency establishes a barrier to learning. Their handwriting is usually characterized by slow copying, inconsistencies in letter formation, mixtures of different letters and styles, and poor legibility even in the native language. Teachers should realize that dysgraphia is a disorder and is not the result of laziness, not caring, not trying, or just carelessness in writing. Specific symptoms of the disorder are the following:

- inconsistencies in letter formation; mixture of upper and lower cases, of print and cursive letters
- unfinished words or letters
- generally illegible writing (despite time given to the task)
- talking to self while writing
- watching hand while writing
- inconsistent position on page with respect to margins and lines
- slow copying or writing
- omitted words in writing
- inconsistent spaces between letters and words
- struggle to use writing as a communications tool
- cramped or unusual grip on pencil
- unusual body, wrist, or paper position

Dysgraphia is a neurological disorder stemming from several causes that can be broadly classified into three main categories (Heilman, 2002): (1) *Dyslexic dysgraphia* appears in individuals who have difficulty or are unable to make a phoneme-to-grapheme conversion, that is, unable to convert the sounds of language to the letters that represent them, (2) *motor dysgraphia* results when the individual has problems controlling the muscles of the hands, wrists, and fingers, and (3) *spatial dysgraphia* is caused by deficits in the spatial processing systems of the brain's right hemisphere.

Dysgraphia cannot be diagnosed just by looking at a sample of handwriting. A qualified clinician must directly test the individual. Determining which type of dysgraphia a child has requires the assessment of various factors, such as fine motor coordination, writing speed, organization, knowledge and use of vocabulary, spelling, and the degree of attention and concentration. If an ELL is diagnosed with dysgraphia, there are some strategies that teachers can use to help this student. See **Teaching Tip 7.8** for some suggested accommodation strategies.

WHAT'S COMING

We have now examined the aspects of first and second-language acquisition, the difficulties that ELLs face when moving from conversational to academic English in the content areas, and the ways to recognize and address learning difficulties. How do we put this all together? To start, what misconceptions must we overcome in order to design effective programs for ELLs? What are the basics of such programs? What kind of professional development is needed so teachers of ELLs can understand and meet their needs? How do we teach technology skills to ELLs as well as use technology to build their language and literacy skills? For the answers to these questions, turn to our final chapter.

Teaching Tip 7.1: Adapting Instruction in Reading Skills for ELLs Learning to Read English

Learning to read requires the acquisition and development of certain skills that allow the learner to successfully match graphic symbols with sounds to generate understanding and meaning. In English, that means matching the 26 letters of the English alphabet with the 50 or so phonemes that make up the sounds of the language. Teaching these five skills to ELLs requires some adaptation because of their experiences with their native language. Here are some suggestions for those adaptations (Klingner & Geisler, 2008).

- **Phonemic Awareness**
  - Keep in mind that confusion about sounds is a natural result of acquiring a new language and does not necessarily mean a weak ability at auditory discrimination or poor phonemic awareness.
  - Determine which phonemes do not exist in the ELL's native language and help the student discriminate those sounds.
  - Avoid concluding prematurely that an auditory learning disability exists when ELLs struggle with unfamiliar phonemes. Continue their oral practice of these troubling sound combinations.

- **Alphabetic Principle (Phonics)**
  - Direct instruction of the sounds of English is important. Vowel sounds, for example, are pronounced differently in Spanish than in English. When ELLs pronounce a word as they would in Spanish, it sounds incorrect as, for example, saying *feet* instead of *fit.*
  - Pay close attention to English words that have the same sound but various spellings as these can make decoding and spelling very difficult.
  - Point out context clues to help ELLs figure out how to read words and their meaning.

- **Vocabulary Acquisition**
  - Explicitly teach even the common words that ELLs find confusing. These include prepositions (*above, in, on*), pronouns (for example, the *he* in, *John was sick. He hoped he would be able to leave work early.*), and linking words (*however, therefore*).
  - Spend time on words with multiple meanings (*bat, light*).
  - Explain figurative language forms such as similes (*red as a rose, tough as nails, swims like a fish*), metaphors (*a sea of troubles, solid as a rock*), and idioms (*I'm all ears, get a kick out of it*).
  - Focus on helpful cognates (*animal* is the same in English, French, and Spanish), but beware of false cognates (*embarasada* in Spanish means *pregnant,* not *embarrassed*).

o When ELLs know and understand the underlying concept behind a new vocabulary word, then providing the native language label will facilitate understanding. But if the concept is a new one, then provide the instruction necessary to explain what the word means.

- **Reading Comprehension**

  o Remember that culture can play an influential role in reading comprehension. A student from India, for example, reading about a wedding in the United States will have different expectations about what should be happening in the text.

  o Find ways to get ELLs to comfortably participate in discussing what they have read to ensure that they fully comprehend the text.

  o ELLs may comprehend more than they can express in speech or writing. Allow them to express what they have learned with their native language or through diagrams and demonstrations.

  o Paying too much attention to ELLs' grammatical errors, accents when speaking, or the mechanics of their writing may lead to misconceptions about their degree of comprehension. Also, too many corrections may lead to hesitancy to speak. Focus on content rather than the form of the ELLs' answers.

- **Fluency**

  o Provide ELLs ample opportunities to read aloud in English and get feedback.

  o Ensure that ELLs understand the text and can decode all the words before reading it.

  o Use expert readers to model fluent, expressive reading and help ELLs through echo reading or partner reading.

  o Provide books on tape or on CD to help struggling ELL readers listen and follow along.

  o Avoid assuming that ELLs who read slowly and lack expression have a learning disability. Instead, provide additional opportunities for them to practice oral reading.

Teaching Tip 7.2: Questions for Reflecting on Your Instructional Strategies

Making a decision to refer an ELL is a difficult one at best. The characteristics and behaviors associated with learning a new language can be very similar to those of a learning disability. On the one hand, you do not want to wait too long before addressing the possibility that an ELL may have a learning disability. On the other hand, you also do not want to misjudge an ELL and make an inappropriate referral. Perhaps by answering these questions suggested by Klingner and Geisler (2008) you can gain a greater insight into what is the appropriate step to take with a struggling ELL.

- **How Many Students Are Still Struggling?** If a majority of ELLs are doing well but only a few are struggling, then look at what may be the cause of their difficulties. If the majority of ELLs are struggling, then ask whether your instruction is culturally, linguistically, and pedagogically appropriate for your ELLs. If not, what adjustments can you make to your instruction? Perhaps it means adding more strategies to your repertoire. Instructional approaches must be flexible enough to meet the diverse needs of your ELLs. Also, are you using the ELLs' culture and experience to foster their learning, monitor their behavior, and encourage their communication, motivation, and language development? Be aware that some ELLs may be struggling not because they have an inherent learning disability but because they are in a learning context that is not providing them with enough opportunities to develop their language and literacy skills.

- **How Varied Are My Instructional Practices?** A potential cause of difficulty for ELLs may be the types of literacy and language instruction you are using. The following questions may help you reflect on your instructional practices that focus on literacy and language skills for ELLs.

  o Have I developed a strong and positive relationship with each ELL?
  o Do I personalize my instruction?
  o Do I value the ELLs' cultural and linguistic background?
  o Do I connect my classroom instruction to the ELLs' personal experiences?
  o Do I give sufficient attention to the ELLs' affect, interests, and motivation?
  o Am I giving enough attention to the ELLs' oral language development?
  o Am I aware of the aspects of reading that could be confusing for the ELLs?
  o Did I determine which sounds and letters of the ELLs' first language are different from those of English? If so, am I clarifying misunderstandings and giving sufficient practice?
  o Am I adjusting my instruction to give the ELLs adequate support whenever they do not seem to understand as, for example, explicit instruction at their proficiency level and additional opportunities for practice?

o Are the books I am using at the levels that the ELLs can read and understand?

o Am I preteaching key vocabulary words?

o Am I using multimedia, real items, photographs, charts, and other visuals to help make my instruction comprehensible to ELLs?

o Am I focusing more on the content of the ELLs' responses rather than the form when I am checking for comprehension?

o Do I provide multiple and varied ways for ELLs to demonstrate what they have learned?

If the answer to most of these questions is yes and there are still a few ELL students who are struggling, then it may be time to consider referring them for additional support. You can do so by using two criteria suggested by researchers: (1) assess the individual ELL's rate of progress in comparison with that of similar peers, and (2) determine whether that ELL is attaining the content learning objectives (Compton, Fuchs, Fuchs, & Bryant, 2006).

Teaching Tip 7.3: Questions to Determine the Linguistic Appropriateness of an ELL Assessment

Accurately assessing an ELL's language proficiency and learning problems requires test instruments that closely match the dialect and language register of the student being tested. The following questions should be asked to determine the linguistic appropriateness of an assessment instrument (Solano-Flores, 2008).

- Is the test language similar to the language of instruction?
- Do the test norms reflect the variety of dialects within the language spoken by the test taker?
- Is the dialect used in the test determined to be the most socially acceptable dialect in the language used in the test?
- Is the dialect of the language used in the test compatible with the dialect used by the test taker?
- Does the test avoid the use of colloquial terms with unusual meanings?
- Are the word meanings found on the test similar to their use in colloquial language?
- Does the test taker understand the meaning of expressions typically found only in tests as, for example, *none of the above*?
- Are the test questions in conflict with the test taker's previous experiences as, for example, understands the difference between a comma and a decimal point in numbers?
- Is the number of test items with unfamiliar expressions low?

Count the number of yes and no answers and use that result to determine if the assessment instrument is appropriate for reliably and validly determining an ELL's English language proficiency and/or learning difficulty.

Teaching Tip 7.4: Questions for
Deciding if Struggling ELLs Have a Learning Disability

The answers to these questions will help an evaluating team decide if there is sufficient evidence to warrant a determination that an ELL has a learning disability (Wilkinson et al., 2006).

- **Early Intervention**

  o What is the student's present level of performance?

  o How was instruction modified, and what were the results?

  o What interventions did the problem-solving team, in cooperation with the teacher and family (or caregivers), decide to implement, and what procedures were identified for determining and documenting their effectiveness?

  o What were the results of the intervention, and do any difficulties remain?

  o Is additional problem solving needed, or should a special education referral be considered?

  o Have all results of the early intervention been adequately documented?

- **Referral**

  o What factors other than the presence of a disability may explain the academic and behavioral difficulties (e.g., exclusionary clause)?

  o What other alternatives should be considered to resolve the student's difficulties before requesting a Full and Individual Evaluation (FIE)?

  o What are the current unresolved questions and concerns?

- **Assessment**

  o What procedures will be used to address the issues identified by the referral committee?

  o What additional procedures are needed to establish eligibility?

  o How will the FIE incorporate best practices in the assessment of English language learners (ELLs)?

  o How do FIE outcomes correlate with referral concerns?

  o What are the student's strengths and weaknesses?

- **Multidisciplinary Team**

  o Does the multidisciplinary team (MDT) include members with the necessary expertise (e.g., who understand cultural and linguistic diversity) to involve parents meaningfully or to interpret for the families?

  o Did the FIE incorporate best practices in the assessment of ELLs?

  o Does the MDT have any remaining questions after the FIE results have been considered? If so, specify the additional action or information needed to resolve these questions.

o Has the MDT considered all potential factors contributing to the student's difficulties as FIE results are interpreted?

o Has the MDT documented data that address the exclusionary clause?

o If the student is found to have a learning disability, what data other than the presence of an IQ–achievement discrepancy support the decision?

Teaching Tip 7.5: Strategies for Teaching ELLs With Reading Difficulties

When working with ELLs who have reading difficulties, the following strategies may make the instructional process somewhat easier and more successful for them as well as for other students in the class.

General Strategies

- Make your classroom expectations clear by using simple language and any visual devices that the ELLs comprehend.
- Ensure that classroom procedures are orderly, structured, and predictable.
- Remember that many struggling ELLs can learn to read. They just need different kinds of instructional strategies.
- Be constructive and positive. Labeling can often be disabling when you label the child rather than the behavior. Avoid labels that undermine the instructional environment and adversely affect the child's self-concept and performance.
- Honor the diversity in the class and use it whenever possible in the reading.
- Recognize that ELL struggling readers will take up to three times longer to complete work and will tire quickly.
- Avoid appeals to "try harder." The brains of ELL struggling readers are already expending extra mental effort while decoding print in English, and these appeals will not improve performance. What is needed is slower speed with clearer comprehension.
- Determine and then compliment their abilities, and teach through their strengths. Plan lessons so the ELL students experience a sense of accomplishment rather than failure.

In the Elementary Classroom

- Get a complete explanation of the ELL's history of problems encountered when learning to read in the native language as well as in English.
- Select scientifically researched reading strategies and use a multisensory approach.
- Recognize the frustration these students feel struggling to read in a new language.
- Recognize that reading performance in English may be below the child's potential despite any learning disability.
- Remember that the child learns in different ways, but can learn.
- Realize that the child may have behavioral and self-esteem problems as a result of cultural differences.

- Maintain contact with the child's parents (or caregivers) and give them periodic progress reports.
- Make suggestions of what they can do with the child at home to complement your classroom strategies.
- Ensure that other non-ELL classmates understand the nature of reading problems and cultural differences so that the ELL child is not bullied or mocked.
- Assign a buddy (peer tutor) to help the struggling reader in the class and school.
- Encourage the child to point out his or her own talents and strengths.

In the Secondary Classroom

- Get a complete explanation of the ELL student's history of reading problems in the native language (if possible) and in English.
- Use a multisensory approach in classroom instruction.
- Recognize the compounded frustrations of an ELL teenager trying to learning English and with reading problems.
- Remember that ELL students with dyslexia or other reading difficulties learn in different ways, but they can learn.
- Realize that ELL teenagers may have problems with their self-esteem.
- Recognize that these students may have behavior or truancy problems.
- Realize that these students often have a significant gap between their performance and their potential and not all due to reading and language problems.
- Use diagrams and graphic organizers when teaching. Advanced organizers that contain important notes in simple language about the lesson are also very helpful.
- Maintain contact with the ELL student's parents (or caregivers) and give them periodic progress reports. Make suggestions of what they can do with the student at home to complement your classroom strategies.
- Ensure that these ELL students' legal rights are adhered to when they take tests.
- Students with mild dyslexia often develop coping strategies in elementary school. Be aware that these strategies may be inadequate for the complex and multifaceted secondary curriculum.
- Ensure that any remedial materials are relevant to the maturity and not the academic level of the student.
- Be aware that ELL struggling readers can have great difficulty reading an unseen text aloud in class. Asking them to do this can adversely affect their self-esteem.

Teaching Tip 7.6: Strategies for
Teaching ELLs With Mathematics Difficulties

Teachers of ELLs with mathematics difficulties should help these students identify their strengths and weaknesses in both English language skills and mathematics. After identification, teachers, parents (or caregivers), and other support people can work together to develop instructional strategies that will help the ELL learn mathematics more effectively. Having a student peer as a tutor can allow the ELL and the tutor to focus specifically on the difficulties that student is having. Other strategies to consider using include the following (Sousa, 2008):

- **Problem-Solving Instruction and Task Analysis:** Give explicit instruction in the steps necessary to solving a mathematical problem, including the following:

  o What kind of problem is this?

  o What information is the problem looking for?

  o What cue words (e.g., *take away, altogether*) are used in the problem?

  o The cue words suggest what kind of operation?

  o Must I perform these operations in a special order?

  o Did I get an answer that seems correct?

  o Did I recheck the problem to make sure I understand it, and is there anything I missed?

- **Reciprocal Peer Tutoring:** Ask students to pair up, choose a team goal to work toward, tutor each other on mathematics problems, and then individually work a sheet of drill problems. The students get points for correctly solving the problems and for making progress on working toward their identified goal.

- **Model-Lead-Test Strategy Instruction:** Teach the students in three stages to use learning strategies independently:

  o Model the correct use of the strategy.

  o Lead the students as they practice correct use of the strategy.

  o Test the students' independent use of it. Once students attain a score of 80 percent correct on two consecutive tests, instruction on the strategy stops.

- **Explicit Vocabulary Building and Random, Recurrent Assessments:** Use brief assessments to help students build basic subject-specific vocabulary in mathematics and also to gauge the students' retention of vocabulary.

- **Monitor Progress Through Charts:** Use both group and individual achievement awareness charts to build awareness of the students' progress and to stimulate motivation. Emphasize progress so that even those students working at different levels of proficiency can chart significant gains.

- **Teacher Think-Alouds:** Use explicit explanations of steps involved in problem solving by modeling metacognitive thought, that is, by explaining your own thought process as you solve a problem.

- **Student Think-Alouds:** Ask students to describe the steps of problem solving, paying attention to their content and not so much on the mechanics of their English.

- **Tactile, Concrete Experiences of Mathematics:** Use three-dimensional objects in mathematics instruction such as geometrical shapes, coins, or blocks to form various geometrical shapes.

- **Daily Relooping of Previously Learned Material:** Bring in previously learned material to build on each day so that students have a base knowledge to start with, and their learned structures are constantly reinforced.

- **Value of Estimation:** Model estimation for the students as a way to begin solving mathematics problems and provide them with repeated opportunities to practice it. Because these students often have difficulty with *exact* calculations, estimation may increase their confidence to continue with a problem if their first guess seems sensible.

- **Technology:** Use technology that decreases dependence on language skills. Calculators and numerous tutorial programs on CDs and Internet sites can be very helpful. Some of them may even be in the ELL's native language. See the **Resources** section for helpful Internet sites.

- **Rewrite Word Problems:** Word problems pose a particularly difficult challenge for ELLs with mathematics disabilities. First they must be able to read and understand the English to determine the nature of the problem and then decide what mathematical operations are required to solve it. Rewriting word problems with simpler vocabulary and using diagrams or other visuals may lead to more success in solving these types of problems.

Teaching Tip 7.7: Strategies for
Teaching Science to ELLs With Learning Difficulties

Here are some strategies for teaching science to ELLs who have learning difficulties.

- **Hands-On, Active Participation:** Science is about doing and exploring. Design activities so that students are actively involved in developing the project or experiment. This hands-on participation is important because it can often make it easier for the ELLs to understand the specialized science vocabulary that accompanies an investigation.

- **Use Visuals:** Bring two-dimensional or three-dimensional visuals into the classroom to enhance your instruction in the science concept.

- **Use Pictures to Demonstrate Steps:** Use a series of pictures to demonstrate the steps in a project or experiment so that students get a visual image of what they need to do.

- **Modeling or Demonstration:** Demonstrate how to do a lab or experiment before having the students try it on their own. Be sure to emphasize and model the safety precautions that must be taken during the experiment.

- **Use Prereading Strategies:** Give an overview of a science unit, preview the main ideas, and connect the topic to the students' background knowledge (positive transfer).

- **Preteach Vocabulary:** Identify and explain key science vocabulary words prior to working with the lesson or unit. Ask the students to define the words for you as best they can to ensure they understand the terms.

- **Teach How to Pick Out the Main Idea and Justify It:** Teach the ELLs how to pick out the main idea of a paragraph or text reading and explain why it is the main idea. This can be done as a class or in small groups to build consensus of what the main idea is.

| K
What We
Know | W
What We
Want to Know | L
What We
Learned |
|---|---|---|
| | | |

- **"KWL" Chart:** Use the "know (K), want to know (W), learned (L)" chart as a form of self-monitoring in which students are taught to list what they know already about a topic, what they want to know, and what they learned.

- **Peer Tutoring:** Ask students to work in pairs with one student tutoring the other student on a particular science concept. After some time, ask for one student from each pair to report any ideas that need to be clarified or questions to be answered.

Teaching Tip 7.8: Accommodation
Strategies for ELLs With Writing Difficulties

Accommodation strategies help bypass writing difficulties and reduce the impact that writing has on the learning process so that ELL students can focus more on the content of their writing. The accommodations can adjust the rate and volume of writing, the complexity of the task, and the tools used to create the final product. Here are some accommodation strategies in each of these areas (MacArthur, 2009; Sousa, 2007).

- Allow more time for students to complete written tasks, such as note taking, written tests, and copying. Also, allow these students to begin written projects earlier than others. Consider including time in the student's schedule for acting as an aide, and then have the student use that time for making up or starting new written work.

- Encourage developing keyboarding skills and using the computer. Students can begin to learn keyboarding as soon as they attain adequate English proficiency. However, they may need time and more practice to adjust to an English keyboard. Encourage them to use word-processing programs and assign a native English-speaking peer to help them. Teaching hand-writing is still important, but students may produce longer and more complex writing with a computer.

- Have students prepare worksheets in advance, complete with the required headings, such as name, date, and topic. Provide a standard template with this information already on it.

- Provide partially completed outlines and ask students to fill in the missing details. This is a valuable, but not burdensome, exercise in note taking.

- Allow students to dictate to another student. One student (scribe) writes down what another student says verbatim and then allows the dictating student to make changes without help from the scribe.

- Correct poor spelling in first drafts, but do not lower the grade because of it. However, make clear to the ELLs that spelling does eventually count, especially in assignments completed over time.

- Reduce copying of printed work. Avoid having students copy over something already printed in a text, like entire mathematics problems. Provide a worksheet with the text material already on it or have the students just write down their original answers or work.

- Allow students to use abbreviations in some writing, such as b/4 for *before,* b/c for *because,* and w/ for *with.* These are also helpful shortcuts during note taking.

- Allow students to use print or cursive writing. Many students with dysgraphia are more comfortable with print (manuscript) letters. However, students should still be encouraged to use cursive writing. It eliminates the need to pick up a pencil and deciding where to replace it after each letter. Cursive has very few reversible letters, a typical source of confusion for students with dysgraphia. It eliminates word-spacing problems and allows the writing process to flow more easily.

- Teach and model for students the stages of writing, such as brainstorming, drafting, editing, and proofreading.

- Encourage students to use a spell checker. Using the spell checker decreases the demands on the writing process, lowering frustration and diverting more energy to thought production. For students who also have reading difficulties, concurrently using a computer reading program also decreases the demands on the writer.

- Have students proofread after a delay in time when they are more likely to catch writing errors. This way, they will see what they actually wrote rather than what they thought they wrote.

- Allow students to use lined and graph paper. Lined paper helps students keep their writing level across the page. Have younger students use graph paper for mathematics calculations to keep columns and rows straight. Older students can turned lined paper sideways for column control.

- Allow students to use different writing instruments. Students should use the writing instrument they find most comfortable. Some students have difficulty writing with ballpoint pens, preferring thin-line marker pens that have more friction with the paper. Others prefer mechanical pencils.

- Have pencil grips available in all styles. Even high school students enjoy these fun grips and some like the big pencils usually associated with primary school.

- Allow some students to use speech recognition programs. For students with very difficult writing problems, using a speech recognition program within a word-processing program allows them to dictate their thoughts rather than type them. However, this is not a substitute for learning handwriting.

CHAPTER 7

Key Points to Ponder

Jot down on this page key points, ideas, strategies, and resources you want to consider later. This sheet is your personal journal summary and will help to jog your memory.

_____

_____

_____

_____

_____

_____

_____

_____

_____

_____

_____

_____

_____

_____

_____

Chapter 8

Putting It All Together

It should be clear by now that it is a relatively easy task for children to learn their first language. Even learning a second language is not much more difficult if it occurs simultaneously with the first language. In fact, learning two languages at the same time—that is, becoming bilingual—establishes neural circuits that will greatly facilitate acquiring a third language in adulthood. However, learning a second language between the age of 5 to 12 years is a somewhat more difficult task, and still more difficult after that. In school, students who are learning English as their second language must not only acquire academic literacy in order to learn subject-area content, but they must also navigate two cultures. School represents a formidable daily task, both socially and academically. In addition to the pressures that all adolescents experience, ELLs also experience a myriad of other strains: an inability to express oneself in a familiar language, and family expectations for academic success. ELLs who are immigrants may also feel a loss of identity, friends, and culture. Furthermore, many ELLs spend the entire instructional day in mainstream classrooms where the majority of students speak English as their native language and instruction occurs in English. Faced with these challenges, what can teachers of ELLs do to help them acquire English successfully and achieve academically?

THE DIVERSITY OF ENGLISH LANGUAGE LEARNERS

For mainstream content teachers without a background in English as a Second Language instruction, determining the appropriate teaching methods and goals for these students poses a significant and unique challenge. Classroom teachers facing these challenges will benefit from understanding some basic information about the characteristics of the nonnative speaker and the impact of English learners on classroom interactions. It is difficult to make generalizations about ELL students because they come from such diverse backgrounds. Some students will learn English more quickly than others. The reasons for this do not always reflect intelligence or motivation, but rather they are related to the following factors, some of which we have discussed in greater detail in previous chapters:

- **Age.** We have noted that the older the students, the more difficult it is for them to acquire the second language naturally. Research has shown that children younger than 12 usually acquire languages more quickly than older children.
- **Native Language.** ELL students' fluency in their first language directly impacts their acquisition of English. Also important are the proximity of speech sounds for oral communication (phonemes) and whether or not the first language uses Roman letters (graphemes) for written communication (see Chapter 3).
- **Literacy of Parents.** The level of literacy of the ELLs' parents affects the acquisition of written language. Some students' parents are illiterate in their native language. The students of these parents may have a tougher time learning how to read and write in English.
- **Reason for Immigrating.** Gaining knowledge of why, when, and from where a student's family immigrated can help teachers understand the psychological implications of the move. For example, refugee status immigrants may be escaping violence, war, or political or religious persecution. These issues may surface in the classroom and the teacher needs to be prepared for that possibility.

In the preceding chapters, we have discussed the neural processes involved in acquiring first and second languages, the strategies that teachers of ELLs might consider in teaching the basic skills of learning English, the approaches to helping ELLs read in the content areas, and the ways to recognize and address problems faced by ELLs with learning disabilities. Extracting from all that information, this chapter puts together the basic framework for the understandings that need to be in place when designing the curricular, instructional, and assessment programs for the growing population of ELLs in our schools.

MISCONCEPTIONS ABOUT ELLs
AND ENGLISH LANGUAGE ACQUISITION

Before we look at this framework, we need to dispel some common misconceptions that exist regarding ELLs and how they acquire English (Harper & de Jong, 2004; Klingner, de Schonewise, de Onis, & Barletta, 2008). These misconceptions persist largely because many teachers, especially in secondary schools, have not had sufficient training in understanding the nature of second-language acquisition and the unique needs of ELLs. Despite their good intentions, this lack of adequate training results in teachers making classroom decisions that may not be the most effective for their ELL students' academic achievement.

If you work with ELL students in any capacity, you might find this review of misconceptions helpful.

- **Misconception: Exposing ELLs to English and having them interact with native English speakers will result in learning English.** It may seem logical to assume that exposing ELLs to language and opportunities for interaction with English speakers would be the basic and adequate conditions for learning English as a second language. If ELLs are exposed to comprehensible English and provided with meaningful opportunities to interact in English, why would they not naturally develop English language skills the same way native speakers develop their first language? They would not for the following reasons:

  > Answer to statement #1 on page 6 of the Introduction

  o Recall from Chapter 2 that although there are some important similarities between the processes of learning a first and a second language, there are also important differences, especially for older learners. Mere exposure to English (or any other target language) is not sufficient to develop the grade-level language proficiency that ELLs need to master the abstract concepts and complex language of secondary school classrooms and textbooks.

  o Developing advanced language skills requires ELLs to pay conscious attention to the grammatical, morphological, and phonological aspects of the English language. ELLs need not only exposure to academic English, but also direct instruction in the relationships between the forms and functions of the language.

  o Older ELLs have more advanced cognitive skills, such as memory and analytic reasoning, and can therefore draw upon a more sophisticated linguistic and conceptual base than young children. Thus, ELLs can be active participants in their own language-learning process.

  Unless carefully designed, cooperative learning activities may not provide ELLs in-depth language experiences.

  o Interaction between ELLs and native English speakers does not necessarily occur naturally or comfortably in mainstream classrooms. When such interactions do occur, they are often limited to brief exchanges in conversational English that do not provide the opportunities to develop academic language.

  o Unless carefully designed, cooperative learning activities may not provide ELLs in-depth language experiences, such as being able to question, agree, disagree, offer an opinion, or ask for clarification.

- **Misconception: All ELLs learn English in the same way and at the same rate.** Here, too, it may seem logical to conclude that because all children speak their native language, their brain will acquire the second language through the same linguistic pathways and at the same rate. You may note that many ELL students acquire social English quickly and easily yet struggle with academic language and literacy. Thus, a common misunderstanding is that all ELLs will develop social language skills before academic language skills. Older ELLs, however, who are already liter-

Answer to statement #2 on page 6 of the Introduction

ate and have a strong foundation in their native language may not follow this pattern, but the reverse. For some students, too, social and emotional factors may inhibit the development of social language proficiency while academic language skills progress more quickly. Consequently, it is important to keep the following in mind:

o When ELLs make errors while practicing their new language, there may be many factors at play other than a cognitive disorder or developmental problem.

o Your own experiences with learning a second language may have limited application to students' struggles with the structure of English.

o Be aware of the common writing errors that ELLs make. These include problems with verb tenses, plural and possessive forms of nouns, subject/verb agreement, and the use of articles (Ferris, 2002). Many of these errors are developmental and may be influenced by the student's native language.

o An ELL's rate of learning English may be affected by prior education, native language literacy level, and personal factors, such as personality, aptitude, and motivation.

o Some ELLs learn English better through written text while others learn English primarily through oral communication. These different types of learners require different kinds of support when learning to write in English.

o Although some ELLs have much in common with native English speakers from diverse socioeconomic, racial, or ethnic backgrounds, they do not follow the same learning path or timeline for English language development.

o The language acquisition process takes several years and there are no shortcuts.

• **Misconception: Teaching methods that are successful with native English speakers also will be successful with ELLs.** Many of the curricular, instructional, and assessment decisions that teachers make are based on district, state, and national standards. Despite the awareness of the needs of ELLs and the state and national mandates to help their academic progress, most of these standards are based on approaches for a diverse student population of native English speakers. In middle and high schools, the standards assume that the ELLs have reached sufficient levels of proficiency in oral language and literacy skills in

Answer to statement #3 on page 6 of the Introduction

English to participate in language-rich content classrooms. Although standards generally allow ELLs to use their native language when possible, their recommendations do not specify the knowledge and skills content-area teachers need to relate to classes with linguistic diversity. Therefore, consider the following:

o Benchmarks in the content areas that are based on native English speakers can be inappropriate for ELLs who often follow a different developmental route and rate in language and literacy when learning English. Oral and written language development, for instance, may occur simultaneously in ELLs, and some ELLs may be able to read English before they can speak it.

o Most content-area teachers expect their ELLs to have at least minimal reading skills and are unprepared for the basic literacy needs of some ELLs. They assume that reading intervention programs designed for low-literacy native English speakers are also appropriate for ELLs who do not read well in English. However, although ELLs in secondary schools generally have limited English vocabularies and reduced reading fluency and comprehension in English, they typically do not have the basic decoding difficulties displayed by many struggling native English readers. Consequently, interventions aimed at improving decoding skills may be inappropriate for many ELLs.

o Recall from Chapter 2 that reading skills and strategies developed in an ELL's native language can transfer to the learning of English. But this may not occur automatically and ELLs may need targeted instruction and extended practice in applying their native language literacy skills to English. Keep in mind, also, that the ELLs' native languages and writing systems (e.g., alphabetic, syllabic, logographic) differ in important ways from English.

o It may seem that process approaches to writing will address the ELLs' writing needs along with those of native English-speaking students. Without linguistic and cultural modifications for ELLs, process-oriented approaches to instruction using literature logs and dialogue journals may not be successful. ELLs may have different understandings of paraphrase and citation conventions and lack experience with peer review, revising, and teachers' indirect forms of feedback.

o Most ELL students do not have the same quick grasp of what sounds right or best in English as their peers who are native speakers. It is important to be aware of the basic differences in native language-to-English word order in phrases and sentences, and of the differences in the purpose and position of a topic sentence in paragraphs.

- **Misconception: Using visuals and other nonverbal tools in instruction helps ELLs avoid the language demands in school.** Nonverbal instructional tools, such as visuals, charts, graphic organizers, hands-on activities, and role play, can help make very complex information comprehensible to ELLs. These supports also help in reducing the language demands of content learning. However, these nonverbal tools should not be used *in place of* academic language

Answer to statement #4 on page 6 of the Introduction

instruction but *in addition* to it. And just because ELLs have a broad understanding of content ideas and concepts, we cannot assume that they automatically have the ability to use English to carry out academic tasks effectively (Leung & Franson, 2001).

- **Misconception: Assessments of ELLs' native language proficiency provide an accurate picture of linguistic proficiency.** Assessments administered to young ELLs characterize some children as "non-nons," meaning that they are limited in both their native language and English. Yet researchers have pointed out that there are numerous flaws in these assessments and that too many of these children are misidentified as having low-level ability in both languages (MacSwan, Rolstad, & Glass, 2002). Some ELL educators suggest that these assessments of students' native language proficiency be abandoned and replaced with home language surveys, brief parent interviews, and a second-language assessment.

  > Answer to statement #5 on page 6 of the Introduction

- **Misconception: The more time ELLs spend in receiving English instruction, the faster they will learn it.** As logical as this statement sounds, it is not supported by research. Studies have consistently shown that a strong foundation in the ELL's native language is more conducive to successful English language acquisition than placement in an English-only environment (e.g., August & Hakuta, 1997; August & Shanahan, 2006; Slavin & Cheung, 2005). These findings further show that students who are taught using at least some of their native language perform significantly better on standardized tests in English reading than similar students taught only in English.

  > Answer to statement #6 on page 6 of the Introduction

- **Misconception: Errors in English may cause problems and should be avoided.** It is natural for ELLs to make errors when learning English. These errors should not be interpreted as signs of developmental delay or a learning disability. The types of errors that ELLs make vary depending on the characteristics of their native language, so an ELL who speaks Spanish will make different errors than one who speaks Chinese. As ELLs gain proficiency in English, they may resort to code-switching. In this practice, the ELL combines two languages in one phrase or sentence, or switches back and forth between two languages in a conversation. (Code-switching between Spanish and English is called Spanglish. For example, *Te veo ahorita, me voy de shopping para el mall* for *See you later, I'm going shopping in the mall.*) This is not a sign of language confusion or errors, but rather a normal result of the brain's accommodation to two language systems and an indication of its ability to shift between them (Genesee & Nicoladis, 2006). Code-switching in fact may indicate mastery of two languages rather than limited proficiency in either one.

  > Answer to statement #7 on page 6 of the Introduction

Unless educators address these misconceptions, their curriculum, instruction, and assessment practices will only partially meet the needs of ELLs in their classrooms. ELLs should be integrated into the academic goals and discourse of the classroom. Language and content learning goals for ELLs should be coordinated with those for native speakers of English. See **Teaching Tip 8.1** for recommendations on how to overcome common misconceptions about ELLs and second-language acquisition.

BASIC COMPONENTS FOR ELL INSTRUCTION

Teaching ELL students, including those with learning disabilities, needs to center around four basic components, as shown in Figure 8.1 (Rodriguez, 2009).

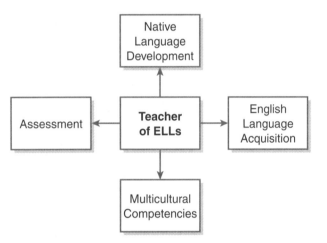

Figure 8.1 Effective instruction for ELLs should include the four components shown in this diagram. (Adapted from Rodriguez, 2009.)

- **Developing the Native Language.** Developing the ELLs' native language will also help in developing their second language. Total-English immersion programs are not as effective as those that transition from the ELLs' L1 to English over time. Contrary to some beliefs, ELLs can develop *both* their native and English language and literacy skills as they are acquiring their new language. The more teachers know about how to connect common characteristics from the ELLs' L1 to English, the more successful they can be in teaching them English and content material.

- **Acquiring the English Language.** It is important to know about the cerebral processes at work as the ELL brain learns English, and how L1 transfer can both help and hinder the ELL's comprehension of the phonological, morphological, syntactic, and semantic characteristics of English. Moreover, ELLs build two English language constructs, conversational and academic. This distinction has important implications for language learners in academic environments.

We noted in previous chapters that how quickly and how easily an ELL will acquire English is closely related to the degree of similarity between English and the ELL's native language. Table 8.1 shows the effect that an ELL's native language can have on learning English.

Table 8.1 Effect of an ELL's Native Language on Learning the English Language

ELL's Native Language	Assisting Factors of English	Impeding Factors of English
Spanish, Italian, Portuguese, French, Haitian Creole	• Uses Latin alphabet • Large number of phonetic and written cognates • Many similar phonemes • Similar syntactic structure: subject/verb/object	• Deep orthography makes pronunciation and spelling rules unreliable • Adjectives come before nouns they modify, not after • Pronouns agree with gender of subject, not gender of noun • No diacritical marks to indicate change in pronunciation
Russian (also Bulgarian and Ukranian)	• Similar number of consonant sounds	• Uses Latin alphabet instead of Cyrillic alphabet • Deep orthography makes pronunciation and spelling rules unreliable • Phonemes not in Russian (e.g., 22 vowel and diphthongs sounds compared to Russian's 5) • Fairly fixed word order • Uses articles; Russian does not
Arabic	• Some phonetic cognates, but written in Latin alphabet	• Uses Latin alphabet instead of Arabic alphabet • Read from left to right, not from right to left • Typical word order is subject/verb/object instead of verb/subject/object • Phonemes not in Arabic (e.g., 22 vowel and diphthong sounds compared to Arabic's 8) • Punctuation rules more rigid • Stress patterns unpredictable • Adjectives come before nouns they modify, not after
Chinese (Cantonese and Mandarin)	• Written left to right as in modern Chinese writing • Adjectives come before noun they modify	• Words are composed from abstract letters, not from a logographic symbol • More vowel sounds than in Cantonese and Mandarin • Changes in pitch and tone used to indicate emphasis or emotion, not to distinguish word meanings • Verb/tense system more complicated

(Continued)

(Continued)

ELL's Native Language	Assisting Factors of English	Impeding Factors of English
Korean	• Koreans have daily exposure to Latin alphabet • Written left to right as in modern Korean writing	• Uses Latin alphabet instead of Korean alphabet (hangul) • More consonant and vowel sounds than in Korean • Stress patterns important to meaning, unlike stressless Korean • Extensive use of auxiliary verbs that do not exist in Korean • Verb/tense system more complicated • Typical word order is subject/verb/object instead of subject/object/verb
Vietnamese	• Uses Latin alphabet as in modern Vietnamese • Written left to right • Typical word order is subject/verb/object	• Uses no diacritical marks that are plentiful in Vietnamese writing • Changes in pitch and tone used to indicate emphasis or emotion, not to distinguish word meanings • Adjectives come before nouns they modify, not after • Verb/tense system more complicated
Hmong	• Uses Latin alphabet • Written left to right • Typical word order is subject/verb/object	• Adjectives come before nouns they modify, not after • Subject-verb agreement required • Changes in pitch and tone used to indicate emphasis or emotion, not to distinguish word meanings • Verb/tense system more complicated • Difficult to discriminate ending consonants such as "d" and "t"
Tagalog	• Uses Latin alphabet • Stress used to differentiate words with same spelling but different meanings	• Phonemes not in Tagalog (e.g., 22 vowel and diphthongs sounds compared to Tagalog's 11) • Typical word order is subject/verb/object, not verb/subject/object or verb/object/subject • Verb/tense formations very different • No diacritical marks to indicate change in pronunciation

ELL's Native Language	Assisting Factors of English	Impeding Factors of English
Japanese	• Some modern commercial Japanese uses Latin alphabet • Modern Japanese written from left to right, but traditional Japanese is written from top to bottom and from right to left • Large number of English words used in Japanese	• Uses Latin alphabet instead of logographic symbols or syllabary script • English diphthong sounds are difficult to differentiate • Typical word order is subject/verb/object instead of subject/object/verb • Uses auxiliary verbs; nonexistent in Japanese • Uses articles; Japanese does not • Different rules of syntax
Navajo	• Uses Latin alphabet	• Function of adjectives and many nouns in English provided by verbs in Navajo • No diacritical marks • Verb/tense formations very different • Orthography rules very different • Typical word order is subject/verb/object instead of subject/object/verb

Researchers believe that, on average, ELLs may take two years to become fluent in interpersonal communications. Academic language, however, takes far longer—at least five to seven years. Many people seriously underestimate how long it takes to fully develop academic language skills in a second language, so it is understandable that many teachers dispute these numbers. They hear their ELLs talking to other students socially in reasonably accurate English, and often with little or no accent. It appears these students know English well enough to comprehend all that is happening in their content classrooms, and to participate fully without any special modifications. Thus, many students are released prematurely from ESL courses only to be mainstreamed into classes for which they are not yet prepared to succeed. However, the ELLs need to reach the level of English required to comprehend academic content and to participate in activities and assignments.

Remember that the ELLs' informal communication is not reflective of academic language proficiency. Appropriate emphasis must be placed on acquiring academic English so that ELLs can master the text-centered and lecture-prone content-area classes found in secondary-level schools. When we modify existing lessons to address the ELLs' specific language needs, we integrate these

An ELL's informal communication is not reflective of academic language proficiency.

students into the class and curriculum, instead of creating a separate and less rigorous curriculum for them. Furthermore, this focus on academic language also benefits the native English-speaking students who may be struggling with reading or writing. From this perspective, considering the needs of ELLs' in lesson planning has potential benefits for other students as well.

- **Building Multicultural Competencies.** Not only must ELLs acquire English, but they must also adapt to a new culture with its own set of mores, social rules, conventions, and associated expectations for behavior. We need to recognize these challenges as well and help ELLs make the social and cultural adjustments needed to feel welcome in school. Part of feeling welcomed means that the ELLs' native culture is respected. Cultural differences can be a source of misunderstanding for teachers and their ELLs. People of all cultures express themselves both verbally and nonverbally. Nonverbal cues in one culture may represent something entirely different in another. For example, in Western cultures, when a student smiles at the teacher, it often indicates understanding. However, in many Asian cultures, smiling may camouflage confusion or frustration. Teachers who are educated about their ELL students' cultural mores communicate that they value their students' heritage. Moreover, students whose native culture is valued have a greater sense of self-worth and higher academic achievement levels.

- **Assessing Progress in Language and Literacy Skills in Both the Native and English Languages.** Continuous monitoring of progress in both the L1 and English is needed to ensure that ELLs gain linguistic proficiency in both their languages. Assessing progress in academic English is especially important so that the ELLs achieve grade-level reading proficiency as soon as possible. Although assessment should be continuous, it should also be informal and not so intrusive as to cause undue anxiety.

This approach ensures that effective classroom instruction for ELLs addresses their social, cultural, academic, linguistic, and cognitive backgrounds. It also places a heavy demand on the capabilities and training of those who teach ELLs.

Professional Development for ELL Teachers

For decades, educational research has shown that of all the factors affecting a student's achievement, the quality of teaching is among the most important. In other words, the quality of learning rarely exceeds the quality of teaching. As the population of ELLs continues to grow, so will the demand for ELL teachers. In a number of school districts now, the ELL enrollment is increasing faster than the availability of fully

> *The quality of learning rarely exceeds the quality of teaching.*

trained ELL teachers. Consequently, many teachers currently assigned to ELLs are not adequately trained for the job. They work hard and they are well-intentioned, but unless they are able to competently address the learning challenges that ELLs face, they cannot be fully effective.

What constitutes a fully trained ELL teacher? Rodriguez (2009) recommends that teachers specializing in working with ELLs should be able to demonstrate competencies in the following:

- Knowledge of methods for monitoring students' linguistic and literacy progress
- Ability to use various types of formal and informal assessment procedures
- Knowledge of assessment information to make instructional decisions, plan individual student programs, and suggest appropriate learning environments
- Proficiency in two languages (or the availability of personnel to communicate in students' primary languages)
- Understanding the nature of bilingualism and the process of becoming bilingual
- Understanding structural differences between the child's primary language and second language
- Ability to develop curriculum that integrates language content
- Identify approaches of students' learning profile
- Planning strategies to respond positively to the diversity of behaviors involved in cross-cultural environments and classrooms
- Incorporating multicultural activities, materials, and techniques related to content-area curriculum.

This is an impressive list of competencies, reflecting the complex nature of the teaching and learning processes involved in successful second-language acquisition.

What Other Teachers Can Do

Chronic underachievement in the content areas plagues many ELL students. Chapter 5 offered numerous suggestions for content-area teachers who have English learners in their classrooms, especially in the areas of language arts, social studies, mathematics, and science. Although the suggestions may seem overwhelming for content-area teachers who already have a full plate, just taking a few minutes to incorporate some effective strategies can make a big difference in the ELLs' comprehension and achievement in any class. See **Teaching Tip 8.2** for general ideas to consider when planning lessons for all classes that include ELLs.

In addition to using strategies that are effective with ELLs, it is also important that content teachers become partners with their students' English as a Second Language (ESL) teachers. ELLs are moving between the two worlds of their ESL classroom and their content classrooms. They have to work harder and they need more support than the average native English-speaking student who has an age-appropriate command of the English language. The focused language instruction that ELLs receive in their ESL classroom is critical, but it also reduces the time they spend in the content classroom. Consequently, content teachers should provide the ESL teacher with the main ideas, the content-specific vocabulary, and the sentence structures related to upcoming lessons. The ESL teacher can use this information as a basis for academic language instruction for ELLs in the ESL classroom. With this content-based approach to ESL instruction, ELLs have opportunities to practice listening, speaking, reading, and writing English. By sharing this information with the ESL teacher, content teachers establish a link for ELLs between what they learn in ESL and what they learn in the content classroom. As a result of this collaboration between teachers, the ELLs will spend more time on content-related information.

Models of Coteaching

Schools that have designed programs to help ELLs improve their academic English often pair teachers of ELLs with mainstream or content-area teachers in the same classroom. This coteaching arrangement can occur in various formats. Honigsfeld and Dove (2008) suggest the five following models of coteaching that can be used with ELLs in different group combinations.

One Group of Students (Whole class)

1. *One lead teacher and one teacher teaching to an objective.* In this format, the mainstream or content-area teacher and the ELL teacher take turns assuming the lead role. As one leads, the other may, if needed, provide mini-lessons to individuals or small groups to preteach or clarify a particular concept or skill.
2. *Two teachers teach the same content.* With this format, both teachers conduct a whole-class lesson and work together to teach the same lesson at the same time.

Two Groups of Students (Within the class)

3. *Two teachers teach the same content.* Here students are divided into two learning groups. The teachers do parallel teaching, presenting the same content using appropriate differentiated learning strategies.

4. *One reteaches while the other teaches alternative information.* Flexible grouping puts together students by proficiency level for specific content. The composition of the student groups changes as needed.

Multiple Student Groups (Within class)

5. *Two teachers monitor and teach.* With multiple groupings, both teachers can monitor and facilitate student work while also assisting selected students with their specific learning needs.

Coteaching not only helps ELLs progress academically but also invites cooperation among teaching colleagues and on-the-job professional development in ways that are not often found in schools today.

Avoid Watering Down the Curriculum

Content teachers may believe that they are helping their ELLs when they create lessons with low-level, ostensibly easier concepts and language, and simpler worksheets than for their non-ELL students. However, this practice results in watered-down content and denies ELLs access to the grade-level curriculum. The negative effects of a watered-down curriculum for ELLs multiply as they are promoted through the grade levels without the basic foundational knowledge they need. Rather than simplifying the curriculum content for ELLs, it may be more effective for the content teacher to focus their efforts instead on determining the major concepts and processes in the curriculum that English learners must know and sharing this information with the students' ESL teachers. These concepts, along with the appropriate academic language, can then become the main focus for our ELLs, supported by their ESL teacher. By helping the ELLs focus on the most important concepts, content teachers bring the task down to manageable size without watering down the curriculum. Valuable time is spent on the most important material, and as a result, the workload is less overwhelming and more productive for both students and teachers.

Enhancing ELL Literacy

One of the major goals of school programs for ELLs is to enhance their literacy in both their native and English languages. We noted earlier that the literacy of the ELLs' parents can have an impact on written language acquisition. Pransky (2009) suggests that ELLs can come from *literacy-oriented communities* or *non-literacy-oriented communities*. In the former, parents are well-educated and they prepare their children for success in school and in society. They also interact with their children in ways that develop their children's critical thinking, conversational skills, and vocabulary. By contrast, a non-literacy-oriented community may value education, but the parents may have less formal education and spend less time interacting with their young children in ways that develop adultlike thinking and language skills. Both communities turn out intelligent, able children. However, a literacy orientation is more matched to what schools expect and non-literacy-oriented children will have difficulty keeping up academically.

One way to get an idea of an ELL's native and English language literacy exposure is to consider using a short survey that asks them about the kinds of materials they read and write outside of school. Gottlieb (2006) suggests that the survey ask whether the ELLs read and write any of the following and whether they do so in their native language, English, or both:

Read:
- newspapers
- magazines
- brochures/pamphlets
- maps or directions
- street names and signs
- information on the Internet
- short stories
- books

Write:
- e-mails
- memos or notes
- information on papers or forms
- lists
- letters to family members or friends
- short stories
- poetry or song

Although one must always use caution in interpreting self-reported information, this type of survey can give teachers some insight into their ELLs' language and literacy practices as well as their educational background and experiences. The results can help teachers estimate whether an ELL comes from either a literacy-oriented or a non-literacy-oriented community.

Helping the non-literacy-oriented ELL requires the teacher to focus on developing certain cognitive skills. These include:

- Developing standard dialect skills
- Increasing vocabulary
- Building strong metacognitive skills
- Developing a sophisticated level of personal narrative
- Developing a strong executive function
- Organizing semantic memory
- Fostering comfort with abstract and generalization
- Creating effective internal scripts

Suggestions are shown in **Teaching Tip 8.3** on how to accelerate the academic achievement of students from non-literacy-oriented communities.

Using Technology

Many ELLs get their first exposure to the English language through media rather than through formal schooling. Television, movies, the Internet, radio, and popular music are appealing sources of entertainment. Although teachers may be wary about using these forms of technology in the classroom, their appeal to students cannot be denied. Well-planned and appropriate use of technology in and out of the classroom can make a significant difference in how fast and how well ELLs learn academic as well as conversational English. Furthermore, activities involving technology can challenge ELLs by promoting critical thinking and enhancing executive functions such as analyzing, critiquing, and making judgments about competing ideas. The key words here are "well-planned" and "appropriate."

Using technology should not be a goal in itself. To avoid frustration, it requires quality professional development for teachers along with systemic integration of content. As new technology tools enter the classroom, they need to be evaluated with all students in mind. Some teachers continue to use only classic technologies in their classrooms, such as the overhead projector, videos, or television. But integrating technology means more than simply using the overhead to display information, a computer to input grades, or using the Internet to do research. It is about using technology as a tool to *enhance* teaching, learning, and multisensory experiences, providing a myriad of pathways for students at varying levels. For elementary ELLs, for example, using technology to engage in actual activity may lead to improved language skills by increasing their vocabulary, their ability to share their own and their peers' feelings, and hence feel accepted in their new environment.

Does Multitasking With Technology Reduce Attention Span?

Before looking at applications of technology to ELL language development, we should address one serious question that often arises about technology and student learning: Does multitasking with the many forms for technology reduce a student's attention span? Teachers understandably worry whether adding more technology time in the classroom is counterproductive because it may be lessening the time that the students can focus on the learning objective at hand. Although there are no formal or reliable studies to date that test this notion, scientists can make some suppositions based on what is already known about brain growth and development.

We know that the brain is constantly changing and that it is very sensitive to stimuli in its environment. If children are sitting in front of a computer or television screen for long periods of time, pressing buttons and getting reactions quickly, their brain may get accustomed to rapid responses. At the same time, they gain little practice in concentrating for long periods and this could affect how they handle the relatively sedate school environment. Science is just beginning to look at whether the brain can become better at multitasking over time just by doing it. There is no evidence yet that multitasking shortens attention span. On the contrary, when students find something of great interest through technology, they will often spend many hours with it. So although technology does not yet appear to shorten attention span, it does place many demands on it. The question facing the students is not how *long* they can focus on an appealing topic, but *which* topic they should choose.

Answer to statement #8 on page 6 of the Introduction

Advantages of Using Technology With ELLs

Although all students can benefit from appropriate use of technology, ELLs may benefit in ways that can make their acquisition of English and adjustment to a new culture somewhat easier. Here are some of the advantages to using technology:

- **Encourages Learner-Centered Classrooms.** Technology provides students access to information that was once under the control of teachers. By allowing ELLs to integrate technology, such as using the Internet or working as a team on a project, teachers provide students with opportunities to enhance and extend their learning to higher levels of cognitive involvement. When technology involves students in complex authentic tasks, the results can be student-centered cooperative learning, increased teacher-student and peer interaction, and more positive attitudes toward learning. As students solve a problem requiring

> Some educators are concerned that using technology in the classroom will reduce attention span.

  research on the Internet, they are working closely as a team, allowing for greater interaction and sense of responsibility for the team. Instead of the student sitting alone at a desk with a book, collaboration allows learners to take an active role in helping each other to accomplish a learning task. When technology is used as a resource to improve learning, and not just to increase productivity, the role of teachers, learners, and even the learning process itself changes. This transformation to student-centered classroom marks a new role for the teacher as a facilitator. As both teachers and facilitators, they help ELLs construct their own meaning.

- **Enriches Learning Experiences.** Learning through technology activities shifts the learning process itself. The Internet transforms the way we view information and changes how we obtain and use it. With billions of webpages, the Internet contains rich sources of information and engages the user's brain in imaginative ways. It is a tool that can enrich learning by allowing ELLs access to meaningful content. They can take a virtual tour of the National Gallery of Art to view and analyze renowned artwork. They can use information from numerous databases rather than be limited to the textbook and local resources. They can collaborate online with classrooms around the world. They can be paired with global experts. These activities accelerate content learning by providing relevant information that is not solely dependent on learning English. Through experiences such as these, ELLs have the opportunities to participate in an engaged learning environment and learn at higher levels.

- **Allows for Immediate Communication and Feedback.** Classes in today's schools should allow for more social interaction, learner communication, and cooperation, all skills of especially high value to ELLs. The teacher is not the only expert because ELLs often have their own experiences that they incorporate as part of learning. With technology, ELLs can control and self-direct their learning and get immediate feedback. They no longer depend on direct teacher instruction, which may limit the student to passive listening and watching the teacher.

- **Is Intrinsically Motivating.** Technology can often provide the context for a learning task that helps the ELL student to grasp meaning without relying solely on the English language. At the same time, the ELL gains meaning of the English vocabulary associated with the learning task thus providing the motivation to learn and move on. Technology increases the ELLs' autonomy, allows for more responsibility, promotes equal opportunities in a nonsexist environment, and encourages student cooperation with peers. By using the modern tools of technology, ELLs can learn and interact with the multicultural world, extend their language skills, and not be embarrassed for not knowing all the answers, thereby building their self-confidence.

Challenges of Using Technology With ELLs

Although developing excellent technological skills will make a major difference in the lives and futures of our ELL students, there are several challenges that educators face when trying to help ELLs achieve this competency (Robertson, 2008).

- **Language.** To use instructional technology effectively and efficiently, ELLs need to have the language skills and vocabulary necessary to understand how to use the technology.
- **Limited Access.** Many ELLs may not have access to a computer or the Internet in their home. They also may be unaware of the technology opportunities available through their school or library, or they may be unable to get to the library on a regular basis.
- **Varying Levels of Experience.** The level of experience that ELLs have with computers can vary from one student who learned to use the computer as a toddler to another who is sitting in front of a computer for the first time. These differences in level of experience require that teachers develop their own ability to differentiate technology instruction for their students. The good news is that technology often can help teachers differentiate instruction for their ELLs.
- **School Facilities.** Although many schools have invested heavily in technical equipment, many have not—including numerous schools serving ELLs.
- **Staying Up to Date.** It is very difficult for teachers to keep up with the new jargon associated with technology tools, the digital information overload, and the latest technical trends, plus trying to determine how these things all relate to their students.

Despite these challenges, teachers (even those with limited technical know-how) can use technology to help ELLs build their technical skills and digital literacy. See **Teaching Tip 8.4** for strategies for helping ELLs use technology and **Teaching Tip 8.5** for ways to use technology to build ELLs' language skills.

GIFTED AND TALENTED ELLs

Because of the inherent language barriers, ELLs have fewer opportunities compared to their native English-speaking peers to be identified by teachers as gifted and talented students (Aguirre, 2003). Giftedness and talent in ELLs manifest in ways that are part of these students' linguistic, ethnic, and cultural backgrounds. Identification procedures, therefore, should focus on a broader conception of giftedness and include nontraditional approaches that consider the students' culture. Researchers suggest that there are several barriers to identifying ELL students as gifted and talented (Bernal, 2002; Harris, Rapp, Martinez, & Plucker, 2007).

- **Poor Communication.** Teachers of gifted and talented students and teachers of other special populations, such as ELL students, may not communicate with each other thereby reducing opportunities to observe and know ELLs in various educational settings. Teacher collaboration allows multiple sources to discuss individual students and increases the likelihood of identifying ELLs who have exceptional gifts and talents.
- **Lack of Explicit Policies.** Many school districts do not have explicit policies regarding the proper identification of gifted students from underrepresented groups, including ELLs.
- **Avoiding the Issue.** Gifted program coordinators and district administrators may be reluctant to address this underrepresentation of ELLs because of limited financial and physical resources to accommodate additional students in gifted and talented programs.
- **Concern for Compromising the Program.** Parents and school personnel may worry that gifted programs may be compromised if students who do not meet traditional testing requirements are admitted. These concerns often contribute to the unwillingness to change the current identification procedures.
- **Low Expectations for ELLs.** Some educators believe that acquiring English is such a difficult challenge that they have low expectations of culturally and linguistically diverse students. As a result, educators may overlook students who demonstrate culturally relevant gifts and talents that are not recognized or appreciated by the majority culture.

Identifying Gifted and Talented ELLs

Educators should recognize that different cultures stress specific academic and intellectual abilities and talents, so the ways that ELLs express giftedness and intellect are directly related to their cultural values (Esquivel & Houtz, 1999). The parents of ELLs often are not aware of the services for gifted children, and some parents do not speak or read English, thus making it challenging for them to be advocates for their child's education. For parents to be involved, they need to feel welcomed and understood in a new and complex educational system. Thus, school staff members should develop awareness about the relationships that parents have with schools in their country of origin.

Use of Intelligence Tests With ELLs

The identification and placement of children in gifted and talented programs has traditionally been based on scores on a verbal or nonverbal test of intelligence. Verbal IQ tests require mastery of oral, writing, and reading skills in English—a distinct disadvantage for ELLs. Cognitive assessments are available in various languages. However, to be valid, the assessment's norms must be appropriate for the individual student's country of origin and linguistic history. If the student has not had the same amount of language exposure as the norming group, the results may not accurately reflect the ELL's abilities (Rhodes, Ochoa, & Ortiz, 2005). Thus, relying primarily on standardized tests to identify ELLs as gifted students may not be appropriate and may well be the main cause of ELLs' underrepresentation in these programs (Bernal, 2002).

Although several nonverbal tests of intelligence exist, research on the validity and reliability of their use with ELL populations has been limited. One recent study compared the validity of three nonverbal tests for the purpose of identifying academically gifted ELLs (Lohman, Korb, & Lakin, 2008). Nearly 1,200 elementary children (approximately 40% ELLs) were administered the Raven Standard Progressive Matrices (Raven), the Naglieri Nonverbal Ability Test (NNAT), and Form 6 of the Cognitive Abilities Test (CogAT). Results showed the following:

- U.S. national norms for the Raven substantially overestimated the number of high-scoring children.
- The NNAT overestimates the number of both high-scoring and low-scoring children.
- Primary-level ELL children score especially poorly on the NNAT.
- ELL children scored lower than non-ELL children on the three nonverbal tests.

Apparently, none of the nonverbal tests predict achievement for ELL students very well. Despite the diverse nature of intelligence and giftedness, many school districts use test scores, including IQ scores, in the decision to place students in gifted and talented programs (Ford & Grantham, 2003). As long as standardized tests in English are used in lieu of more authentic assessment procedures, few ELL students are likely to be identified as gifted. Although there are no universally accepted valid and reliable identification procedures for identifying gifted and talented ELLs, the collection of data from observing the interaction of students with varied learning opportunities can provide a better profile for identification. See **Teaching Tip 8.6** for some recommendations for identifying gifted and talented ELLs.

Answer to statement #9 on page 6 of the Introduction

CONCLUSION

Schools are enrolling ELLs at increasing rates. As these students cross the threshold, all educators need to be ready to provide them with the greatest opportunity for social and academic success. School staff should be taught about the cultures of their students. New identification and assessment strategies should be employed by the school district based on the values or particular culture of the child. By doing so, we ensure that not only will no child be left behind, but that all students will have the opportunity to move forward to reach their full potential.

By now you may realize that all the answers to the *What Do You Already Know* test in the **Introduction** are false.

Teaching Tip 8.1: Strategies to Overcome Misconceptions About ELLs and L2 Acquisition

We are often unaware how misconceptions we have about certain student populations guide our decision making in the classroom. Therefore, it is important to recognize what misconceptions exist about ELLs and second-language acquisition in order to ensure that our curricular, instructional, and assessment decisions are based on sound research. Here are strategies to consider to overcome common misconceptions.

- **Use reciprocal teaching.** Reciprocal teaching (see Chapter 5) has been used successfully as a participation structure with ELLs where strategy roles are modeled by the teacher, who highlights the language needed to perform each role. Strategy roles are practiced by the students, then assigned to and rotated among individuals in small groups.
- **Provide frequent opportunities to practice academic language.** Exposure and interaction are simply not enough for ELLs to learn academic language. They need explicit opportunities to practice using the new language to negotiate meaning in interactive settings.
  - o Draw their attention to the structure of the English language that is used in specific academic contexts and provide appropriate feedback that ELLs can use to further their oral and written academic language development.
  - o Provide ELLs with opportunities to respond to challenging questions through response formats appropriate to these students' oral proficiency levels such as yes/no, either/or, short answer, or extended response options.
  - o When responding to ELLs' journal writing, rephrase their errors to clarify ideas, provide input on the grammatical form, or suggest a more appropriate word or phrase rather than ignoring errors entirely or correcting all writing errors directly on the journal entries (Cloud, Genesee, & Hamayan, 2000; de Jong & Derrrick-Mescua, 2003).

- **Ensure that teaching strategies are appropriate for ELLs.** Remember that ELLs spend most of the school day in classrooms with content-area teachers and that these classrooms offer great potential to develop academic language skills in English. Acting on this opportunity, however, requires an understanding of the language-learning needs of ELLs as well as the language demands of the subject areas. Many teachers (especially secondary-level mathematics, science, or social studies teachers) do not think of themselves as language teachers.
  - o For example, the KWL chart discussed in previous chapters is a useful instructional tool. But bear in mind that its usage assumes that the ELLs possess the language skills to participate in the various steps of the activity (i.e., stating facts, proposing ideas, asking questions). When using KWL charts and other instructional tools, ensure that the language demands of these tasks are addressed as well as the cultural assumptions that may prohibit effective ELL participation.

o When using cooperative learning structures, ensure that ELLs can actively and appropriately participate by paying attention to the language demands and the required tasks.

- **Support ELLs' literacy learning in English.** All teachers can contribute to ELLs' literacy learning in English.

  o Build on their existing word recognition skills or on their knowledge of cognates. For learners who are literate in nonalphabetic languages (such as Chinese and Korean), give greater attention to developing letter-to-sound associations.

  o Before an assignment, include discussions aimed at eliciting and linking the ELLs' related background knowledge as well as hands-on experiences that invite key questions and highlight key vocabulary. In this way, you identify important concepts, vocabulary, and questions before your lecture or reading begins.

- **Plan for both the conceptual and linguistic development of ELLs.** Because ELLs are simultaneously acquiring content and language proficiency, plan both conceptual and linguistic development for these students.

  o Identify the language demands of their content area that may be particularly challenging for ELLs. For example, Chapter 5 discussed how mathematics teachers need to recognize that the vocabulary of mathematics poses special challenges for ELLs. Specialized terms may be unfamiliar to these students, such as *equation* and *denominator,* along with the specialized use of common terms such as *table, column,* and *round* for which ELLs may have learned meanings that do not apply to mathematics. Every content area has similar language hurdles for ELLs.

  o Include ways to reduce the language demands for ELLs (i.e., provide comprehensible input) while simultaneously providing opportunities for ELLs to develop the necessary academic language skills. Graphic organizers are an effective means of understanding text structure and of supporting the development of academic writing proficiency in various content areas. Students construct graphics from text using knowledge structures such as classification, description, and sequence, add key vocabulary words to represent concepts, and draw links to specify relationships among concepts. They then write expository prose using the conceptual and linguistic scaffolding provided in the graphic.

  o Consider using a planning sheet for listing activities that develop language skills as well as content. Here is an example of a planning sheet that a mathematics teacher could use to ensure that the language objectives are included in this lesson on triangles.

Language Activities	Content Activities & Assessment
Content objective: Classifying triangles as right, obtuse, or acute **Language Activities:** *Listening:* Explain 3 types of triangles *Speaking:* Ask students to describe the 3 types of triangles *Reading:* Read pp. 56–58 in text *Writing:* Write what they learned in their math journals	Students will classify triangles as right, obtuse, or acute. Evaluate based on content mastery revealed by proficiency level (e.g., beginning students explain in words, pictures, and actions; more advanced students include explanatory text incorporating language objectives.

- **Understand the factors that contribute to ELLs' behavior.** Learning a second language is a complex process subject to individual learner variables. Consequently, an ELL's behavior often cannot be reduced to a simple explanation.

  o For instance, rather than attributing an ELL's continued silence to a lack of motivation or ability, consider other possibilities such as culture shock or a response to discriminatory language practices in school.

  o Examine the linguistic and cultural assumptions underlying the activities of ELLs.

  o Consider a wide range of factors when trying to understand and explain the behaviors of ELLs. These include (1) affective factors, such as personality, motivation, and attitude, (2) cultural and educational background, (3) literacy level in their native language, (4) age, and (5) approaches to learning.

  o Learn more about ways that other cultures structure their children's educational experiences and explore ways that languages are similar and different.

Teaching Tip 8.2: General Ideas to Consider When Planning Lessons for ELLs

All teachers can create an effective learning environment for their ELLs. Select four or five of the following ideas—especially those you have never tried—and implement them in your content-area or mainstream classroom. Although all students will benefit from any of these ideas, you may notice improvement in the ELLs' classroom participation and comprehension of content.

Before the Lesson

- Assess the English language proficiency of your ELLs. Be realistic about what you expect the ELLs to do during and after the lesson.
- Plan ahead. Think about how you will make the content comprehensible to your ELLs by considering the following questions:
    - How will you link the content to the ELLs' previous knowledge?
    - How will you build the background information so ELLs can establish a context for the new learning? Is there a video or a passage to read aloud about your topic at the beginning of the lesson?
    - How will you develop content-area vocabulary? What visuals will you need?
- Consider activities that address visual, auditory, and kinesthetic learning modalities.
- Include teaching aids such as maps, charts, pictures, and flashcards before the lesson is taught.
- Add vocabulary word banks to student activities.
- Rewrite any text so that the concepts are paraphrased in simpler English. Eliminate non-essential details.
- Find nonfiction books in the library written at a lower reading level about the topic or unit you are going to teach.

During the Lesson

- Determine what the ELLs already know about the topic and build on it.
- Introduce concrete concepts and vocabulary first. Move to abstract concepts only when these are firmly in place.
- When speaking, simplify your vocabulary and sentence structure, avoiding idioms that may confuse the students.

- Demonstrate highlighting techniques so that students can highlight important information.
- Provide concrete examples and real-world experiences when possible.
- Give the ELLs in advance any questions that you will ask during class so that they can prepare their responses.
- Teach students how to categorize their information using graphic organizers. Create semantic and story maps so students can see relations between and among topics.
- Check for understanding regularly and review and repeat important concepts and vocabulary as appropriate.
- Teach ELLs to find the definitions for key vocabulary in the text.
- Help ELLs become acquainted with their textbooks (table of contents, glossary, index, etc.).
- Use think-alouds to model your thinking processes and procedures for students.
- Tape-record important parts of your lesson and give the tapes to ELLs to reinforce their learning.

After the Lesson

- Ask non-ELL classmates to make copies of their notes for ELLs to use.
- Have ELLs watch videos or listen to tapes about your current lesson using the closed-captioned feature.
- Provide follow-up activities that reinforce vocabulary and concepts.
- Have students work in small groups or pairs so that language and concepts are reinforced.
- Adjust the homework assignments to your ELLs' level of English language proficiency.
- Modify assessments so that your ELLs have various opportunities and modalities to show what they have learned.

Teaching Tip 8.3: Fostering a Literacy Orientation in ELLs

ELLs from non-literacy-oriented homes are likely to have a difficult time in school because they have not had practice in the thinking and language skills typically found in children from literacy-oriented homes. Here are some suggestions for fostering this practice in ELLs who have not naturally acquired it (Pransky, 2009).

- **Developing Standard Dialect Skills.** The dialect that ELLs speak can strongly affect others' perceptions of those students' intelligence and organizational and writing skills. The standard dialect is the one of formal schooling.

  o Be more explicit and sensitive when encouraging students to use standard dialect. One way is to focus attention on how language is used in the classroom as contrasted with how it is used in the ELLs' home communities as, for example, in song.

  o Be careful how you communicate language differences to students. If ELLs think you are calling their English wrong—especially if it is the way their family uses it—this may erode self-esteem, motivation, and the sense of belonging to the school and class.

- **Increasing Vocabulary.** Chapter 3 noted the importance of vocabulary in language acquisition and especially in learning to read. Studies show large vocabulary gaps between children of different social classes (Beck, McKeown, & Kucan, 2002). ELLs from non-literacy-oriented homes know very few descriptive synonyms in English for common words, yet they need such words to succeed academically.

  o Create a variety of word-centered activities, such as index card games, age-appropriate and adapted TV game shows, word sorts, graphic organizers, and word clusters. Recycle words periodically, especially synonyms. These activities help to build the ELLs' vocabulary and to think about semantic constructions in English.

- **Building Strong Metacognitive Skills.** Metacognition, you will recall, means being aware of your own thinking processes. Although all children develop metacognitive skills over time, children from a literacy-oriented home develop them at younger ages.

  o Use puzzles and skill games to strengthen the ELLs' metacognition skills. As you watch students tackle puzzles, you get a sense of how they solve other problems. Use that information to help them develop metacognitive skills when making decisions about puzzles and when learning content.

  o Coach students to focus on the processes of their own thinking by drawing on material they already know well. For example, suppose a student is working on a multistep mathematics problem using an unsystematic approach. Point out that the approach is the main issue, not the mathematics.

Putting It All Together **231**

o Ask students to reflect on their learning—not on the content, but on the process. What did they do well, and how did they know? What successful way of thinking will they be sure to repeat tomorrow?

o Ask ELLs to write entries in their journals about how they solve problems successfully in nonschool activities and give an example.

- **Developing a Sophisticated Level of Personal Narrative.** Because the narrative form is not the same across all cultures, ELLs from various cultures bring differing forms of narrative to the class discourse. Regardless of culture, however, the narrative sophistication with which we link our thoughts does transfer across different languages. ELLs with underdeveloped narrative skill have difficulty understanding grade-level texts.

o Be knowledgeable about the power of narrative and be able to recognize language features that signal narrative stages, and how to help ELLs develop their narrative skills.

- **Developing a Strong Executive Function.** Executive function occurs in the front part of the brain and is the ability to skillfully manage and process multiple sources of information. As with metacognition, all children eventually develop executive function, but it occurs faster in a literacy-oriented environment.

o Use graphic representations to symbolize ways of thinking or steps in problem solving. The picture of a magnifying glass, for example, can mean that students should look for important words. Icons on computer screens are excellent examples of graphic representations for a task.

- **Organizing Semantic Memory.** Semantic memory is knowledge of facts and data and can be based on a taxonomy or hierarchy. For any student, a well-organized semantic memory is essential for success in formal schooling. For example, if during a lesson a teacher says *dog*, a student with a good semantic memory might call up something like animal–mammal–four legs–barks. Students who lack an organized semantic memory tend to learn more slowly and appear to have difficulties in reading and writing, particularly with expository text (Booth, Bebko, Burman, & Bitan, 2007).

o Semantic memory is built on a strong vocabulary. Incorporate vocabulary activities that deepen comprehension of word meanings, such as Venn diagrams.

o Expand the ELLs' familiarity with attributes and their categories. For example, challenge early-elementary-age students to compare and contrast different objects, such as square to rectangle to triangle, or animals to plants.

- **Fostering Comfort With Abstraction and Generalization.** Being comfortable with abstract ideas is essential to reading content texts and for independent academic success. The ability to generalize enables learners to independently create broader meaning from a specific learning activity.

○ Whenever ELLs have difficulty generalizing their learning at school, ask them to reflect on related out-of-school experiences. This will help them realize how often they do generalize.

○ Provide examples in the classroom of how they can abstract the essence of what they learned in one specific situation, relate that learning to a set of new circumstances, and apply their previous learning successfully.

- **Creating Effective Internal Scripts.** When beginning a new learning task, we use subvocalized speech to orient ourselves to the situation and to get organized. For example, when asked to complete an exploratory task, a literacy-oriented ELL might say: *This is similar to a problem we faced last week. I think I remember how we solved that one. I'll get started.* But a non-literacy-oriented ELL might be confused and wonder: *Where is the teacher? I am not sure what I am to do here.*

○ Ask students to practice their internal speech by using a learning journal to reflect on what they did successfully—or unsuccessfully—and what they hope to do in the same way or improve on when faced with a similar task or concept. Use prompts like: *The next time I have this type of problem, I plan to . . .*

○ Encourage students who do not have task-oriented internal speech to refer to their learning journal before they start on their tasks.

Underachieving ELLs will develop literacy-oriented skills in those classrooms that encourage them, but not quickly enough to close the achievement gap. These suggested strategies will guide students in these practices systematically and consistently and apply them directly to their class assignments. By organizing schooling for non-literacy-oriented ELLs around the development of these skills, they will be able to achieve as highly as literacy-oriented students.

Teaching Tip 8.4: Strategies
for Helping ELLs Use Technology

For ELL students learning technology, it is particularly important to focus on instructional strategies that are commonly used in other content areas, such as academic language development and meaningful interaction with the content. Here are some practical strategies for making technology more accessible to ELL students (Langer de Ramirez, 2010; Robertson, 2008).

- **Build Vocabulary.** There are so many words specific to technology. For example, an ELL may know that a mouse is an animal, but may not know that the word also refers to the tool we use to move a computer's cursor. To effectively teach technical vocabulary:
  - *Find out what students know.* Arrange students into small groups (perhaps with peers who speak the same native language) and give them a list of new words. Ask them to discuss which words they know, and to write down multiple meanings so that you can help clarify appropriate usage. After students have discussed the list, ask the groups to share their ideas with the whole group.
  - *Review the basics.* Present a very basic introduction to technological vocabulary words that students are likely to encounter, including parts of the computer (mouse and screen), items that students may see on their screen (cursor and menu), and verbs referring to what they will be doing when they use the computer (click, double-click, scroll, cut, paste, highlight, undo, etc.).
  - *Use visuals, props, and demonstrations.* For ELL students, be sure to demonstrate the meaning of the technology vocabulary word with a visual prop or an action. Drawing programs allow students to combine graphics with labeling, thus building up their English vocabulary and improving their spelling.
  - *Check for comprehension.* Ask students to demonstrate the meaning of new words for you to ensure they understand. Consider asking them to quiz each other in pairs, and to write definitions in their own language or use drawings to demonstrate comprehension.

- **Use Handouts.** ELLs may have difficulty trying to follow along on their own computers while the teacher demonstrates the steps on a computer screen projected in the front of the class. Students who fall behind may get lost and will need to ask for help to catch up.
  - Give ELLs handouts with visuals of the computer screen so that they can easily follow you. Many school technology departments may have these types of visuals readily available. To create your own visual handouts, capture a picture of the screen and paste it into a Word document.

- **Create Simple Assignments for Beginners.** When learning a new technology skill, ELLs should work with known information. For example, students learning how to use a word-processing program should write about something with which they are familiar, rather than having to research a new topic while also learning how to use the program. In this way, the students can concentrate more effectively on applying their new technology skills. Once they have some proficiency in the program, they can be challenged to create documents using newly learned information.

- **Extend Practice Time.** Because many ELLs have limited interaction with computers, they may need more time to master basic computer skills, such as
  - guiding and clicking with the mouse
  - double-clicking
  - dragging
  - scrolling
  - using the control, alternate, escape, and arrow keys
  - using various search engines

ELLs are trying to make meaning of the instructions given in a second language, while also figuring out how to use the technology. If class time is limited, the extra practice time may need to take place in an afterschool technology class. This may be an opportunity to pair a non-ELL student who is technologically competent with an ELL student who is developing computer skills.

- **Use Pairs and Small Groups for Rehearsal and Transfer.** One of the advantages of ELLs working with each other and non-ELLs in pairs and small groups is that they have opportunities to practice their English vocabulary and literacy skills. This practice is called *rehearsal* and it increases retention of learning. Moreover, learning is reinforced when we use it to socially construct knowledge. If students are exposed to new information, vocabulary, and technology all at the same time, they will learn some of it and forget some of it. Instead, get a small group of students to use the new information, vocabulary, and technology to build something together or to solve a problem. In this way, they learn it and remember it by discussing different approaches to a problem, activating their prior knowledge (transfer), and learning from each other.
  - For example, if a group of students has typed information for a brochure into a word-processing program and now wants to move one paragraph to another area, one student may suggest they delete the paragraph and type it in the new space. Another student may suggest that it would be better to cut the paragraph and paste it to the new area. By working together the students learn from each other and make decisions as a group that will lead to a higher-quality product. This type of interactive learning involves rehearsal and transfer and also helps ELLs develop their English language skills.

- **Provide Relevant Learning Objectives.** Students get excited and motivated about using computers and technology when they are applying their technology skills to content they are interested in.

  o Establish meaningful objectives for the ELLs using technology. For example, if students are learning how to make a brochure, ask them to consider creating it about their home country. Students who want to make movies may want to create their own music group and pretend they are going on tour of several countries.

  o Introduce the technology with very basic, well-known information so all students can understand it. Give general guidelines to ensure the quality of the project, but allow students some options for individuality. For example, you may require that a brochure project have one photo, a clear purpose and title, three paragraphs of text, and contact information. This sets the minimum parameters for a successful project, but allows students to focus on an area of their own interest.

- **Teach Students to Check Their Electronic Sources.** Students can receive enormous amounts of information electronically, and they may be apt to accept the information because they do not have time to verify it. ELLs may be particularly susceptible to accepting information they receive electronically because they may come from a culture where written information is considered reliable.

  o Check with the school librarian or technology specialist to determine if they have orientation sessions about search engines and popular research sites, how to best conduct a search, and how to evaluate information once they find it.

  o Lead the students through a discussion and investigation as to the origin of news. Support the development of good online research skills by teaching them how to determine if information is accurate and relevant to their needs.

Teaching Tip 8.5: Strategies for Using
Technology to Build ELLs' Language Skills

There are many ways you can use technology with ELLs to support the development of their language and literacy skills. For example (Kottler, Kottler, & Street, 2008):

- Encourage ELLs to watch television in English. Soap operas, situation comedies, and music videos are good ways for students to sensitize themselves to English sounds and usage.
- Use audio recordings to help ELLs with pronunciation. They can listen to tapes of native English speakers in order to improve their pronunciation.
- Consider videotaping particularly difficult lessons. Save them so the ELLs can play them back later at their own pace. Also, the ELLs can make videos as part of their assignments and get involved in activities that require technical skills rather than reading skills. By periodically taping their activities, ELLs can see how well their language skills are developing over time.
- Encourage young ELLs who are learning to read English to use computers to improve their reading level and fluency.
  - Programs that include puzzles, games, and stories provide practice in word building that supports learning to read. Even in first grade, ELL students can learn to use presentation programs, such as PowerPoint, to demonstrate the sequencing in a story they have read or to create their own story.
  - Later, word-processing programs with all their spell- and grammar-checking features allow the ELLs to concentrate on their message without being slowed down by handwriting and looking up words in the dictionary.
- E-mail offers ELLs opportunities to communicate with others all over the world. ELLs can exchange e-mails with those who speak their native language as well as native English speakers in various countries. Determine whether your school has the capability to do videoconferencing between your classroom and those in other countries so the students can actually see the ones they send their e-mails to.
- Take advantage of Microsoft Word's readability feature. For example, before you ask the ELLs to read an article on the Internet, copy and paste it into Microsoft Word. Run the readability test to decide if the text is appropriate or too difficult for your ELLs to understand. (To run readability, click the Microsoft Office button, then Word Options, then Proofing.)

Teaching Tip 8.6: Recommendations for Identifying Gifted and Talented ELLs

Various authentic procedures exist for identifying gifted and talented ELLs. These include but are not limited to the following (Sarouphim, 2002):

- Classroom observations
- Checklists and rating scales
- Portfolio evaluations
- Teacher nominations
- Problem-solving-based assessments
- Teaching within the testing situation
- Interviews with parents and communities
- Self-identification
- Alternative testing

Harris et al. (2007) has adapted a three-tiered procedure developed by Coleman (2003) for identifying gifted and talented students.

- **Tier I: Conduct a general screening or student search.**
  - Implement a schoolwide (or districtwide) screening system that is applied to every student in the general and the ELL population.
  - Use multiple criteria to obtain a complete picture of students' talent and potential.
  - All assessments must be administered in the ELL's native language (many of these are available commercially) as well as in English. Policymakers and researchers should test the reliability and validity of translated assessments in an effort to make future gifted screenings and assessments accessible to non-English speakers.
  - Give multiple screening procedures (e.g., curriculum-based assessment, identification of learning characteristics, assessment of nonverbal cognitive abilities) from multiple sources (e.g., teachers, parents, peers, grades, self-report) at multiple times throughout the year.
  - Implement multifaceted assessment procedures so that information is gathered (a) from multiple sources (caregivers/families, teachers, students, and others with significant knowledge of the ELLs), (b) in different ways (e.g., observations, performances, products, portfolios, interviews), and (c) in different contexts (e.g., in-school and out-of-school settings).
  - Provide information about the gifted program and identification practices of the district to parents in their native language. Include characteristics to look for in their child that might indicate giftedness as well as the procedures for notifying the district's gifted coordinator if such traits are observed.

○ Ensure that the screening process is ongoing throughout the school year so that ELLs who enter the school system at different times in the school year have a chance to participate in the assessment and identification process.

○ Establish a district task force to monitor the referral and identification procedures for accountability.

- **Tier II: Review students for eligibility.**

  ○ Consider for the second tier those ELLs who demonstrated potential based on the Tier I screening process.

  ○ Carry out professional development of regular classroom teachers and especially language instruction program teachers (such as ESL teachers) aimed at recognizing talent in ELL students.

  ○ Review data by a team of school personnel that includes teachers of the gifted and talented and ELL teachers. Parents (or caregivers) and general education teachers should be active members of the team.

  ○ After reviewing the data for each student, decide whether to (a) collect additional data about the student, or (b) immediately place the student in the program for gifted and talented children.

- **Tier III: Match students to services.**

  ○ Offer appropriate educational services to ELL students with demonstrated high potential that may include an alternate placement (e.g., class for gifted and talented students) or enriched services (e.g., afterschool class).

  ○ Individualize specific curricular programming for the ELL's unique strengths. Thoughtful and creative planning for ELLs who are gifted and talented often requires very specialized consideration of appropriate services.

  ○ Consider setting aside a certain number of slots for ELL students to increase their representation in gifted and talented programs.

The successful identification of gifted and talented ELL students involves an emphasis on authentic identification procedures carried out by competent school personnel and supported by the proactive and dedicated leadership of school administrators.

CHAPTER 8

Key Points to Ponder

Jot down on this page key points, ideas, strategies, and resources you want to consider later. This sheet is your personal journal summary and will help to jog your memory.

_____

_____

_____

_____

_____

_____

_____

_____

_____

_____

_____

_____

_____

_____

_____

Glossary

Academic language fluency. The ability to use spoken English (or any other language) with such complexity that one's academic performance is not impaired.

Affixes. Prefixes (e.g., *pre-*, *re-*, and *un-*) and suffixes (e.g., *-able, -ful,* and *-or*) added to root words.

Alphabetic principle. The understanding that spoken words can be broken down into phonemes, and that written letters represent the phonemes of spoken language.

Aphasia. The reduction or loss of language ability as a result of damage to the brain.

Axon. A long fiber that transmits signals from one neuron to another.

Bilingual education. A program for English learners in which they receive instruction in their native language for part of the school day so they can learn grade-level content and succeed academically.

Broca's area. A region of the brain located behind the left temple that is associated with speech production, including vocabulary and probably syntax and grammar.

Cloze. An oral or written assessment technique whereby the student uses context clues to provide a word or words that have been omitted from a sentence.

Code-switching. The practice of combining two languages in one phrase or sentence or going back and forth between languages in a conversation.

Cortex. The surface of the brain (sometimes called gray matter) containing the neurons and their connections (synapses) with other neurons.

Dendrite. The branched extension from the cell body of a neuron that receives impulses from nearby neurons through synaptic contacts.

Dialect. A variation of a language through vocabulary, grammar, pronunciation, and the rules of discourse.

Diphthong. A complex sound of two letters that begins with one vowel sound gliding over to another vowel sound, such as the *oi* sound in *moisture* and the *ow* sound in *cow.*

Dyscalculia. A condition that causes persistent problems with processing numerical calculations.

Dyslexia. Also known as severe reading disability, this is a learning disorder characterized by persistent problems in reading and writing.

Early Modern English. The English of Shakespeare's time, spoken from about 1450 to 1700 AD.

English language learners (ELLs). Students whose native language is not English and whose proficiency in the English language prevents them from learning grade-level content that is taught in academic English.

Fluency. The ability to quickly and accurately speak, read, and write a language.

Frontal lobe. The front part of the brain that monitors higher-order thinking, directs problem solving, and regulates the excesses of the emotional system.

Functional magnetic resonance imaging (fMRI). An instrument that measures blood flow to the brain to record areas of high and low neuronal activity.

Grammar. The formal set of rules that determines the way words and sentences are correctly used in a particular language.

Grapheme. The smallest part of written language that represents a single phoneme in the spelling of a word. A grapheme may be just one letter, such as *b, d, g,* and *s,* or several letters, as in *ck, sh, igh,* and *th.*

Graphic organizer. A visual representation of knowledge, concepts, or ideas, such as with charts, diagrams, and timelines.

Idiom. A figurative phrase whose meaning cannot be interpreted literally, such as *it's raining cats and dogs* and *he's going bananas.*

Instructional congruence. A teaching strategy that makes meaningful connections to the knowledge, perspectives, and behavior that ELLs bring to the classroom.

Intonation. The rise and fall in the pitch of one's voice while speaking.

KWL charts. A visual tool used prior to instruction whereby the teacher finds out what the students already know (K), what they want to know (W), and, after instruction, what they have learned (L).

L1. An individual's first (or native) language.

L2. An individual's second language, which for ELLs is English.

Language proficiency. An individual's ability to understand, process, and use a language through listening, speaking, reading, and writing.

Linguistic feature. A language form used in sentence construction such as a prepositional phrase, subordinate clause, relative clause, and active and passive voices.

Linguistic misalignment. A situation whereby the linguistic features, dialect, and register of an assessment do not match those of the student being assessed.

Manipulatives. Objects, such as pegs, blocks, puzzle pieces, models, and Cuisinere rods, that students use to foster the learning of abstract concepts, especially in mathematics.

Metacognitive strategies. Teaching techniques that ask students to think about their own mental processes when dealing with a learning task.

Mental lexicon. The dictionary in the brain that contains a person's intuitive knowledge of words and their meanings.

Mirror neurons. Clusters of neurons in the brain that fire not only when experiencing a task or emotion but also when seeing someone else experience the same task or emotion.

Morphemes. The smallest meaningful units into which words can be separated, as *in-describ-able* and *un-conscious-ness*.

Morphology. The set of grammar rules that direct how words are built out of pieces (morphemes).

Native language. Usually, the first language an individual acquires, also referred to as L1.

Neural network. A collection of interconnected brain cells that process information and may send signals to other networks.

Neuron. The basic cell making up the brain and nervous system, consisting of a cell body, a long fiber (axon) that transmits impulses, and many shorter fibers (dendrites) that receive them.

Old English. Also called Anglo-Saxon, this was the language spoken from about 450 to 1100 AD, after the tribes from Germany invaded England.

Orthography. The written system that describes a spoken language. Spelling and punctuation represent the orthographic features of written English.

Positron emission tomography (PET). A process that traces the metabolism of radioactively tagged sugar in brain tissue, producing a color image of cell activity.

Phoneme. The smallest unit of sound that makes up a spoken language. For example, the word *go* has two phonemes, */guh/* and */oh/*. The English language has about 44 phonemes. Some phonemes are represented by more than one letter.

Phonemic awareness. The ability to hear, identify, and manipulate phonemes in spoken syllables and words.

Phonics. The study of phoneme-to-grapheme relationships in a language.

Phonological awareness. A recognition that oral language can be divided into smaller components, such as sentences into words, words into syllables and, ultimately, into individual phonemes.

Phonology. The study of the sound patterns of a language, including how the sounds can be combined as well as the patterns of stress, timing, and intonation.

Pronunciation. The uttering of the sound or sounds of a word.

Prosody. The rhythm, cadence, accent patterns, and pitch of a language.

Register. A language used for a specific situation or context.

Rehearsal. The reprocessing of information in working memory.

Reliability. The extent to which an assessment instrument produces consistent results over time when measuring similar students in similar circumstances.

Response to Intervention (RTI). A method of determining whether students have learning difficulties by assessing their responses to the methods, strategies, curriculum, and interventions they encounter.

Scaffolding. A temporary support system for an ELL that should be removed when the student reaches the appropriate level of proficiency in a particular skill or content.

Second-language acquisition. The developmental process of learning a new language, generally English, and also referred to as L2.

Semantics. The study of how meaning of a language is derived from words and other text forms.

Sequential bilingual. An individual who enters school as monolingual and begins to acquire a second language.

Sheltered instruction. A set of instructional strategies and techniques used to help ELLs with limited proficiency in English learn academic content that is taught in English. Another goal is to promote English-language proficiency as the ELLs learn academic content.

Simultaneous bilingual. An individual who is exposed to two languages at the same time very early in life, and who gains proficiency in both.

Stress. The emphasis placed on a syllable in pronunciation so that it is longer, louder, more articulated, or higher in pitch, as in *MEX-i-co* or *Al-a-BAM-a*.

Syntax. The rules and conventions of grammar that govern the order of words in phrases, clauses, and sentences.

Transfer. The influence that past learning has on new learning, and the degree to which new learning will be useful in the learner's future.

Validity. The extent to which an assessment instrument accurately measures in a student what it is intended to measure.

Wernicke's area. A region of the brain, usually located in the left hemisphere, thought to be responsible for sense and meaning in one's native language.

Working memory. The temporary memory wherein information is processed consciously.

References

Abedi, J., & Lord, C. (2001). The language factor in mathematics tests. *Applied Measurement in Education, 14,* 219–234.

Abella, R., Urrutia, J., & Shneyderman, A. (2005). An examination of the validity of English language achievement test scores in an English Language Learner population. *Bilingual Research Journal, 29,* 127–144.

Abu-Rabia, S., & Kehat, S. (2004). The critical period for second language pronunciation: Is there such a thing? Ten case studies of late starters who attained a native-like Hebrew accent. *Educational Psychology, 24,* 77–98.

Abutalebi, J., & Green, D. (2007). Bilingual language production: The neurocognition of language representation and control. *Journal of Neurolinguistics, 20,* 242–275.

Aguirre, N. (2003). ESL students in gifted education. In J. A. Castellano (Ed.), *Special populations in gifted education: Working with diverse gifted learners* (pp. 17–27). Boston: Allyn & Bacon.

Alfassi, M. (2004, March–April). Reading to learn: Effects of combined strategy instruction on high school students. *The Journal of Educational Research, 97,* 171–184.

Amaral, O. M., Garrison, L., & Klentschy, M. (2002). Helping English learners increase achievement through inquiry-based science instruction. *Bilingual Research Journal, 26*(2), 213–239.

Anderson, R. T. (2001). Lexical morphology and verb use in child first language loss: A preliminary case study. *International Journal of Bilingualism, 5,* 377–401.

Arbib, M. A. (2009, November). Mirror system activity for action and language is embedded in the integration of dorsal and ventral pathways. *Brain and Language.* Available online at www .sciencedirect.com.

Au, T. K., Knightly, L. M., Jun, S.-A., & Oh, J. S. (2002). Overhearing a language during childhood. *Psychological Science, 13,* 238–243.

August, D., & Hakuta, K. (1997). *Improving schooling for language minority children: A research agenda.* Washington, DC: National Academy Press.

August, D., & Shanahan, T. (Eds.). (2006). *Developing literacy in second-language learners: Report of the National Literacy Panel on Language-Minority Children and Youth.* Mahwah, NJ: Erlbaum.

Baker, K., & de Kanter, A. A. (1981). *Effectiveness of bilingual education: A review of the literature* (Final draft report). Washington, DC: Department of Education, Office of Planning, Budget, and Evaluation.

Baker, W., & Trofimovich, P. (2005). Interaction of native- and second-language vowel system(s) in early and late bilinguals. *Language and Speech, 48,* 1–27.

Baker, W., Trofimovich, P., Flege, J. E., Mack, M., & Halter, R. (2008). Child-adult differences in second-language phonological learning: The role of cross-language similarity. *Language and Speech, 51*(4), 317–342.

Banks, J. (2006). *Cultural diversity and education: Foundation, curriculum and teaching* (5th ed.). Boston: Pearson.

Barcroft, J. (2002). Semantic and structural elaboration in L2 lexical acquisition. *Language Learning, 52*(2), 323–363.

Barrera, M. (2008, June). Assessment of culturally and linguistically diverse learners with disabilities: Introduction to the special series. *Assessment for Effective Intervention, 33,* 132–134.

Barron, V., & Menken, K. (2002). *What are the characteristics of the bilingual education and ESL teacher shortage?* Washington, DC: National Clearinghouse for English Language Acquisition and Language Instruction Educational Programs.

Beal, C. R., Adams, N. M., & Cohen, P. R. (2010). Reading proficiency and mathematics problem solving by high school English language learners. *Urban Education, 45*(1), 58–74.

Beatty, J. (2001). *The human brain: Essentials of behavioral neuroscience.* Thousand Oaks, CA: Sage Publications.

Beck, I., McKeown, M., & Kucan, L. (2002). *Bringing words to life.* New York: Guilford Press.

Bedore, L. M., & Peña, E. D. (2008). Assessment of bilingual children for identification of language impairment: Current findings and implications for practice. *The International Journal of Bilingual Education and Bilingualism, 11*(1),1–29.

Bernal, E. M. (2002). Three ways to achieve a more equitable representation of culturally and linguistically different students in GT programs. *Roeper Review, 24,* 82–88.

Bialystok, E., Craik, F. I. M., Klein, R., & Viswanathan, M. (2004). Bilingualism, aging, and cognitive control: Evidence from the Simon Task. *Psychology and Aging, 19,* 290–303.

Bialystok, E., McBride-Chang, C., & Luk, G. (2005, November). Bilingualism, language proficiency, and learning to read in two writing systems. *Journal of Educational Psychology, 97*(4), 580–590.

Biemiller, A., & Boote, C. (2006). An effective method for building meaningful vocabulary in primary grades. *Journal of Educational Psychology, 98,* 44–62.

Bischoff-Grethe, A., Proper, S. M., Mao, H., Daniels, K. A., & Berns, G. S. (2000). Conscious and unconscious processing of nonverbal predictability in Wernicke's area. *Journal of Neuroscience, 20,* 1975–1981.

Bleakley, H., & Chin, A. (2008). What holds back the second generation? The intergenerational transmission of language human capital among immigrants. *Journal of Human Resources, 43*(2), 267–298.

Bloch, C., Kaiser, A., Kuenzli, E., Zappatore, D., Haller, S., Franceschini, R., et al. (2009, February). The age of second language acquisition determines the variability in activation elicited by narration in three languages in Broca's and Wernicke's area. *Neuropsychologia, 47,* 625–633.

Booth, J. R., Bebko, G., Burman, D. D., & Bitan, T. (2007). Children with reading disorder show modality independent brain abnormalities during semantic tasks. *Neuropsychologia, 45*(4), 775–783.

Booth, J. R., Wood, L., Lu, D., Houk, J. C., & Bitan, T. (2007, February). The role of the basal ganglia and cerebellum in language processing. *Brain Research, 1133,* 136–144.

Bortfeld, H., Wruck, E., & Boas, D. A. (2007, January). Assessing infants' cortical response to speech using near-infrared spectroscopy. *Neuroimage, 34,* 407–415.

Buchweitz, A., Mason, R. A., Hasegawa, M., & Just, M. A. (2009, January). Japanese and English sentence reading comprehension and writing systems: An fMRI study of first and second language effects on brain activation. *Bilingualism* (Cambridge, England), *28,* 141–151.

Bunch, G. C., Abram, P. L., Lotan, R. A., & Valdés, G. (2001). Beyond sheltered instruction: Rethinking conditions for academic language development. *TESOL Journal, 10*(2/3), 28–33.

Burman, D. D., Bitan, T., & Booth, J. R. (2008). Sex differences in neural processing of language among children. *Neuropsychologia, 46*(5), 1349–1362.

Burnham, D., Kitamura, C., & Vollmer-Conna, U. (2002). What's new pussycat? On talking to babies and animals. *Science, 296,* 1435.

Calderón, M. (2004). *Standards-based writing for English language learners.* Los Angeles: Los Angeles County Office of Education.

Calderón, M. (2007). *Teaching reading to English language learners, Grades 6–12.* Thousand Oaks, CA: Corwin.

Calderón, M., Hertz-Lazarowitz, R., & Slavin, R. (1998). Effects of bilingual cooperative integrated reading and composition on students making the transition from Spanish to English reading. *The Elementary School Journal, 99,* 153–166.

Calderón, M., & Minaya-Rowe, L. (2003). *Designing and implementing two-way bilingual programs.* Thousand Oaks, CA: Corwin.

Callahan, R. M. (2005). Tracking and high school English learners: Limiting opportunity to learn. *American Educational Research Journal, 42*(2), 305–328.

Capps, R., Fix, M., Murray, J., Passel, J. S., & Herwantoro, S. (2005). *The new demography of America's schools: Immigration and the No Child Left Behind act.* Washington, DC: The Urban Institute.

Carasquillo, A., Kucer, B., & Abrams, R. (2004). *Beyond the beginnings: Literacy interventions for upper elementary English language learners.* Clevedon, UK: Multilingual Matters.

Carlo, M. S., August, D., McLaughlin, B., Snow, C. E., Dressler, C., Lippman, D. N., et al. (2004). Closing the gap: Addressing the vocabulary needs of English language learners in bilingual and mainstream classrooms. *Reading Research Quarterly, 39*(2), 188–215.

Celedón-Pattichis, S. (2003). Constructing meaning: Think-aloud protocols of ELLs on English and Spanish word problems. *Educators for Urban Minorities, 2*(2), 74–90.

Cheour, M., Ceponiene, R., Lehtokoski, A., Luuk, A., Allik, J., Alho, K., et al. (1998, September). Development of language-specific phoneme representations in the infant brain. *Nature Neuroscience, 1,* 351–353.

Cheung, A., & Slavin, R. E. (2005, Summer). Effective reading programs for English language learners and other language-minority students. *Bilingual Research Journal, 29,* 241–267.

Chiang, Y., & Schmida, M. (2002). Language identity and language ownership: Linguistic conflicts of first-year university writing students. *Enriching ESOL Pedagogy,* 393–409.

Chouinard, P. A., & Goodale, M. A. (In press). Category-specific neural processing for naming pictures of animals and naming pictures of tools: An ALE meta-analysis. *Neuropsychologia.*

Cibrowski, J. (1993). *Textbooks and students who can't read them.* Cambridge, MA: Brookline Books.

Clements, A. M., Rimrodt, S. L., Abel, J. R., Blankner, J. G., Mostofsky, S. H., Pekar, J. J., et al. (2006, August). Sex differences in cerebral laterality of language and visuospatial processing. *Brain and Language, 98,* 150–158.

Cloud, N., Genesee, F., & Hamayan, E.V. (2000). *Dual language instruction: A handbook for enriched education.* Boston: Heinle & Heinle.

Coggins, P. E., III, Kennedy, T. J., & Armstrong, T. A. (2004, April). Bilingual corpus callosum variability. *Brain and Language, 89,* 69–75.

Coleman, M. R. (2003). The identification of students who are gifted. *ERIC Digest.* (ERIC Document Reproduction Service No. ED480431).

Collins, A. M., & Loftus, E. F. (1975, November). A spreading-activation theory of semantic processing. *Psychological Review, 82,* 407–428.

Collins, M. (2005). ESL preschoolers' English vocabulary acquisition from storybook reading. *Reading Research Quarterly, 40,* 406–408.

Collins, M. F. (2010). ELL preschoolers' English vocabulary acquisition from storybook reading. *Early Childhood Research Quarterly, 25*(1), 84–97.

Compton, D. L., Fuchs, D., Fuchs, L. S., & Bryant, J. D. (2006). Selecting at-risk readers in first grade for early intervention: A two-year longitudinal study of decision rules and procedures. *Journal of Educational Psychology, 98,* 394–409.

Conboy, B. T., Sommerville, J. A., & Kuhl, P. K. (2008, September). Cognitive control factors in speech perception at 11 months. *Developmental Psychology, 44,* 1505–1512.

Coop, S., & Reich, G. A. (2008, November–December). New immigrants, new challenges: High school social studies teachers and English language learner instruction. *The Social Studies, 99,* 235–242.

Cooper, G. (Ed.). (1987). *Red tape holds up bridge, and more flubs from the nation's press.* New York: Perigee Books.

Crosson, B., McGregor, K., Gopinath, K. S., Conway, T. W., Benjamin, M., Chang, Y.-L., et al. (2007, June). Functional MRI of language in aphasia: A review of the literature and the methodological challenges. *Neuropsychological Review, 17,* 157–177.

Cruz, M. (2004). Can English language learners acquire academic English? *English Journal, 93*(4), 14–17.

Daisey, P., & José-Kampfner, C. (2002). The power of story to expand possible selves for Latina middle school students. *Journal of Adolescent and Adult Literacy, 45*(7), 578–587.

Damasio, H., Grabowski, T. J., Tranel, D., Hichwa, R. D., & Damasio, A. (1996). A neural basis for lexical retrieval. *Nature, 380,* 499–505.

Dapretto, M., & Bookheimer, S. Y. (1999). Form and content: Dissociating syntax and semantics in sentence comprehension. *Neuron, 2,* 427.

Dehaene, S. (2009). *Reading in the brain.* New York: Viking.

Dehaene, S., Molko, N., Cohen, L., & Wilson, A. J. (2004). Arithmetic and the brain. *Current Opinion in Neurobiology, 14*(2), 218–224.

Dehaene-Lambertz, G. (2000). Cerebral specialization for speech and non-speech stimuli in infants. *Journal of Cognitive Neuroscience, 12,* 449–460.

de Jong, E.J., & Derrick-Mescua, M. (2003). Refining preservice teachers' questions for second language learners: Higher order thinking for all levels of language proficiency. *Sunshine State TESOL Journal, 2*(2), 29–37.

Denton, C. A., Anthony, J. L., Parker, R., & Hasbrouck, J. (2004). Effects of two tutoring programs on the English reading development of Spanish–English bilingual students. *The Elementary School Journal, 104,* 289–305.

DeStigter, T., Aranda, E., & Eddy, L. (1997). The *Tesoros* literacy project: Treasuring students' lives. *English Journal, 86*(6), 89–92.

Diaz-Rico, L. (2000). Intercultural communication in teacher education: The knowledge base for CLAD teacher credential programs. *The CATESOL Journal, 12*(1), 145–161.

Dong, Y. R. (2009, April). Linking to prior learning. *Educational Leadership, 66,* 26–31.

Duff, P. A. (2001). Language, literacy, content, and (pop) culture: Challenges for ESL students in mainstream courses. *The Canadian Modern Language Review, 58*(1), 103–132.

Ecke, P. (2004). Language attrition and theories of forgetting: A cross-disciplinary review. *International Journal of Bilingualism, 8*(3), 321–354.

Edmonds, L. M. (2009, March). Challenges and solutions for ELLs: Teaching strategies for English language learners' success in science. *The Science Teacher, 76,* 30–33.

Ehri, L. (1998). Grapheme-phoneme knowledge is essential for learning to read words in English. In J. Metsala & L. Ehri (Eds.), *Word recognition in beginning literacy* (pp. 3–40). Mahwah, NJ: Erlbaum.

Eimas, P. D., Siqueland, E. R., Jusczyk, P., & Vigorito, J. (1971). Speech perception in infants. *Science, 171,* 303–306.

Ernst-Slavit, G., Moore, M., & Mahoney, C. (2002). Changing lives: Teaching English and literature to ESL students. *Journal of Adolescent & Adult Literacy, 46*(2), 16–28.

Esquivel, G. B., & Houtz, J. C. (1999). *Creativity and giftedness in culturally diverse students.* Cresskill, NJ: Hampton Press.

Fadiga, L., Craighero, L., & Olivier, E. (2005, March). Human motor cortex excitability during the perception of other's action. *Current Opinion in Neurobiology, 15,* 213–218.

Ferris, D. R. (2002). *Treatment of error in second language student writing.* Ann Arbor: University of Michigan Press.

Figueroa, R. A., & Newsome, P. N. (2006). The diagnosis of LD in English learners? Is it nondiscriminatory? *Journal of Learning Disabilities, 39,* 206–215.

Flavell, J. H. (1979). Metacognition and cognitive monitoring: A new area of cognitive development enquiry. *American Psychologist, 34,* 906–911.

Flege, J. E., Bohn, O.-S., & Jang, S. (1997). Effects of experience on non-native speakers' production and perception of English vowels. *Journal of Phonetics, 25,* 437–470.

Ford, D. Y., & Grantham, T. C. (2003). Providing access for gifted culturally diverse students. *Theory into Practice, 42,* 217–225.

Francis, D., Lesaux, N., & August, D. (2006). Language of instruction. In D. August & T. Shanahan (Eds.), *Developing literacy in second-language learners. Report of the National Literacy Panel on language-minority children and youth* (pp. 365–413). Mahwah, NJ: Lawrence Erlbaum.

Francis, N., & Kucera, H. (1982). *Frequency analysis of English usage: Lexicon and grammar.* Boston: Houghton Mifflin.

Friederici, A. D., Friedrich, M., & Christophe, A. (2007, July). Brain responses in 4-month-old infants are already language specific. *Current Biology, 17,* 1208–1211.

Galuske, R. A. W., Schlote, W., Bratzke, H., & Singer, W. (2000). Interhemispheric asymmetries of the modular structure in human temporal cortex. *Science, 289,* 1946–1949.

Gazzaniga, M. S., Ivry, R. B., & Mangun, G. R. (2002). *Cognitive neuroscience: The biology of the mind* (2nd ed.). New York: Norton.

Genesee, F., Lindholm-Leary, K., Saunders, W., & Christian, D. (2006). *Educating English language learners.* New York: Cambridge University Press.

Genesee, F., & Nicoladis, E. (2006). Bilingual first language acquisition. In E. Hoff & M. Shatz (Eds.), *Handbook of language development* (pp. 324–342). Oxford, England: Blackwell.

Geva, E., & Yaghoub-Zadeh, Z. (2006). Reading efficiency in native English-speaking and English-as-a-second-language children: The role of oral proficiency and underlying cognitive-linguistic processes. *Scientific Studies of Reading, 10,* 31–57.

Ghosh, S. S., Tourville, J. A., & Guenther, F. H. (2008, September–October). A neuroimaging study of premotor lateralization and cerebellar involvement in the production of phonemes and syllables. *Journal of Speech, Language, and Hearing Research, 51,* 1183–1202.

Gibson, C. J., & Gruen, J. R. (2008). The human lexinome: Genes of language and reading. *Journal of Communication Disorders, 1,* 409–420.

Goh, C. (2008). Metacognitive instruction for second language listening development: Theory, practice and research implications. *RELC Journal, 39*(2), 188–213.

Goh, C., & Yusnita, T. (2006). Metacognitive instruction in listening for young learners. *ELT Journal, 60,* 222–232.

Gottlieb, M. (2006). *Assessing English language learners.* Thousand Oaks, CA: Corwin.

Grabe, E., Rosner, B. S., García-Albea, J. E., & Zhou, X. (2003). Perception of English intonation by English, Spanish, and Chinese listeners. *Language and Speech, 46*(4), 375–401.

Green, D. W., Crinion, J., & Price, C. J. (2007, July). Exploring cross-linguistic vocabulary effects on brain structures using voxel-based morphometry. *Bilingualism* (Cambridge, England), *10,* 189–199.

Greene, J. P. (1998). *A meta-analysis of the effectiveness of bilingual education.* Claremont, CA: Thomas Rivera Policy Institute.

Guiller, J., & Durndell, A. (2007, September). Students' linguistic behaviour in online discussion groups: Does gender matter? *Computers in Human Behavior, 23,* 2240–2255.

Gunn, B., Biglan, A., Smolkowski, K., & Ary, D. (2000). The efficacy of supplemental instruction in decoding skills for Hispanic and non-Hispanic students in early elementary school. *The Journal of Special Education, 34,* 90–103.

Guo, T., & Peng, D. (2006). ERP evidence for parallel activation of two languages in bilingual speech production. *NeuroReport, 17,* 1757–1760.

Gutiérrez, R. (2002). Beyond essentialism: The complexity of language in teaching mathematics to Latina/o students. *American Educational Research Journal, 39*(4), 1047–1088.

Hall, C. J. (2002). The automatic cognate form assumption: Evidence for the parasitic model of vocabulary development. *International Review of Applied Linguistics, 40,* 69–87.

Hampton, E., & Rodriguez, R. (2001). Inquiry science in bilingual classrooms. *Bilingual Research Journal, 25*(4), 417–434.

Harper, C., & de Jong, E. (2004, October). Misconceptions about teaching English-language learners. *Journal of Adolescent & Adult Literacy, 48,* 152–162.

Harris, B., Rapp, K. E., Martinez, R. S., & Plucker, J. A. (2007, Fall). Identifying English language learners for gifted and talented programs: Current practices and recommendations for improvement. *Roeper Review, 29,* 26–29.

Hart, B., & Risley, T. R. (2003). The early catastrophe. The 30 million word gap by age 3. *American Educator, 27,* 4–9.

Hayes-Harb, R. (2007). Lexical and statistical evidence in the acquisition of second language phonemes. *Second Language Research, 23*(1), 65–94.

Hazan, V., & Barrett, S. (2000). The development of phonemic categorization in children aged 6–12. *Journal of Phonetics, 28,* 377–396.

Heilman, K. M. (2002). *Matter of mind: A neurologist's view of brain-behavior relationships.* New York: Oxford University Press.

Helman, L. A. (2004). Building on the sound system of Spanish: Insights from the alphabetic spellings of English-language learners. *The Reading Teacher, 57,* 452–460.

Hernandez, A. E., & Li, P. (2007, July). Age of acquisition: Its neural and computational mechanisms. *Psychological Bulletin, 133,* 638–650.

Himmele, P., & Himmele, W. (2009). *From the language-rich classroom: A research-based framework for teaching English language learners.* Alexandria, VA: ASCD.

Hirsh, K. W., Morrison, C. M., Gaset, S., & Carnicer, E. (2003). Age of acquisition and speech production in L2. *Bilingualism: Language and Cognition, 6,* 117–128.

Honigsfeld, A., & Dove, M. (2008). Coteaching in the ESL classroom. *The Delta Kappa Gamma Bulletin, 74*(2), 8–14.

Hoover, J. J., & Barletta, L. M. (2008). Considerations when assessing ELLs for special education. In J. K. Klingner, J. J. Hoover, & L. M. Baca (Eds.), *Why do English language learners struggle with reading?* (pp. 93–108). Thousand Oaks, CA: Corwin.

Hsiao, J. H., & Shillcock, R. (2005, October). Foveal splitting causes differential processing of Chinese orthography in the male and female brain. *Cognitive Brain Research, 25,* 531–536.

Huang, J. (2004). Socialising ESL students into the discourse of school science through academic writing. *Language and Education, 18*(2), 97–119.

Huang, J., & Morgan, G. (2003). A functional approach to evaluating content knowledge and language development in ESL students' science classification texts. *International Journal of Applied Linguistics, 13*(2), 234–262.

Hufferd-Ackles, K., Fuson, K., & Sherin, M. (2004). Describing levels and components of a math-talk learning community. *Journal for Research in Mathematics Education, 35*(2), 81–116.

Hull, R., & Vaid, J. (2007). Bilingual language lateralization: A meta-analytic tale of two hemispheres. *Neuropsychologia, 45*(9), 1987–2008.

Iacoboni, M., Molnar-Szakacz, I., Gallese, V., Buccino, G., Mazziotta, J. C., & Rizzolatti, G. (2005). Grasping the intentions of others with one's own mirror neuron system. *PloS Biology, 3,* e79.

Individuals with Disabilities Education Improvement Act (IDEA) of 2004, PL 108–446, 20 U.S.C. §§ 1400 *et seq.*

International Association for the Evaluation of Educational Achievement (IEA). (2007). *Trends in International Mathematics and Science Study (TIMSS), 2007.* Amsterdam, Netherlands: Author.

Jacobs, C. L. (2001). Those kids can't read this book—It's too thick. *English Journal, 90*(6), 33–37.

Janzen, J. (2008). Teaching English language learners in the content areas. *Review of Educational Research, 78*(4), 1010–1038.

Jaušovec, N., & Jaušovec, K. (2009, November). Gender related differences in visual and auditory processing of verbal and figural tasks. *Brain Research, 1300,* 135–145.

Jenkins, J. (2004). Research in teaching pronunciation and intonation. *Annual Review of Applied Linguistics, 24,* 109–125.

Jiménez, R. T. (1997). The strategic reading abilities and potential of five low-literacy Latina/o readers in middle school. *Reading Research Quarterly, 31*(3), 224–243.

Jiménez, R. T., & Gaméz, A. (1996). Literature-based cognitive strategy instruction for middle school Latina/o students. *Journal of Adolescent and Adult Literacy, 40*(2), 84–91.

Joseph, J., Noble, K., & Eden, G. (2001). The neurobiological basis of reading. *Journal of Learning Disabilities, 34,* 566–579.

Kauffmann, D. (2007). *What's different about teaching reading to students learning English.* Washington, DC: Center for Applied Linguistics.

Klingner, J. K., Barletta, L. M., & Hoover, J. J. (2008). Response to intervention models and language learners. In J. K. Klingner, J. J. Hoover, & L. M. Baca (Eds.), *Why do English language learners struggle with reading?* (pp. 37–56). Thousand Oaks, CA: Corwin.

Klingner, J. K., de Schonewise, E. A., de Onis, C., & Barletta, L. M. (2008). Misconceptions about the second language acquisition process. In J. K. Klingner, J. J. Hoover, & L. M. Baca (Eds.), *Why do English language learners struggle with reading?* (pp. 17–35). Thousand Oaks, CA: Corwin.

Klingner, J. K., & Geisler, D. (2008). Helping classroom reading teachers distinguish between language acquisition and learning disabilities. In J. K. Klingner, J. J. Hoover, & L. M. Baca (Eds.), *Why do English language learners struggle with reading?* (pp. 57–73). Thousand Oaks, CA: Corwin.

Kohnert, K., Bates, E., & Hernández, A. (1999). Balancing bilinguals: Lexical-semantic production and cognitive processing in children learning Spanish and English. *Journal of Speech, Language and Hearing Research, 42,* 1400–1413.

Kottler, E., Kottler, J. A., & Street, C. (2008). *English language learners in your classroom: Strategies that work.* Thousand Oaks, CA: Corwin.

Kovács, Á. M., & Mehler, J. (2009, April). Cognitive gains in 7-month-old bilingual infants. *Proceedings of the National Academy of Sciences USA, 106,* 6556–6560.

Kovelman, I., Baker, S. A., & Petitto, L-A. (2008, January). Bilingual and monolingual brains compared: A functional magnetic resonance imaging investigation of syntactic processing and a possible "neural signature" of bilingualism. *Journal of Cognitive Neuroscience, 20,* 153–169.

Kovelman, I., Shalinsky, M. H., Berens, M. S., & Petitto, L.-A. (2008, February). Shining new light on the brain's "Bilingual Signature": A functional near infrared spectroscopy investigation of semantic processing. *Neuroimage, 39,* 1457–1471.

Krashen, S. (2004). *The power of reading.* Westport, CT: Libraries Unlimited.

Kroll, J. F., Bobb, S. C., Misra, M., & Guo, T. (2008, July). Language selection in bilingual speech: Evidence for inhibitory processes. *Acta Psychologica (Amst.), 128,* 416–430.

Lager, C. A. (2006). Types of mathematics–language reading interactions that unnecessarily hinder algebra learning and assessment. *Reading Psychology, 27,* 165–204.

Lai, C. S., Fisher, S. E., Hurst, J. A., Vargha-Khadem, F., & Monaco, A. P. (2001). A forkhead-domain gene is mutated in a severe speech and language disorder. *Nature, 413,* 519–523.

Langer de Ramirez, L. (2010). *Empower English language learners with tools from the web.* Thousand Oaks, CA: Corwin.

Lardiere, D. (2009). Some thoughts on the contrastive analysis of features in second language acquisition. *Second Language Research, 25*(2), 173–227.

Lavigne, F., & Darmon, N. (2008, November). Dopaminergic neuromodulation of semantic priming in a cortical network model. *Neuropsychologia, 46,* 3074–3087.

Layton, C. A., & Lock, R. H. (2002). Sensitizing teachers to English language learner evaluation procedures for students with learning disabilities. *Teacher Education and Special Education, 25*(4), 362–367.

Lee, H., & Jung, W. S. (2004). Limited-English-Proficient (LEP) students and mathematical understanding. *Mathematics Teaching in the Middle School, 9*(5), 269–272.

Lee, O. (2005). Science education with English language learners: Synthesis and research agenda. *Review of Educational Research, 75*(4), 491–530.

Lee, O., Maerten-Rivera, J., Penfield, J. D., LeRoy, K., & Secada, W. G. (2008). Science achievement of English language learners in urban elementary schools: Results of a first-year professional development intervention. *Journal of Research in Science Teaching, 45*(1), 31–52.

Leonard, C. M. (2001). Imaging brain structure in children: Differentiating language disability and reading disability. *Learning Disability Quarterly, 24,* 158–176.

Lesaux, N., & Siegel, L. (2003). The development of reading in children who speak English as a second language. *Developmental Psychology, 39,* 1005–1019.

Leung, C., & Franson, C. (2001). England: ESL in the early days. In B. Mohan, C. Leung, & C. Davison (Eds.), *English as a second language in the mainstream: Teaching, learning and identity* (pp. 153–164). New York: Longman.

Liang, J., & van Heuven, V. J. (2004, December). Evidence for separate tonal and segmental tiers in the lexical specification of words: A case study of a brain-damaged Chinese speaker. *Brain and Language, 91*(3), 282–293.

Linan-Thompson, S., Vaughn, S., Prater, K., & Cirino, P. T. (2006, September–October). The response to intervention of English language learners at risk for reading problems. *Journal of Learning Disabilities, 39,* 390–398.

Lohman, D. F., Korb, K. A., & Lakin, J. M. (2008, Fall). Identifying academically gifted English language learners using nonverbal tests: A comparison of the Raven, NNAT, and CogAT. *Gifted Child Quarterly, 52,* 275–296.

López, O. S. (2010, May). The digital learning classroom: Improving English language learners' academic success in mathematics and reading using interactive whiteboard technology. *Computers & Education, 54,* 901–915.

Lovett, M. W., De Palma, M., Frijters, J., Steinbach, K., Temple, M., Benson, N., et al. (2008, July/August). Struggling readers interventions for reading difficulties: A comparison of response to intervention by ELL and EFL. *Journal of Learning Disabilities, 41,* 333–352.

Lucas, T., McKhann, G., & Ojemann, G. (2004). Functional separation of languages in the bilingual brain: A comparison of electrical stimulation language mapping in 25 bilingual patients and 117 monolingual control patients. *Journal of Neurosurgery, 101,* 449–457.

MacArthur, C. A. (2009). Writing disabilities: An overview. *LDOnline* [Online]. Available at http://www.ldonline.org/article.

MacSwan, J., Rolstad, K., & Glass, G. (2002). Do some school-age children have no language? Some problems of construct validity in the Pre-LAS Espanol. *Bilingual Research Journal, 26*(2), 395–420.

McCardle, P., Mele-McCarthy, J., Cutting, L., Leos, K., & D'Emilio, T. (2005). Learning disabilities in English language learners—identifying the issues. *Learning Disabilities Research and Practice, 20*(1), 1–5.

McCrostie, J. (2007). Investigating the accuracy of teachers' word frequency intuitions. *RELC Journal, 38*(1), 53–66.

McLaughlin, B., Blanchard, A., & Osanai, Y. (1995). *Assessing language development in bilingual preschool children.* (National Clearinghouse of Bilingual Education Program Information Guide Series, No. 22). Washington, DC: National Clearinghouse of Bilingual Education.

Merino, B. J., & Hammond, L. (2002). Writing to learn: Science in the upper-elementary bilingual classroom. In M. J. Schleppegrell & M. C. Columbi (Eds.), *Developing advanced literacy in first and second languages* (pp. 227–244). Mahwah, NJ: Lawrence Erlbaum.

Midgley, K. J., Holcomb, P. J., & Grainger, J. (2009, May). Language effects in second language learners and proficient bilinguals investigated with event-related potentials. *Journal of Neurolinguistics, 22,* 281–300.

Morris, D., Bloodgood, J. W., Lomax, R. G., & Perney, J. (2003). Developmental steps in learning to read: A longitudinal study in kindergarten and first grade. *Reading Research Quarterly, 38,* 302–328.

Nation, I. S. P. (2001). *Learning vocabulary in another language.* Cambridge, UK: Cambridge University Press.

National Center for Education Statistics (NCES). (2009a). *The Nation's Report Card: Mathematics 2009* (NCES 2010–451). Washington, DC: Institute of Education Sciences, U.S. Department of Education.

National Center for Education Statistics. (2009b). *The Nation's Report Card: Mathematics 2009* (NCES 2010–451). Washington, DC: Institute of Education Sciences, U.S. Department of Education.

National Center for Education Statistics. (2009c). *The Nation's Report Card: Reading 2009* (NCES 2010–458). Washington, DC: Institute of Education Sciences, U.S. Department of Education.

National Clearinghouse for English Language Acquisition (NCELA). (2005). *The biennial report to Congress.* Washington, DC: U.S. Department of Education.

National Clearinghouse for English Language Acquisition (NCELA). (2006). *The growing numbers of limited English proficient students: 1993/94-2003/04.* Washington, DC: U.S. Department of Education.

National Council of Teachers of English (NCTE). (2006). *NCTE position paper on the role of English teachers in educating English language learners (ELLs)*. Urbana, IL: Author.

National Joint Committee on Learning Disabilities (NJCLD). (2005). *Responsiveness to intervention and learning disabilities*. Available online at: www.nasponline.org.

National Reading Panel. (2000). *Teaching children to read: An evidence-based assessment of the scientific research literature on reading and its implications for reading instruction*. Washington, DC: National Institute of Child Health and Human Development.

Newman-Norlund, R. D., Frey, S. H., Petitto, L.-A., & Grafton, S. T. (2006, December). Anatomical substrates of visual and auditory miniature second language learning. *Journal of Cognitive Neuroscience, 18,* 1984–1997.

Oh, J. S., Jun, S.-A., Knightly, L. M., & Au, T. K. (2003). Holding on to childhood language memory. *Cognition, 86,* B53–B64.

Opitz, C. (2004). Language attrition and language acquisition in a second-language setting. *International Journal of Bilingualism, 8*(3), 395–398.

Ovando, C. J., Combs, M. C., & Collier, V. P. (2006). *Bilingual & ESL classrooms: Teaching in multicultural contexts* (4th ed.). New York: McGraw-Hill.

Pallier, C., Dehaene, S., Poline, J.-B., LeBihan, D., Argenti, A.-M., Dupoux, E., et al. (2003). Brain imaging of language plasticity in adopted adults: Can a second language replace the first? *Cerebral Cortex, 13,* 155–161.

Paulesu, E., Demonet, J. F., Fazio, F., McCrory, E., Chanoine, V., Brunswick, N., et al. (2001, March). Dyslexia: Cultural diversity and biological unity. *Science, 291,* 2165–2167.

Pawan, F. (2008, August). Content-area teachers and scaffolded instruction for English language learners. *Teaching and Teacher Education, 24,* 1450–1462.

Perie, M., Grigg, W., & Dion, G. (2005). *The Nation's Report Card: Mathematics 2005* (NCES 2006-453). Washington, DC: U.S. Department of Education, National Center for Education Statistics.

Perie, M., Grigg, W., & Donahue, P. (2005). *The Nation's Report Card: Reading 2005* (NCES 2006-451). Washington, DC: U.S. Department of Education, National Center for Education Statistics.

Pilonieta, P., & Medina, A. L. (2009, October). Reciprocal teaching for the primary grades: "We can do it, too!" *The Reading Teacher, 63,* 120–129.

Pinker, S. (1994). *The language instinct: How the mind creates language.* New York: William Morrow.

Pinker, S. (1999). *Words and rules: The ingredients of language.* New York: Basic Books.

Porcaro, C., Zappasodi, F., Barbati, G., Salustri, G., Pizzella, V., Rossini, P. M., et al. (2006, July). Fetal auditory responses to external sounds and mother's heart beat: Detection improved by Independent Component Analysis. *Brain Research, 1101,* 51–58.

Post, B., Marslen-Wilson, W. D., Randall, B., & Tyler, L. K. (2008, October). The processing of English regular inflections: Phonological cues to morphological structure. *Cognition, 109,* 1–17.

Pranksy, K. (2009, April). Supporting English language learners. *Educational Leadership, 66,* 74–78.

Pu, Y., Liu, H.-L., Spinks, J. A., Mahankali, S., Xiong, J., Feng, C.-M., et al. (2001, June). Cerebral hemodynamic response in Chinese (first) and English (second) language processing revealed by event-related functional MRI. *Magnetic Resonance Imaging, 19,* 643–647.

Rampey, B. D., Dion, G. S., & Donahue, P. L. (2009). *NAEP 2008 Trends in Academic Progress in Reading and Mathematics (NCES 2009-479).* Washington, DC: National Center for Education Statistics, U.S. Department of Education.

Reyes, P., & Fletcher, C. (2003). Successful migrant students: The case of mathematics. *Journal of Curriculum and Supervision, 18,* 306–333.

Rhodes, R. L., Ochoa, S. H., & Ortiz, S. O. (2005). *Assessing culturally and linguistically diverse students: A practical guide.* New York: The Guilford Press.

Robertson, K. (2008). Preparing ELLs to be 21st-century learners. Available online at http://colorincolorado.org.

Rodriguez, D. (2009, July). Meeting the needs of English language learners with disabilities in urban settings. *Urban Education, 44,* 452–464.

Rodriguez-Fornells, A., van der Lugt, A., Rotte, M., Britti, B., Heinze, H. J., & Munte, T. F. (2005). Second language interferes with word production in fluent bilinguals: Brain potential and functional imaging evidence. *Journal of Cognitive Neuroscience,17,* 422–433.

Rolstad, K., Mahoney, K., & Glass, G. (2005). The big picture: A meta-analysis of program effectiveness research on English language learners. *Educational Policy, 19,* 572–594.

Rossell, C. H., & Baker, K. (1996). The educational effectiveness of bilingual education. *Research in the Teaching of English, 30*(1), 7–74.

Roux, F.-E., Lubrano, V., Lauwers-Cances, V., Tremoulet, M., Mascott, C. R., & Demonet, J. F. (2004). Intra-operative mapping of cortical areas involved in reading in mono- and bilingual patients. *Brain, 127,* 1796–1810.

Rowe, M. L., Özçaliskàn, S., & Goldin-Meadow, S. (2008, January). Learning words by hand: Gesture's role in predicting vocabulary development. *First Language, 28,* 182–199.

Samway, K. D. (2006). *When English language learners write: Connecting research to practice, K–8.* Portsmouth, NH: Heinemann.

Sánchez, M. T., Parker, C., Akbayin, B., & McTigue, A. (2010). *Processes and challenges in identifying learning disabilities among students who are English language learners in three New York State districts.* Washington, DC: U.S. Department of Education, Institute of Education Sciences.

Sarouphim, K. M. (2002). DISCOVER in high school: Identifying gifted Hispanic and Native American students. *Journal of Secondary Gifted Education, 14,* 30–38.

Saunders, W. M. (1999). Improving literacy achievement for English learners in transitional bilingual programs. *Educational Research and Evaluation, 5*(4), 345–381.

Saunders, W., Foorman, B., & Carlson, C. (2006). Do we need a separate block of time for oral English language development in programs for English learners? *Elementary School Journal, 107,* 181–198.

Saunders, W. M., & Goldenberg, C. (1999). Effects of instructional conversations and literature logs on limited- and fluent-English-proficient students' story comprehension and thematic understanding. *The Elementary School Journal, 99*(4), 277–301.

Savage-Rumbaugh, S., & Lewin, R. (1994). *Kanzi: The ape at the brink of the human mind.* New York: Wiley.

Schleppegrell, M. J., & Achugar, M. (2003). Learning language and learning history: A functional linguistics approach. *TESOL Journal, 12*(2), 21–27.

Schmitt, N. (2008). Review article: Instructed second language vocabulary learning. *Language Teaching Research, 12*(3), 329–363.

Serafini, S., Gururangan, S., Friedman, A., & Haglund, M. (2008, March). Distinct and overlapping cortical areas for bilingual naming and reading using cortical stimulation—Case report. *Journal of Neurosurgery: Pediatrics, 1,* 247–254.

Shay, S. (2008). *The history of English: A linguistic introduction.* Washington, DC: Wardja Press.

Shaywitz, B. A., Shaywitz, S. E., & Gore, J. (1995). Sex differences in the functional organization of the brain for languages. *Nature, 373,* 607–609.

Short, D. (2002). Newcomer programs: An educational alternative for secondary immigrant students. *Education and Urban Society, 34*(2), 173–199.

Shyyan, V., Thurlow, M. L., & Liu, K. K. (2008, June). Instructional strategies for improving achievement in reading, mathematics, and science for English language learners with disabilities. *Assessment for Effective Intervention, 33,* 145–155.

Siegler, R. S., & Opfer, J. E. (2003). The development of numerical estimation: Evidence for multiple representations of numerical quantity. *Psychological Science, 14*(3), 237–243.

Silverman, R., & Hines, S. (2009, May). The effects of multimedia-enhanced instruction on the vocabulary of English-language learners and non-English-language learners in pre-kindergarten through second grade. *Journal of Educational Psychology, 101,* 305–314.

Singh, L. (2008, February). Influences of high and low variability on infant word recognition. *Cognition, 106,* 833–870.

Siok, W. T., Niu, Z., Jin, Z., Perfetti, C. A., & Tan, L. H. (2008, April). A structural-functional basis for dyslexia in the cortex of Chinese readers. *Proceedings of the National Academy of Sciences USA, 105*(14), 5561–5566.

Slabakova, R. (2009). Features or parameters: Which one makes second language acquisition easier, and more interesting to study? *Second Language Research, 25*(2), 313–324.

Slater, W. H., & Horstman, F. R. (2002). Teaching reading and writing to struggling middle school and high school students: The case for reciprocal teaching. *Preventing School Failure, 46,* 163–166.

Slavin, R. E. (1995). *Cooperative learning: Theory, research and practice* (2nd ed.). Boston: Allyn & Bacon.

Slavin, R. E., & Cheung, A. (2003). *Effective programs for English language learners: A best-evidence synthesis.* Baltimore, MD: Johns Hopkins University, CRESPAR.

Slavin, R. E., & Cheung, A. (2005). A synthesis of research on language of reading instruction for English language learners. *Review of Educational Research, 75,* 247–281.

Snow, C. E., Burns, M. S., & Griffin, P. (Eds.). (1998). *Preventing reading difficulties in young children.* Washington, DC: National Academy Press.

Solano-Flores, G. (2008). Who is given tests in what language by whom, when, and where? The need for probabilistic views of language in the testing of English language learners. *Educational Researcher, 37,* 189–199.

Solari, E. (2007). *Improving reading comprehension of English learners through listening comprehension instruction.* Santa Barbara, CA: University of California Linguistic Minority Research Institute.

Sommer, I. E., Aleman, A., Somers, M., Boks, M. P., & Kahn, R. S. (2008, April). Sex differences in handedness, asymmetry of the Planum Temporale and functional language lateralization. *Brain Research, 1206,* 76–88.

Sousa, D. A. (2005). *How the brain learns to read.* Thousand Oaks, CA: Corwin.

Sousa, D. A. (2006). *How the brain learns* (3rd ed.). Thousand Oaks, CA: Corwin.

Sousa, D. A. (2007). *How the special needs brain learns* (2nd ed.). Thousand Oaks, CA: Corwin.

Sousa, D. A. (2008). *How the brain learns mathematics.* Thousand Oaks, CA: Corwin.

Swaab, T. Y., Baynes, K., & Knight, R. T. (2002, December). Separable effects of priming and imageability on word processing: An ERP study. *Cognitive Brain Research, 15,* 99–103.

Swanson, E. A., & Howerton, D. (2007, May). Influence vocabulary acquisition for English language learners. *Intervention in School and Clinic, 42,* 290–294.

Thierry, G, & Wu, Y. J. (2007, July). Brain potentials reveal unconscious translation during foreign-language comprehension. *Proceedings of the National Academy of Sciences USA, 104,* 12530–12535.

Thomas, W., & Collier, V. (1997). *School effectiveness for language minority students.* Alexandria, VA: National Clearinghouse for Bilingual Education.

Tong, F., Lara-Alecio, R., Irby, B., Mathes, P., & Kwok, O. (2008, December). Accelerating early academic oral English development in transitional bilingual and structured English immersion programs. *American Educational Research Journal, 45,* 1011–1044.

Torres-Velasquez, D., & Lobo, C. (2004/2005). Culturally responsive mathematics instruction. *Teaching Children Mathematics, 11*(5), 249–255.

Tremblay, A. (2009). Phonetic variability and the variable perception of L2 word stress by French Canadian listeners. *International Journal of Bilingualism, 13*(1), 35–62.

Trofimovich, P., & Baker, W. (2006). Learning second-language suprasegmentals: Effect of L2 experience on prosody and fluency characteristics of L2 speech. *Studies in Second Language Acquisition, 28,* 1–30.

Twain, M. (1876, 1996). *A tramp abroad.* New York: Oxford University Press.

U.S. Department of Education, Institute of Education Sciences. (n.d.). *Early childhood longitudinal study, kindergarten class of 1998-99 (ECLS-K).* Washington, DC: Author.

Valaki, C. E., Maestu, F., Simos, P. G., Zhang, W., Fernandez, A., Amo, C. M., et al. (2004). Cortical organization for receptive language functions in Chinese, English, and Spanish: A cross-linguistic MEG study. *Neuropsychologia, 42*(7), 967–979.

Vandergrift, L., Goh, C., Mareschal, C., & Tafaghodatari, M. H. (2006). The Metacognitive Awareness Listening Questionnaire (MALQ): Development and validation. *Language Learning, 56,* 431–462.

Vandervert, L. (2009). The emergence of the child prodigy 10,000 years ago: An evolutionary and developmental explanation. *The Journal of Mind and Behavior, 30,* 15–32.

van Garderen, D. (2004). Reciprocal teaching as a comprehension strategy for understanding mathematical word problems. *Reading and Writing Quarterly, 20*(2), 225–229.

van Heuven, W. J. B., Schriefers, H., Dijkstra, T., & Hagoort, P. (2008, November). Language conflict in the bilingual brain. *Cerebral Cortex, 18,* 2706–2716.

Vaughn, S., Cirino, P. T., Linan-Thompson, S., Mathes, P. G., Carlson, C. D., Cardenas-Hagan, E., et al. (2006). Effectiveness of a Spanish intervention and an English intervention for English-language learners at risk for reading problems. *American Educational Research Journal, 43*(3), 449–487.

Ventureyra, V. A. G., Pallier, C., & Yoo, H.-Y. (2004). The loss of first language phonetic perception in adopted Koreans. *Journal of Neurolinguistics,17,* 79–91.

Verdugo, D. R., & Belmonte, I. A. (2007, February). Using digital stories to improve listening comprehension with Spanish young learners of English. *Language, Learning & Technology, 11,* 87–101.

Verdugo, R. R., & Flores, B. (2007, February). English-language learners: Key issues. *Education and Urban Society, 39,* 167–193.

Villegas, A., & Lucas, T. (2002). *Educating culturally responsive teachers: A coherent approach.* Albany: State University of New York.

Wallentin, M. (2009, March). Putative sex differences in verbal abilities and language cortex: A critical review. *Brain and Language, 108,* 175–183.

Wang, J., Spencer, K., & Xing, M. (2009, March). Metacognitive beliefs and strategies in learning Chinese as a foreign language. *System, 37,* 46–56.

Wilkinson, C. Y., Ortiz, A. A., Robertson, P. M., & Kushner, M. I. (2006, March–April). English language learners with reading-related LD: Linking data from multiple sources to make eligibility determinations. *Journal of Learning Disabilities, 39,* 129–141.

Willig, A. C. (1985). A meta-analysis of selected studies on the effectiveness of bilingual education. *Review of Educational Research, 55*(3), 269–318.

Wright, L. (1997). Enhancing ESL reading through reader strategy training. *Prospect, 12*(3), 15–28.

Yedlin, J. (2003). *Teacher talk and writing development in an urban, English-as-a-second-language, first-grade classroom.* Unpublished doctoral dissertation, Harvard Graduate School of Education.

Yeung, H. H., & Werker, J. F. (2009, November). Learning words' sounds before learning how words sound: 9-month-olds use distinct objects as cues to categorize speech information. *Cognition, 113,* 234–243.

Zhang, D., & Goh, C. (2006). Strategy knowledge and perceived strategy use: Singaporean students' awareness of listening and speaking strategies. *Language Awareness, 15,* 199–219.

Zwiers, J. (2006). Integrating academic language, thinking, and content: Learning scaffolds for non-native speakers in the middle grades. *Journal of English for Academic Purposes, 5*(4), 317–333.

Resources

Organizations

Center for Applied Linguistics

The center seeks to improve the teaching of English as a second/foreign language, promotes teaching of less-commonly-taught languages, and conducts research to enhance the educational process.

> 4646 40th Street, NW
> Washington, DC 20016
> Phone: (202) 362-0700
> Fax: (202) 362-3740
> Web: http://www.cal.org

Center for Language Minority Education and Research

Promotes equity in schools and society, and explores equity and access issues in oppressed communities.

> California State University, Long Beach (CSULB)
> 1250 Bellflower Boulevard, ED-1, Room 18
> Long Beach, CA 90840-2201
> Phone: (562) 985-5806
> Fax: (562) 985-4528
> Web: http://www.clmer.csulb.edu

Center for Research on Education, Diversity and Excellence (CREDE)

This site is sponsored by the University of California at Berkeley, Graduate School of Education, and focuses on improving the education of students whose ability to reach their potential is challenged by language or cultural barriers, race, geographic location, or poverty. CREDE provides educators with a range of tools to help them implement best practices in the classroom, including publications, multimedia products, and professional development services.

University of California, Santa Cruz

1156 High Street

Santa Cruz, CA 95064

Phone: (408) 459-3500

Fax: (408) 459-3502

Web: http://crede.berkeley.edu

Center for the Mathematics Education of Latinos/as

Addresses the needs of Hispanic students by developing an integrated model that connects mathematics teaching and learning to the cultural, social, and linguistic contexts of Latino/a students and by increasing the number of mathematics educators and teachers with this integrated knowledge.

Department of Mathematics

University of Arizona

617 N. Santa Rita

Tucson, AZ 85721

Phone: (520) 626-7606

Web: http://www.math.arizona.edu/~cemela/english

National Association for Bilingual Education

Ensures equality of educational opportunity through research, professional development, public education, and legislative advocacy.

1030 15th St., NW, Suite 470

Washington, DC 20005

Phone: (202) 898-1829

Fax: (202) 789-2866

Web: http://www.nabe.org

National Clearinghouse for English Language Acquisition (NCELA).

This organization collects, coordinates, and conveys a broad range of research and resources to support an inclusive approach to high-quality education for ELLs. It supports high-quality networking among state-level administrators of Title III programs and serves other stakeholders involved in ELL education, including teachers and other practitioners, parents, university faculty, administrators, and federal policymakers.

2011 Eye St. NW, Suite 300

Washington, DC 20006

Phone: (800) 321-6223; (202) 467-0867

Fax: (800) 531-9347; (202) 467-4283

Web: http://www.ncela.gwu.edu

Teachers of English to Speakers of Other Languages, Inc. (TESOL)

Develops the expertise of those involved in teaching English to speakers of other languages while respecting the individuals' native-language rights.

1600 Cameron Street, Suite 300
Alexandria, VA 22314
Phone: (703) 836-0774
Fax: (703) 836-7864
Web: http://www.tesol.org

Internet Sites

(Note: All Internet sites were active at time of publication.)

California Department of Education

Web: http://www.cde.ca.gov/sp/el/
This site contains information on education issues, instructional resources, lesson plans, curriculum, and designing a standards-based accountability system for evaluating programs for ELL students.

¡Colorín Colorado!

Web: www.colorincolorado.org
This is a free site for the educators and parents of English language learners, offering advice, information, and activities. Although it is mainly aimed at Spanish-speaking families, it is adding content and resources for other languages as well.

Dave's ESL Café

Web: http://eslcafe.com
This site was created by Dave Sperling and hosts forums and activities for ELL students and teachers from around the world. Activities for students include practicing pronunciation, interpreting idioms, and taking tests in various content areas.

Doing What Works

Web: http://dww.ed.gov
This U.S. Department of Education site translates research-based practices into practical tools to improve instruction. The literacy area includes tips for teaching ELLs.

ERIC Clearinghouse on Language and Linguistics

Web: http://www.cal.org/ericcll/digest/
This site contains articles on language learning, using resources from within language-minority communities, model programs, and integrating world language learning with other subject-matter classes.

Everything ESL

Web: http://everythingesl.net
This site is the work of Judie Haynes, an experienced ESL teacher. It contains lesson plans, teaching tips, and links to other resources for English language learners.

Graphic Organizers

Web: http://www.graphic.org
This site offers a wide collection of free, printable, ready-to-use graphic organizers to help students classify ideas and communicate more effectively.

The Internet TESL Journal

Web: http://iteslj.org
This site provides articles, research papers, lessons plans, classroom handouts, teaching ideas, and links for teachers of English as a second language.

Limited English Proficiency

Web: http://www.lep.gov
This is a federal interagency website that acts as a clearinghouse, providing and linking to information, tools, and technical assistance regarding limited English proficiency and language services for federal agencies, recipients of federal funds, users of federal programs and federally assisted programs, and other stakeholders.

Many Things for English Language Learners

Web: http://www.manythings.org
This website is for people who are English language learners and includes quizzes, word games, word puzzles, proverbs, slang expressions, anagrams, a random-sentence generator, and other computer-assisted language-learning activities. The site is noncommercial and has no advertising.

Resources for English as a Second Language

Web: http://www.usingenglish.com
This site offers a large collection of ELL tools and resources for students, teachers, learners, and academics. Helpful tools include a grammar glossary and references of irregular verbs, phrasal verbs and idioms, ELL forums, articles, teacher handouts, as well as useful links and information on English.

Teaching Diverse Learners

Web: http://www.alliance.brown.edu/tdl/index.shtml

This site is operated by the Education Alliance at Brown University and is dedicated to enhancing the capacity of teachers to work effectively and equitably with English language learners (ELLs). This website provides access to information—publications, educational materials, and the work of experts in the field—that promotes high achievement for ELLs.

Language Competency Assessments

Basic Inventory of Natural Languages (BINL), Grades K–12

The Basic Inventory of Natural Languages (BINL) is a measure of oral language proficiency in Arabic, Armenian, Cambodian, Cantonese, Chinese, Creole, Dutch, English, Farsi, Filipino, French, German, Greek, Hindi, Hmong, Ilokano, Inpuiaq, Italian, Japanese, Korean, Laotian, Navajo, Polish, Portuguese, Russian, Spanish, Taiwanese, Tagalog, Toishnese, Ukrainian, Vietnamese, and Yugoslavian, for students in Grades K–12. It can be used for placement and the determination of language dominance. Test-taking skills are not needed by the student because oral language is elicited through the use of large photographic posters. These posters depict scenes from a variety of cultures, which can be discussed without reference to cultural specifics. Testing is done individually and takes 10 minutes.

CHEC Point System, Inc.
1520 N. Waterman Ave.
San Bernadino, CA 92404
Phone: (909) 888-3296
Fax: (909) 384-0519

IDEA Language Proficiency Tests (IPT), Grades PreK–12

The IDEA Language Proficiency Tests (IPT) include normed oral language proficiency tests for students PreK–12, with three levels in both English and Spanish. All three provide designations for non-English- or Spanish-speaking, limited-English- or Spanish-speaking, and fluent-English- or Spanish-speaking students. The tests are individually administered. The IPT Reading and Writing Proficiency Tests are group-administered. They are published in both English and Spanish versions and yield diagnostic reading profiles, percentiles, and NCEs. They can be used as part of the initial identification and program exit process.

Ballard and Tighe
P.O. Box 219
Brea, CA 92822-0219
Phone: (800) 321-4332
Fax: (714) 255-9828

Language Assessment Battery (LAB), Grades K–12

Language Assessment Battery (LAB) is an English-language proficiency test for students in Grades K through 12. It is primarily used to identify, for placement purposes, those nonnative speakers whose English proficiency is not advanced enough to allow English to be used as the primary language of instruction. It can also be used to monitor their progress and for program evaluation purposes. The test has four levels. Except for the speaking test, all sections can be administered in groups, with a total test time of two hours. Short forms of the test are available: The K–2 Short LAB takes about 8 minutes to administer, and the 3-12 Short LAB takes about 10 minutes. A Spanish version of the test was developed with its own norms and is also available in two forms.

Riverside Publishing
8420 W. Bryn Mawr Ave.
Chicago, IL 60631
Phone: (800) 323-9540
Fax: (630) 467-7192

Language Assessment Scales (Oral/Reading and Writing), Grades K–Adult

The Language Assessment Scales (LAS) is published in different forms in English and Spanish: the Pre-LAS, intended for young children approximately four to six years of age; the LAS-O I, for elementary grade levels; the LAS-O II, for secondary levels; and the LAS-A, for adult second-language learners. The tests are individually administered and scored to classify students into five different proficiency levels. They can be used to track annual progress in oral English proficiency and can determine starting level and progress in a first language.

CTB/McGraw-Hill
20 Ryan Road
Monterey, CA 93940
Phone: (800) 538-9547
Fax: (800) 282-0266

Woodcock-Munoz Language Survey, Grades PreK–Adult

The Woodcock-Munoz Language Survey provides information on a student's cognitive and academic language proficiency (the extent to which the student commands the kind of language typically required in school). It is individually administered. It has both English and Spanish forms, each consisting of four subtests, two of which generate a score for oral language ability and two a reading- and writing-ability score. Together, all four constitute a broad language-ability score. A computer scoring and reporting program is available.

Riverside Publishing
8420 W. Bryn Mawr Ave., Suite 1000
Chicago, IL 60631
Phone: (800) 323-9540
Fax: (312) 693-0325

Secondary Level English Proficiency (SLEP) Test, Grades 7–12

The Secondary Level English Proficiency (SLEP) test consists of a listening comprehension section and a reading comprehension section, each of which consists exclusively of multiple-choice items. Therefore, students should have prior experience with this kind of test format. SLEP scores appear in both scale score and percentile forms. Designations are not provided for limited or fluent English proficiency, but guidance is given on what students in different score ranges can be expected to do. Schools can use these guidelines to establish local criteria. The SLEP can be used as part of initial ELL designation, to assess annual progress, and for consideration for program exit. The time required for the entire test is approximately 85 minutes.

Educational Testing Service
P.O. Box 6158
Princeton, NJ 08541
Phone: (609) 771-7206
Fax: (609) 771-7835

The Bilingual Syntax Measure I and II, Grades K–12

The BSM I and BSM II measure second-language oral language proficiency with respect to the syntactic structures in English and Spanish. The BSM I is for students in Grades K–2, and the BSM II is for students in Grades 3–12. Both tests lead to language-proficiency classifications: BSM I has five classifications of English oral language proficiency. BSM II offers two additional classifications. They can be used as part of the initial identification of ELL students needing language support services. The test is individually administered. BSM I takes 10–15 minutes per student and BSM II takes approximately 10–20 minutes per student.

The Psychological Corporation
Harcourt Assessment, Inc.
19500 Bulverde Road
San Antonio, TX 78259
Phone: (800) 211-8378
Fax: (800) 232-1223

Index

Page numbers in **boldface** are in **Teaching Tips**

CORWIN

A SAGE Company

The Corwin logo—a raven striding across an open book—represents the union of courage and learning. Corwin is committed to improving education for all learners by publishing books and other professional development resources for those serving the field of PreK–12 education. By providing practical, hands-on materials, Corwin continues to carry out the promise of its motto: **"Helping Educators Do Their Work Better."**